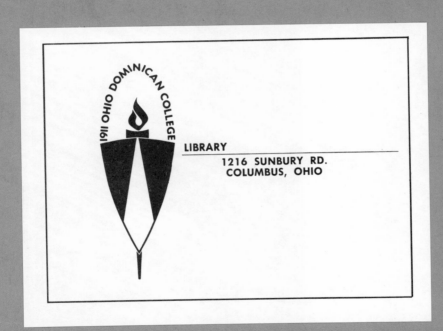

1911 OHIO DOMINICAN COLLEGE

LIBRARY

1216 SUNBURY RD.
COLUMBUS, OHIO

W9-ASG-193

SALT
AND
BITTER
AND
GOOD

AUG 1976
RECEIVED
OHIO DOMINICAN
COLLEGE LIBRARY
COLUMBUS, OHIO
43219

Cora Kaplan

SALT AND BITTER AND GOOD

Three Centuries of English and American Women Poets

Original Portraits by Lisa Unger Baskin

PADDINGTON
PRESS LTD
THE TWO CONTINENTS
PUBLISHING GROUP

For Anne Sexton, 1928-1974

Library of Congress Cataloging in Publication Data

Kaplan, Cora.
   Salt and bitter and good.

   1. Women poets—Biography. 2. English poetry—
History and Criticism. 3. American poetry—History
and Criticism. 4. Women's writings, English.
5. Women's writings, American. I. Title.
PR111.K3   821'.009   73-15027

ISBN 0-8467-0023-9
Library of Congress Catalog Card Number 73-15027
Copyright 1975 Paddington Press Ltd
Printed in the U.S.A.

Designed by Richard Browner

IN THE UNITED STATES
PADDINGTON PRESS LTD
TWO CONTINENTS PUBLISHING GROUP
30 East 42nd Street
New York City, N.Y. 10017

IN THE UNITED KINGDOM
PADDINGTON PRESS LTD
1 Wardour Street
London W1

IN CANADA
distributed by
RANDOM HOUSE OF CANADA LTD
370 Alliance Avenue
Toronto, Ontario

F
821.009
K17e
1975

Contents

98963

Acknowledgments

Charlotte Mew

"The Narrow Door," "Madeleine in Church," "Monsieur Qui Passe," "Fame," "The Farmer's Bride," and "The Quiet House" from *Collected Poems* (1953) by Charlotte Mew. Copyright © The Estate of Charlotte Mew. Reprinted by permission of Duckworth & Co., Ltd.

Amy Lowell

"Streets," "Reaping," "Meeting-House Hill," "The Sisters," and "On Looking at a Copy of Alice Meynell's Poems, Given Me, Years Ago, By A Friend" from *The Complete Poetical Works of Amy Lowell*, copyright © 1914, 1955, by Amy Lowell and by Houghton Mifflin Company. Reprinted by permission of Houghton Mifflin Company.

Elinor Wylie

"Atavism," "Wild Peaches," "A Proud Lady," "Full Moon," "Nebuchadnezzar," "Epitaph," "Let No Charitable Hope," "Cold-blooded Creatures," and "Confession of Faith" from *Collected Poems of Elinor Wylie*. Copyright © 1960 by Edwina C. Rubinstein. Reprinted by permission of Alfred A. Knopf, Inc.

Hilda Doolittle

"Phaedra," "She Contrasts With Herself Hippolyta," "She Rebukes Hippolyta" from *Collected Poems of H.D.* Copyright © 1925, Boni & Liveright, Inc. Copyright (R) 1952 Hilda Doolittle. "Hippolytus Temporizes," "Oread," "Helen," and "Callypso Speaks" from *H.D. Selected Poems*, Grove Press. Copyright 1957 by Norman Holmes Pearson. All poems reprinted by permission of Norman Holmes Pearson.

Marianne Moore

"The Steeple-Jack," "Rigorists," "Silence," and "Sojourn in the Whale" from *The Complete Poems of Marianne Moore*. Copyright © 1951 by Marianne Moore. Reprinted by permission of The MacMillan Company and Faber and Faber Ltd.

Edna St. Vincent Millay

"Never May the Fruit be Plucked," "To the Wife of a Sick Friend," "Justice Denied in Massachusetts," "Dirge Without Music," "Apostrophe to Man," "Intention to Escape From Him," "Theme and Variations," "Say That We Saw Spain Die," "Underground System," "Gazing upon him now, severe and dead," "Love is not blind, I see with single eye," "Admetus, from my marrow's core I do," and "I, being born a woman and distressed" from *Collected Poems* by Edna St. Vincent Millay, Harper & Row. Copyright © 1928, 1934, 1954, 1955, 1962 by Edna St. Vincent Millay and Norma Millay Ellis. Reprinted by permission of Norma Millay Ellis.

Vita Sackville-West

"To Any M.F.H.," "The Owl," "On the Lake," "Sometimes When Night," "The Aquarium, San Francisco," "Sea-Sonnet," and "Black Tarn" from *Selected Poems* (1941) by Victoria Sackville-West. Reprinted by permission of Nigel Nicolson.

Dorothy Parker

"Chant for Dark Hours," "Unfortunate Coincidence," "Symptom Recital," "Fair Weather," "Theory," "Coda," "Interior," and "Of a Woman, Dead Young" from *The Portable Dorothy Parker*, Copyright © 1926, 1928, 1931, 1954, 1956, 1959 by Dorothy Parker. Reprinted by permission of The Viking Press, Inc. and Duckworth & Co., Ltd.

Louise Bogan

"The Frightened Man," "The Crows," "Women," "Cassandra," "Dark Summer," "Hypocrite Swift," "Roman Fountain," "The Dream," "Evening in the Sanitarium," "Animal, Vegetable and Mineral," and "Question in a Field" from *The Blue Estuaries: Poems 1923–1968* by Louise Bogan. Copyright © 1923, 1929, 1930, 1931, 1933, 1934, 1935, 1936, 1937, 1938, 1941, 1949, 1951, 1952, 1954, 1957, 1958, 1962, 1963, 1964, 1965, 1966, 1967, 1968 by Louise Bogan. Reprinted by permission of Farrar, Straus & Giroux, Inc.

Stevie Smith

"Papa Love Baby," "Sunt Leones," "Major Macroo" and "Louise" from *A Good Time Was Had By All* (1937) by Stevie Smith, published by Jonathan Cape, Ltd. "Not Waving But Drowning" from *Not Waving But Drowning* (1957) published by Andre Deutsch, Ltd. and "Seymour and Chantelle" from *Scorpion and Other Poems* (1972) published by Longmans Group, Ltd. All poems by Stevie Smith reprinted by permission of James MacGibbon.

Sylvia Plath

"Aftermath," "Watercolor of Grantchester Meadows," "The Disquieting Muses," "The Stones," from *The Colossus and Other Poems* by Sylvia Plath. Copyright © 1960 by Sylvia Plath and 1967 by Ted Hughes. Reprinted by permission of Alfred A. Knopf Inc. and Olwyn Hughes. "Morning Song," and "The Applicant" from *Ariel* by Sylvia Plath. Copyright © 1965 by Ted Hughes. Reprinted by permission of Harper and Row Inc. and Ted Hughes. "Winter Trees," "The Rabbit Catcher," and "By Candlelight" from *Winter Trees* by Sylvia Plath. Copyright © 1971 by Ted Hughes. Reprinted by permission of Harper and Row Inc. and Olwyn Hughes.

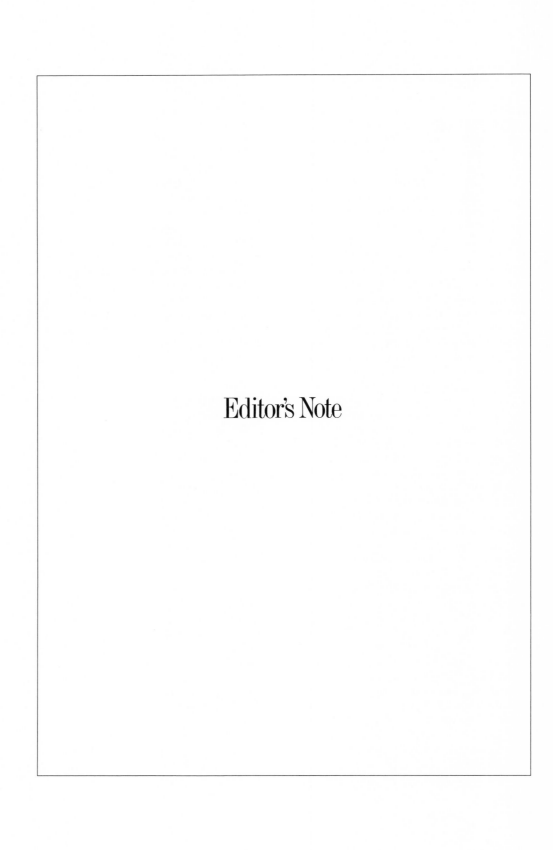

Editor's Note

THIS COLLECTION of women's poetry presents twenty-four poets, none now living, who have written in English over the last three centuries. Some are famous, most are relatively obscure. Each is, in some sense, a representative figure behind whom stand many contemporaries who deserve inclusion in a more comprehensive anthology. This highly selective book has two primary purposes. The first is to give each poet more space than even a large anthology of female poets could allow. The second is to suggest some related perspectives which may contribute toward a new assessment of what it has meant, over some 300 years, to be a woman and a poet.

Although women whom we can identify by name have been writing poetry at least since the fifteenth century, it is in the seventeenth century that a significant number began to identify themselves primarily as poets. The four poets I have chosen from the seventeenth century are very different from each other, but they all share this sense of vocation.

It is always important to explain omissions. In the seventeenth century I have excluded, for reasons of space, several very interesting poets: Anne Killigrew, the court poet who died very young; Margaret Cavendish, Duchess of Newcastle, who wrote eccentric verse fantasies on scientific and philosophical themes; and Mary Lee, Lady Chudleigh, the blunt misanthrope whose poem "To the Ladies" concludes "Value your selves and men despise,/You must be proud, if you'll be wise."

In other periods the issue of selection becomes even more difficult, and the decisions too numerous to detail here. Certain seeming glaring omissions ought, perhaps to be explained. I have left out the poetry of Emily and Charlotte Bronte. Their reputations rest finally on their prose writing, and their verse, except for the few regularly anthologized poems, seems infinitely inferior to their fiction. In two other cases, those of Gertrude Stein and Edith Sitwell, I have felt that I did not have sufficient understanding of or sympathy with their poetry to choose or write confidently. There were several modern American poets about whom I found very little biographical data, and that occasionally led me to omit one poet in favor of another. The last exclusion is simply explained. Anne Sexton's death occurred while this book was in the final stages of preparation; the book is dedicated to her memory.

I have favored poems which, either because of length or because of subjects that do not appeal to male anthologists, have not generally been anthologized. With well-known poets I have also included more familiar lyrics. Poems that deal with women or with the poet's view of nature have been given a slight preference over other themes.

For a much more comprehensive historical anthology readers should turn to *The Women Poets in English*, editor Ann Stanford (New York, 1972). It is to Ms. Stanford's book that I owe my first introduction to many fine women poets.

I hope that readers will go back to the complete works of any poet they have enjoyed. Anthologists have been, but ought not to be, tyrannical arbiters of taste. It is male anthologists, after all, who have made women poets inaccessible to the common reader and, ironically, created the need for collections such as this one.

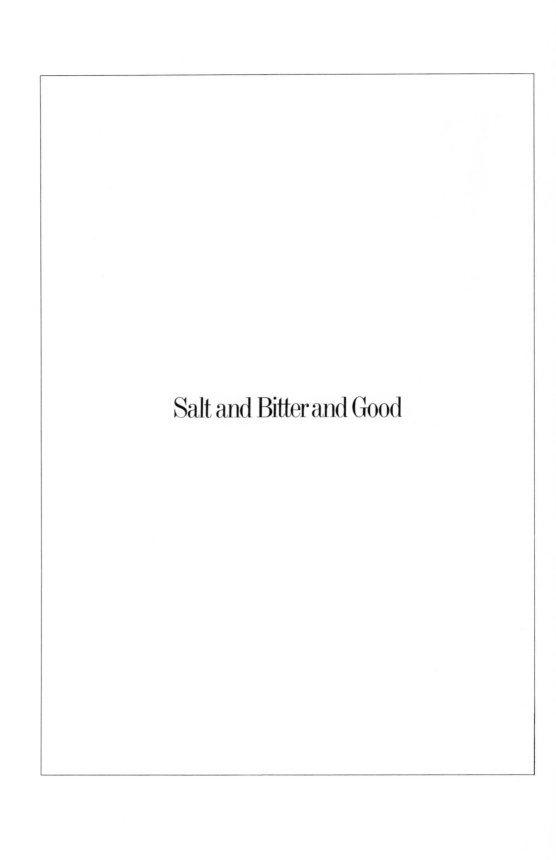

Salt and Bitter and Good

WOMEN'S POETRY vindicates women's experience not so much by praising it, as by questioning and exploring it, by making powerful verbal models that are, in the words of Christina Rossetti, "A pale clear beacon where the storm-drift is—". This perception, long hidden, crystallizes as one reads and arranges the poetry of women in historical sequence, and begins to understand how women poets fought to express a view of the world and the self that was singular to their sex but as comprehensive as any male perspective. In the "Prologue" to "Curse for a Nation," an anti-slavery poem, Elizabeth Barrett Browning conducts a dialogue with a radical "angel" who asks her to write his curse on America. The poet demurs in her own voice.

"To curse, choose men.
For I, a woman, have only known
How the heart melts and the tears run down."

The angel replies:

"Therefore," the voice said, "shalt thou
                             write
  My curse tonight.
Some women weep and curse, I say
(And no one marvels), night and day.

He persuades her to take their part, to

"Weep and write.
A curse from the depths of womanhood
Is very salt, and bitter, and good."

"Salt, and bitter, and good"—Barrett Browning's bravura manifesto for women poets asks them to transform their own suffering and that of their sisters into anger and art, to overturn both the passive model of femininity approved by mid-Victorian society and the connected notion that only men could be political poet-crusaders. The poets in this book, however, have not been chosen because their writings uniformly express a conscious feminist attitude. On the contrary, they are usually in deep conflict both about their "eccentric" choice of vocation and their inferior status, as poets and persons, in relation to the male world. Anne Bradstreet, the Anglo-American Puritan poet, was one of the first to articulate this contradiction. She writes bravely that

I am obnoxious to each carping tongue,
Who sayes, my hand a needle better fits,

but adds, both ruefully and with a faint undertone of irony, that "Men can doe best, and Women know it well." Sylvia Plath, the youngest poet included here, betrays a similar ambivalence in one of her last poems, "Winter Trees." The trees are represented as female, but as heroic metaphors of transcendence, stronger than the human sex to which they are compared:

Memories growing, ring on ring,
A series of weddings.

Knowing neither abortions nor bitchery,
Truer than women,
They seed so effortlessly!
Tasting the winds, that are footless,
Waist-deep in history—

The modern women's movement has generated new insights into the way art reflects the sexual attitudes of a particular culture at a particular time. Critics are more sensitive than they were ten years ago to the special problems that women writers confront. Still, we must wait for a fuller, revised social history of women, as well as some new attempts to understand language as a sexually biased cultural product, before we can make a proper assessment of male and female art. Until then, our literary judgments will inevitably rest on criteria that ignore sexuality and refer to a false "objective" standard which often masks extreme sexual bias about theme and treatment.

To say that we have not come far enough is not to say that no progress has been made. In the past few years several good anthologies of women's verse have appeared, thus relieving the present editor from having to prove that women *did* write poetry before the nineteenth century or that they were capable of producing great poems. Yet the difficulties, psychic and social, of writing and publishing poetry made women peculiarly self-conscious about their endeavors. A look at the sort of *positive* comment which usually introduced them to the public suggests why.

In the preface to the first edition of Anne Bradstreet's poems, published in 1650 and grandly entitled *The Tenth Muse*, John Woodbridge, Bradstreet's brother-in-law, assures us that "Tis the Work of a Woman, honoured and esteemed where she lives, for her gracious courteous disposition, the exact diligence in her place, and discreet mannaging of her family occasions. . . ." Yet even this assurance must be measured against John Winthrop's concern, five years earlier, over another colonial lady:

a godly young woman, and of special parts, who was fallen into a sad infirmity, the loss of her understanding, and reason, which had been growing upon her divers years, by occasion of her giving herself wholly to reading and writing, and written many books.

Woodbridge is merely assuring the public that Anne is neither mad nor disrupting the social order, nor (worst of all) neglecting her domestic duties for poetry. Even John Dryden, in his elegiac "Ode to Anne Killigrew," informs his readers that the young "poetess" was virtuous as well as gifted, and that the chance gift was inherited through the male line: "A soul so charming from a stock so good;/Thy father was transfus'd into thy blood/So wert thou born into the tuneful strain. . . . Such noble vigour did her verse adorn, /That it seem'd borrowed, where 'twas only born." Dryden's insult to Anne Killigrew's talent is the more profound because it was entirely unconscious: he thought he was paying her the ultimate compliment in seeing her neither as a freak nor a plagiarist, but simply as a surrogate son. Anne Killigrew's contemporary and friend, Anne Finch, Countess of Winchilsea, throws another, harsher light on the experience of being a literary lady in Restoration England. Finch tells us that she knew better than to show her poems while she was still at court lest she—like the other Anne?—be ridiculed as a "versifying maid of honour."

Yet the Restoration was a relatively good period for women writers: free, sometimes bitter attacks on male prejudice did find their way into print. Women had profited in a roundabout way from the long dialogue on human rights begun in the Puritan revolution. The Caroline court rejected the political and religious radicalism of the Puritans, but the divine right of kings and its domestic counterpart, the absolute authority of fathers to rule their households, were, for a time, shaky and unfashionable doctrines.

Theaters were open and attitudes towards sexuality were relaxed. Women were just as vulnerable in this permissive atmosphere as they had ever been, but even slightly less repressive attitudes toward the female role in court society meant that a few courageous women dared to write and show their efforts to others. The four seventeenth-century poets included here —Anne Bradstreet, Katherine Philips, Aphra Behn, Anne Finch—thought of themselves as serious poets. They were among the first women to invade the male literary establishment. We know of many women who wrote poems, and others who probably never overcame inhibitions about showing their work to a hostile audience.

Ironically, it may have been the successful infiltration of the arts by a few bold women which contributed to the temporary decline of women poets in the eighteenth century. The men who dominated literary taste in early Hanoverian England—Pope and Gay for example—were especially hostile to bluestocking women. This attitude may have been a backlash against Restoration tolerance and the consequent prominence of a few women writers, but it was more profoundly a reflection of the times. The British Empire was growing, and with it was growing a leisured middle class which included more literate women with time to read—and write. Prose fiction, however, was rapidly replacing poetry as the most popular imaginative literature. Aphra Behn was one of the first true novelists. Women who wanted to scrape a living from literature were more likely to do so by writing novels or memoirs, which would appeal to an audience that craved imaginative release from constricted lives, than by writing poetry. A split developed between the traditional epic function of the poet and the innovative role of the storyteller.

And it was not only in the crowded field of the arts that hierarchies were developing. As the middle class broadened, social distinctions within it became immensely important. "Manners," which so obsessed eighteenth-century society were a way of structuring behavior and relationships in a fragmenting, complex culture in which people were, it seemed, less controlled by religion and fixed notions of authority. For the poor, manners took the form of deference to superiors. For middle-class women, manners meant an elaborate code of social and sexual behavior which rigidly limited their activities outside the home as surely as poverty and ignorance had done, and narrowed the permitted area of female intellectual interests to the field of social relations. When women in the seventeenth century did write poetry they were as likely to write about politics and philosophy, to try epic and didactic verse as men. "Manners," which decreed that it was unfeminine and unseemly to be too interested in such matters, turned women away from precisely those subjects that preoccupied eighteenth-century poets. It took a long century for these attitudes to harden and formalize into a code so strict that to challenge it was a sort of social blasphemy. It is significant that during the brief flare of democratic enthusiasm at the end of the eighteenth century which attracted so many male writers, notions of proper female behavior and appropriate subject matter for female writers became more, not less, genteel. As the skill of the female novelist became recognized, the world of the writer herself became more contracted. Eccentric ambitions were dammed at the source, and it was improper to discuss psychological and sexual disappointment except in the most veiled way, and certainly not in verse which was more personal and revealing than prose fiction.

It is impossible, of course, to account for the dearth of good women poets in the eighteenth and early nineteenth century in some strictly causal way; these observations are meant to provoke, not answer debate. The subject has been hardly touched. It remains true, however, that until Charlotte Smith, who was well known for her novels and her verse, there was no English woman poet as interesting as the Countess of Winchilsea.

"Virtue is praised and starved." Thus wrote Mary Astell, author of the first feminist tract, *A Serious Proposal to the ladies* (1694). She was speaking of the fate of female intellectual endeavor, and her observation was as just for the nineteenth century as for the seventeenth. Two impressive mid-nineteenth century anthologies of female poets were published in America. Caroline May, editor of *The American Female Poets* (1853), introduces her volume by noting that

> One of the most striking characteristics of the present age is the number of female writers, especially in the department of belles lettres. This is even more true of the United States, than of the old world; and poetry, which, is the language of the affections, has been freely employed among us to express the emotions of women's hearts.

She reminded the reader that "It must be borne in mind that not many ladies in this country are permitted sufficient leisure from the cares and duties of home to devote themselves, either from choice, or as a means of living, to literary pursuits." Therefore, she continued, "the themes which have suggested the greater part of the following poems have been derived from the incidents and associations of every-day life." Rufus Griswold, editor of *The Female Poets of America* (1848), prefaced his collection in a very different vein.

> *It is less easy to be assured of the genuineness of literary ability in women than in men. The moral nature of women, in its finest and richest development, partakes of some of the qualities of genius; it assumes, at least, the similitude of that which in men is the characteristic or accompaniment of the highest grade of mental aspiration. We are in danger, therefore, of mistaking for the efflorescent energy of creative intelligence that which is only the exuberance of personal "feelings unemployed." We may confound the vivid dreamings of an unsatisfied heart, with the aspirations of a mind impatient of the fetters of time, and matter, and mortality . . . It does not follow, because the most essential genius in men is marked by qualities which we may call feminine, that such qualities when found in female writers have any certain or just relation to mental superiority.*

While May assumes that "emotions" and the "incidents and associations of every-day life" are legitimate inspiration for the expression of poetic genius, Griswold warns us that such experience is by definition second-rate and therefore incapable of energizing the "creative intelligence." Griswold is echoed, at the end of the century, by William Rossetti in an introduction to Felicia Heman's poetry:

> *One might sum up the weak points in Mrs. Hemans's poetry by saying that it is not only "feminine" poetry (which under the circumstances can be no imputation, rather an encomium) but also "female" poetry; besides exhibiting the fineness and charm of womanhood, it has the monotone of mere sex.*

Edmund Gosse, the influential nineteenth-century critic, begins a laudatory review of Christina Rossetti's poems in *The Critic* of January, 1893 by acknowledging that women have achieved nothing "in the great solid branches of poetry—in epic, in tragedy, in didactic and philosophical verse. . . . The reason is, apparently, that the artistic nature is not strongly developed in her."

All these judgments assume female inferiority and impute to women a very different psychology and sensibility from men, based perhaps on biological determinants. While May describes the difference between men and women poets by referring to the social context of their lives, the male critics are busy setting up categories according to which female feeling and thought are, by definition, incapable of being translated into the highest art. Much critical prejudice against women's writing is based on the male conviction that the central experiences of women's lives—and therefore female perspectives on the world—are trivial. A contempt for subjects considered to be female—"the incidents and associations of every-day life" or "feelings unemployed"—is often disguised as an attack on the form and language of women's poetry.

From the time women began to write verse they were hampered by imperfect education, domestic duties and childbearing. But these practical difficulties, large as they were, were less crippling than the general critical opinion that women who wrote were not only exceptional but "queer," coupled with the equally disabling assumption that nothing mined from the raw material of their lives could be transmuted into great poetry. By the mid-nineteenth century many women had time and privacy in which to write, although they were less able than men to become independent professional writers. What they could not overcome—and here money and social status could be negative assets by providing the illusion of equality and freedom—was the pressure of the stereotyped role into which they were pushed by Anglo-American culture. Griswold's and May's biographical sketches of poets now mostly forgotten—and not worth remembering for their literary accomplishments—tell of child prodigies like Maria Brooks, who "By the time she was twelve . . . had acquired an exquisite skill in music and painting, and could converse easily in many modern languages." Maria Brooks was betrothed at fourteen to a Boston merchant; her anthologized poems include "The Obedient Love of Woman her Highest Bliss." Another lost poet, Eliza Townsend, writes of

> *Woman—that happy, wretched being,*
> *Of Causeless smile, of nameless sigh,*
> *So oft whose joys unbidden spring,*
> *So Oft who weeps, she knows not why.*

Both these women were highly intelligent. Both had early, positive experiences of their ability to learn and to think autonomously. It is an ominous indication of the success of the repressive stereotype that they accept, without visible struggle, the male image of women as obedient if emotionally unstable children.

Certainly one strong factor that has separated good women poets from bad ones was the courage to face the causes of the "nameless sigh" and the uncontrolled weeping, and then to transcend mere analysis by finding adequate, fresh images with which to describe the sources of female "wretchedness." Yet ordinary middle-class Victorian women, brought up in the cult of "true womanhood," were encouraged to see weakness and passivity as virtuous qualities, their tendency to melancholy unalterable, and their domestic prison a refuge. The women's magazines in the first half of the nineteenth century offered these prescriptions month after month. Small wonder that most of the poets collected in Griswold or May wrote about domestic pleasures, the comforts of religion, the beauty of sunsets and the effects—but not the causes—of the discontent that led them to write verse in the first place. Elizabeth Barrett Browning wrote bitterly, in her great feminist poem *Aurora Leigh,* that women were educated to "comprehend husband's talk" and have "Potential faculty in everything/Of abdicating power in it." In defense against this attitude women poets often looked back to classical times, when, it seemed, men allowed women to be heroes and poets. Anne Bradstreet suggests that even the "antic *Greeks*" allowed their women power over poetic language by making poetry "*Calliope's* owne childe." When praise was accorded to the ordinary run of women magazine poets, readers were reminded that the poems were "artless" and that the limitations of the poets' sex rendered them incapable of contributing to "the great solid branches of poetry." They must instead content themselves with writing short verses on nature or the affections—what was commonly described as "lyric" poetry. Small wonder too that rebellious women like Barrett Browning and Mathilde Blind were determined to write long poems and not be satisfied with the award of a blue ribbon for a small lyric gift. When critics did acknowledge that Barrett Browning, Christina Rossetti or Emma Lazarus were fine poets they usually emphasized the isolated nature of the emergence of

female genius, as if to discourage other young women writers. The impact of this sort of criticism was probably not very profound for the individual writer whose connection with other women artists was already established, but it had a strong effect on aspiring poets and on the expectations and attitudes of the general reading public.

"Virtue is praised and starved." It would be comforting if Mary Astell's judgment had lost its relevance sometime in the first two decades of the twentieth century, when English and American women won political rights and a degree of emancipation from the roles decreed by the genteel tradition. That impressive generation of women poets born in the 1880's and 1890's was making major contributions to the development of the "new" poetry. Amy Lowell, Elinor Wylie, Vita Sackville-West, H.D., Edna St. Vincent Millay, Marianne Moore and Louise Bogan were some of the best of this new crop of emancipated, independent women who were choosing without fuss from families or society to be poets. It was a crucial step forward when the least lucrative of the literary professions, and the one in which women had previously had the least success, was attracting female literary talent. It was becoming more and more common in the early twentieth century to see women editing literary magazines and criticizing male poets in the leading journals. It is depressing and surprising therefore to realize how apposite Mary Astell's comment still was by mid-century, and how deeply sexist attitudes were embedded in male assessments of women's verse. The bias is most fairly observed in articles or introductions *praising* a particular female poet in contrast to her sisters. In an almost ecstatic appreciation of Louise

Bogan's verse (*Critical Quarterly*, Summer 1961), the American poet Theodore Roethke has not really progressed much further than Edmund Gosse. He opens his article by noting that

Two of the charges most frequently levelled against poetry by women are lack of range—in subject matter, in emotional tone—and lack of sense of humor.

The reader is prepared for a refutation of these charges; instead, Roethke adds a few of his own:

And one could, in individual instances among writers of real talent, add other aesthetic and moral shortcomings: the spinning-out; the embroidering of trivial themes; a concern with the mere surfaces of life—that special province of the feminine talent in prose—hiding from the real agonies of the spirit; refusing to face up to what existence is; lyric or religious posturing; running between the boudoir and the altar, stamping a tiny foot against God; or lapsing into a sententiousness that implies the author has re-invented integrity; carrying on excessively about Fate, about time; lamenting the lot of the woman; caterwauling; writing the same poem about fifty times, and so on.

None of these complaints is, of course, particularized—if they apply to any poets, they could apply equally to poets of both sexes—but they also beg a lot of questions. What are "the real agonies of the spirit" which women supposedly avoided? Are they agonies that only men can experience? Does one challenge God better in a size ten shoe? Roethke's own poems are about love, mortality, family; he deals with the same themes that engaged most of his contemporaries, male or female. Yet the irrelevant and damning sexual categories he sets up are amazingly typical of the poet-critics' response to women's poetry. The blurbs on Sylvia Plath's books express the same sexist generalizations: "She steers clear of feminine charm, deliciousness, gentility, supersensitivity and the act of being a poet. She simply writes good poetry."— A. Alvarez, (London) *Observer*. Robert Lowell describes Sylvia Plath as "hardly a person at all, or a woman, certainly not another "poetess," but one of those super-real, hypnotic, great classical heroines. This character is feminine, rather than female, although almost everything we customarily think of as feminine is turned on its head." Roethke, Alvarez and Lowell are setting up straw "poetesses" to be knocked down, since almost no women poets "of real talent" succumbed to the described vices. Barrett Browning, Dickinson and Christina Rossetti were no more or less genteel than their male contemporaries. They did, however, see the world from a female perspective.

Increasing independence, the decline of Victorian standards of behavior, the opening of the professions to women, an ever-growing audience of women, the power of women critics and editors in supporting women writers: these developments have, in the twentieth century, resulted in an increase in the numbers of women who choose to write poetry, as well as changing the quality of their verse. More women now insist that their experience of and relation to the world is as significant as that of men. But right through the last and youngest poet in this collection, women did not wholly believe in the equal and separate existence of either themselves or their sensibility, and the many powerful poems in which they assert that they do are often promissory rather than descriptive. Another consequence of the uncompleted struggle to express the central significance of women's experience is that poems which are crucially concerned with that experience are expressed as dilemmas about "universal" human problems. This tactic avoids the judgment of trivialization that greets explorations of "women's matters" in a male-oriented world, but the force and specificity of much women's poetry only reveals itself fully when the necessity for the tactic is understood, and the poems are read *as* women's poetry.

A considerable amount of women's poetry is social or political. This is not surprising, since poets generally observe rather than participate in politics, and women writers have very often been deeply interested and involved in political causes. Elizabeth Barrett Browning is above all a public poet: the love lyrics for which she is now remembered form a very small part of her *oeuvre*. Yet she was severely criticized for writing political verse in her own day—it was unwomanly. Edna St. Vincent Millay also wrote good public poetry which is rarely anthologized, as did many excellent twentieth-century poets not included in this collection. In fact, most of the poetry written by women in the seventeenth century was on public rather than private matters. Where the subject is love, it is distanced in the treatment, so that even Aphra Behn's explicit love lyrics are presented as songs or short narratives. Reinterpreting and reordering our notions about the poetry of women must combine the job of bringing back into public view unknown and forgotten poets with the considerably more strenuous task of reassessing choices of language and subject.

The problem of representing women's poetry in a context that is at once critical, historical and feminist cannot be solved by simple exposure, or by the revaluation of individual reputations. The job is larger and more complex. We must recast our usual ways of thinking about the products of culture in order to understand how language is adapted to express the experience of groups and classes other than the dominant male aristocratic and middle-class culture. For women to write poetry at all was, in most eras, an act of subversion regardless of whether the poetry was critical or accepting of male attitudes. A recognition of this fact has been made difficult by the very success of women's writing. Where the poetry has met the critical standards of men, the poets have often been inserted (usually as minor figures) into already existing periods, movements and genres which have been determined by the predominantly male literary establishment. These categories have some value in describing women's verse but they are not adequate, because they proceed from analyses that disregard women's experience. Running through male-oriented history and values, like a Gulf Stream in the frigid Atlantic, is an alternate but dialectically related history of women. Part of this history is expressed in their use of language and symbols which derive from an economic class experience held in common with men but speak from a very different sex class experience. The "universal" resonance of women's poetry is obvious; what needs to be demonstrated is its particular sexual resonance.

Take, for example, the language of flowers, which in English poetry from the sixteenth century on is frequently used to parallel the stages of human life— bud, bloom, decline and decay. Its particular use by male poets as a way of describing the curve of female sexuality hardly needs example. The analogy is not always hostile to women, nor is it sexist in obvious ways. Male poets also mourn the decline of their own youth and freshness—though they tend to see themselves not as flowers but as more phallic objects like trees, or to image their decline as part of the seasonal cycle—a grander process altogether. But if we consider how vulnerable, passive, fragile and silent flowers are, we see that the metaphor is always subliminally degrading. It makes women important only in their existence as a sensuous object, a function in which their emotional and intellectual response, such as inconstancy or temperament, is the thorn in the rose. Roses, tulips and lilies are favorite symbols for female beauty and sensuality —cupped flowers, they suggest the female sexual parts—and the rose, as a flower which throve well in England and America, was perhaps the most frequently employed. When woman poets began to describe themselves and their sex they very noticeably shied away from the female-flower symbol, although it is used by almost every male contemporary. Mary Astell, however, makes explicit ironic use of the association when she asks women if they wish to be "content to be in the world like Tulips in a garden, to make a fine show and be good for nothing?" When Anne Finch, who is the most skillful poet of nature in the late seventeenth century, does use the rose, she puts it in an aggressively feminist passage which insists on her own prerogatives in art and life. She says that her "hand delights to trace unusual things" . . . "nor will, in fading silks compose, faintly, the inimitable rose." The lines simultaneously pull together and reject the social and literary cliché

of female role. There is deliberate reversal in the use of the verb "trace" for writing and "compose" for embroidery. Contempt for what was regarded as women's only "artistic" outlet is patent in her use of "fading" and "faintly" for needlework, but it is the phrase "unusual things" linked with "inimitable rose" that launches the most successful attack on the complex of associations which reveal women as flower-like imitators of nature. The "inimitable rose" is both the flower and the poet; both are given an individual and positive identity in this skillful passage.

Conscious and/or ironic use of flowers as analogues for the submission, sexual or otherwise, of women, are more common in women's poetry in the nineteenth century. In Christina Rossetti's "Bride Song" the women mourners of the dead, aged virgin bride angrily warn off the tardy bridegroom who arrives "Too late for love, too late for joy" by telling him to keep his hands off the flowers:

Let be these poppies that we strew,
Your roses are too red:
Let be these poppies, not for you
Cut down and spread.

In an extremely sexualized, submissive poem by Dora Greenwell (1821–1882), the woman speaker is a sunflower rather than a rose.

Till the slow daylight pale,
  A willing slave, fast bound to one above,
I wait; he seems to speed, and change, and
                              fail;
  I know he will not move.

I lift my golden orb
  To his, unsmitten when the roses die,
And in my broad and burning disk absorb
  The splendours of his eye.

His eye is like a clear
  Keen flame that searches through me:
                                I must droop
Upon my stalk, I cannot reach his sphere;
  To mine he cannot stoop.

I win not my desire,
  And yet I fail not of my guerdon; lo!
A thousand flickering darts and tongues of
                                fire
  Around me spread and glow.

All rayed and crowned, I miss
  No queenly state until the summer wane,
The hours flit by; none knoweth of my bliss,
  And none has guessed my pain.

I follow one above,
  I track the shadow of his steps, I grow
Most like to him I love
  Of all that shines below.

Even in this poem, with all its troubling masochistic nuances, there is defiance, and a rejection of stereotypical associations of women and flowers. The sunflower is a coarse, common, open flower; Victorian women were supposed to keep themselves shaded from the sun, folded, like the rose. Dora Greenwell's poem—and many others which are less successful but not less disturbing—suggest how the internalization and acceptance of a passive role is involved with language, and with the common or garden symbols used in poetry. In all the women's verse influenced by the Romantic movement—from Charlotte Smith through Alice Meynell and Vita Sackville-West—there is a troubled ambivalence about women's relationship to nature, both tame and wild. In this dynamic, cultivated flowers, like Mary Astell's "Tulips in a garden," are a central image. They represent women as men have made them, mortal flesh, object, passive. Some poets attempt to overturn or at least modify this identification. Elizabeth Barrett Browning, in a minor poem "A Lay of the Early Rose," tells of a white April rose who asks to be let in "Before the rest are free. . . ."

  "For I would lonely stand
  Uplifting my white hand,
On a mission, on a mission,
To declare the coming vision."

The rose falls at the feet of a poet who identifies his plight with hers:

  Poor rose and poet too,
  Who both antedate our mission
  In an unprepared season?

The analogy between the forward rose, in advance of her sisters, and the male poet in the vanguard of sensibility, is cleverly done, though the expression is somewhat pedestrian. In later Barrett Browning, however, flowers are rarely women. She prefers to talk of herself as a sick woman past her first youth rather than as a blown rose. In the last of the *Sonnets from the Portuguese* she reminds Browning of how he brought flowers from the garden to her sick-room where they throve, and she, in return, gave him back thoughts "which on warm and cold days I withdrew/From my heart's ground." The flower-thoughts which she returns are "eglantine" (honeysuckle) and "ivy"—hardy, climbing perennials, not cut flowers.

As women's poetry reflects the growing strength and assurance of women artists in the first part of the twentieth century there is a strong emphasis on women not *as* flowers, but in some kind of critical relationship *to* them. Charlotte Mew describes a blighted, withered girlhood in "The Quiet House" and her speaker, locked away from life, comments that "A rose can stab you across the street."

Alice Meynell, viewing World War I from a peaceful domestic "Summer in England, 1914" uses the rose as a symbol of continuing growth and fertility, of uncaring fecund nature which is oblivious to the horrors of war—"And while the rose made round her cup,/The armies died convulsed." The rose, as the female principle, is active and generative, while the dying male soldiers are dehumanized and passive. H.D.'s Cretan princess, Phaedra, wants to know why westerners must make symbols of the rose instead of loving it, as she does, for "the red, red sweet of it." Perhaps this same desire to separate woman from her floral counterpart is implied in Gertrude Stein's gnomic "A rose is a rose is a rose." In a sexually more liberated age, women are able to confront the fleshy image that both defines and binds. But the intimate connection between women and nature as they themselves see it and as they are seen by men, remains complicated and painful for most women poets. The ability to relate to but remain independent from floral nature is most noticeable in the poets of the 1920's and 1930's, the generation which, at first, felt most caught up in the mood of aesthetic and personal freedom that followed the First World War. Elinor Wylie, Louise Bogan, Edna St. Vincent Millay are able to write with detachment about female passivity without accepting it or giving in to its terrors. As lovers, their women are passionate, active, betrayed and betraying, and they view the passing of their beauty with ironic regret. Louise Bogan says that "Women have no wilderness in them," and Millay begins a sonnet "I know I am but summer to your heart/And not the full four seasons of the year." There is in these statements an emotional distance which poets of the nineteenth century could rarely achieve. In a sense this group of twentieth-century poets made a truce with nature; they acknowledged that women had a special alignment with it, but they did not accept this relationship as fixed, biological, or in any other way overdetermined. They were, as befits a generation that saw women achieve the vote, short skirts and the promise of intellectual and professional parity with men, hopeful. This hopefulness they extended to love, which they still saw as a force for life in spite of man's desire to subjugate women or keep them as a seasonal bloom. These poets had gardens of their own and were determined not to become flowers in them. This truce was, however, a fragile one, which broke down when history did not seem to keep its promise of a steady advance for women in independence and equality. Sylvia Plath, who anticipates the darker, more pessimistic perceptions of the new feminist poets, sees the association of woman and flower as both compelling and threatening. Love, which brings on the nightmare identification between the two, "is the bone and sinew of my curse/The vase, reconstructed, houses/the elusive rose."

The rose, of course, is only one item of natural imagery with sexual connotations. Wild nature, the "rudest scenes" that Charlotte Smith loved, oceans (water in general) and opposite symbols of confined and controlled nature such as shepherds and sheep, often have double and even conflicting meanings in women's poetry. Wild nature was a key to the understanding and release of the transcendent spirit in male romantic poetry. This was, of course, no mere ideal fantasy for the men; for them the late eighteenth and early nineteenth century was a time of enormous advance for the common man and much greater independence—from patronage for example—for the artist. When women explored the same psychological terrain and looked for the same sort of release from contemplating nature they found themselves looking at a graveyard of frustrated ambitions and adolescent aspiration stunted by an essentially unchanged adult role, in a society in which the model of female personality and behavior was becoming more rather than less rigidly defined. No wonder the early romantic impulse in women melted down rather quickly into a pool of tears. Like Alice, they could see the key on the table but they were the wrong shape for the door to the garden. Until twentieth-century social conditions made romantic heroism a real, if slender, possibility for women, wild nature in their poetry generally referred to a patriarchal order where men had authority and the chance of transcendence; and women were denied it. The poet, by the very act of writing, is often seeking to appropriate or control the symbols of nature. When she sees as absolute the failure to do this in life, the poetry reflects failure, and the poet may compare herself to a sheep or a sacrificial lamb. In Charlotte Mew's "Fame" the poet speaker sees herself as a dead white ewe—"the moon's dropt child."

Every writer has a triangular relationship to "words," "self" and "the world." If the psychic and social experience of woman is categorically different from that of man it follows that her experience of language and its meanings will also be different, since language absorbs and, in use, confirms and reflects the social interactions of a given culture. The expression of this distinctive experience of language is a strength, not a weakness, in women's poetry. She does not become a

better poet by straining (as, perhaps, Marianne Moore too often does) to become sexually neuter or masculine in this structure. The best women poets are, or course, as self-conscious about the special sexual implications of the language as are the best male poets. (A general sensitivity to words and their effect is part of what makes a poet.) Even when they may be writing about subjects which are neither reflexive nor personal the poem can take on a new level of meaning when we know the sex of the poet. In Louise Bogan's much-admired "Roman Fountain" the poet says it is "good to strive/To beat out the image whole,/To echo the shout and stammer" of the "man-made" fountain which shapes "the bare/Clear gouts of water in air." The effort and activity when carried out by a woman is not merely heroic—it is revolutionary. Louise Bogan and Sylvia Plath are particularly good examples of women who have been able consistently to convert conventional poetic symbols to a female point of view.

The women represented in this book are the forerunners of the many living writing women poets who are, with greater collective confidence than they have ever had in the past, confronting the problems of language, politics and the consciousness of being female in the context of being women and poets. Sometimes these days that means being black and poor (like Phillis Wheatley) as well. Women are at the front of a continuing effort to alter the elite relationship of art to the culture that produces it. Persons who have been denied their history, or a fair understanding of it are in a weaker position when it comes to changing it. Knowledge of a past struggle for achievement and of links between these poets in their themes and lives gives women today access to their own talents. The recognized existence of a tradition of women poets is as important as any other lost or distorted piece of women's history. Elizabeth Barrett Browning, a fine poet and the greatest single positive influence in the fight for woman's right to *be* a poet, asked her sisters to "Weep and write./A curse from the depths of womanhood/Is very salt, and bitter, and good." Blood and tears are suggested in this passage, and the phrase "the depths of womanhood" is meant to include women's sexuality and all it implies in the assertion of their genius. A living poet, Maxine Kumin, is able to say today, of a woman taking a "Morning Swim"

> *. . . water fell*
> *Through all my doors. I was the well*
> *That fed the lake that met my sea*
> *In which I sang* Abide With Me.

To that triumphant, controlled image of female autonomy and centrality it has been a long swim.

Anne Bradstreet (1612-1672)

IN A CENTURY when the work of major poets was often circulated in manuscript or published only after their death, it is especially remarkable that Anne Bradstreet's *The Tenth Muse Lately Sprung up in America* (1650) ever found its way into print. The poet herself did not desire or engineer the publication of her poems. Her admiring brother-in-law, the Reverend John Woodbridge, took her manuscript to England in 1647 and got it published there. Mistress Bradstreet thus became the first Anglo-American poet to be so honored in her lifetime. Twelve pages of prefatory prose and verse by Woodbridge and others assures the reader of the time that he is not being conned; the poetry is indeed by a woman, and one who is "honoured, and esteemed where she lives, for her gracious demeanour, her eminent parts, her pious conversation, her courteous disposition, her exact diligence in her place, and discreet mannaging of her family occasions . . ." Moreover, the poet has neglected no conventional duty; she produced the work in her spare time, hours "curtailed from her sleep, and other refreshments."

Woodbridge's apologia gives us a glimpse of the hardships under which Mistress Bradstreet wrote and of the strength of her desire to do so. Given her birth and education the desire, at least, is understandable. Anne was brought up in the Earl of Lincoln's household, where her father, Thomas Dudley, was the Earl's steward and friend. She was, presumably, allowed the freedom of the Earl's considerable library. She survived an attack of smallpox at fifteen and at sixteen was married to young Simon Bradstreet, a

friend of her father's and a fellow Puritan. Puritanism accounted for the emigration to New England in 1630 of the whole Dudley family, including the Bradstreets. The Bradstreets moved five times after their arrival in the wilderness colony of Massachusetts Bay, settling finally in the early 1640's in Merrimack (now Andover), Massachusetts. In emigrating, the Dudleys and the Bradstreets moved upward in social status. In the new world they were aristocracy, not merely gentry. But they sacrificed status, if status also means the society, comforts and intellectual milieu of the civilized world. At first Anne's heart "rose" against the wilderness. Her early years in New England were full of childbearing, child care, ill health; she had gradually to subdue her spirit to the rigors of her new environment. She went through a period of religious doubt, a doubt recorded only in her journals. (Heterodoxy of any sort was dangerous in the grim climate of conformity which the new society found necessary for survival.) In these first years Anne Bradstreet must have witnessed and discussed the tragedy of Anne Hutchinson, who was banished from the community, "cast out as unsavory salt," even after recanting her heresies.

By the time she was thirty-eight Mistress Bradstreet had written enough poetry to fill a book. The first edition of *The Tenth Muse* includes almost all of her public poetry—"The Four Elements," "The Four Ages of Man," "The Four Seasons of the Yeare," "The Four Monarchies," "A Dialogue between Old England and New" and "Elegies" and "Epitaphs." These last were dedicated to Du Bartas (the sixteenth-century French poet), Sir Philip Sidney, and Queen

Elizabeth. Most of this collection is the work of a beginner; she imitates the form and subjects of Du Bartas and of Sir Walter Ralegh. The frequently laborious couplets of the early poems were her apprenticeship—the sort of thing a young man of similar talents and circumstances might get through in his early twenties. Her best poetry—the domestic and love lyrics—came later, when the demands of motherhood were lighter.

As the daughter and spouse of the colonial administrators, Anne was privy to all sorts of political debates carried into the home. The long poems are, significantly, political and historical. It is as if she were trying, in verse that reflected the world of men, to reach beyond the frustrations of these housebound, child-oriented years. Yet her distance from that world, and her sometimes scornful judgment of it, surfaces occasionally—in the ''Prologue,'' in her essay on ''Childhood'' in the ''Four Ages,'' and in the poem on Queen Elizabeth.

Both Thomas Dudley and Simon Bradstreet served as Governor of Massachusetts Bay colony. Anne loved them both and it seems that admiration, love and moral support for her literary efforts must have flowed from both of them as well as from Woodbridge. In her best poems Anne records a happy, affectionate domestic life. The lyrics on her husband, her children, her soul, the burning of her house, are freed from the confines of Du Bartas's influence. They owe more to the background of Elizabethan poetry in which she was educated than to the metaphysical tradition with which she was contemporary. The prose meditations which she wrote for her children employ domestic and nursery imagery in a completely unselfconscious way. Here, too, she is very bold in using her own experience as a woman and mother as a model for the virtuous life.

Some children are hardly weaned; although the teat be rubbed with wormwood or mustard, they will either wipe it off, or else suck down sweet and bitter together. So it is with some Christians: let God embitter all the sweets of this life, that so they might feed upon more substantial food, yet they are so childishly sottish that they are still hugging and sucking these empty breasts that God is forced to hedge up their way with thorns or lay affliction on their loins that so they might shake hands with the world, before it bid them farewell.

The Puritan way of life allowed, theoretically at least, no psychological separation of the divine and material world. In her religious and domestic writing Anne Bradstreet often achieves the integration of these things, and perhaps moves toward the much more difficult integration of her role as woman and poet. Against the ''carping tongues'' who would have a woman mad if she read and wrote overmuch, Anne Bradstreet stands eloquent witness to the resiliency of the female intellect and imagination.

The Prologue

1

To sing of wars, of captains, and of kings,
Of cities founded, commonwealths begun,
For my mean pen are too superior things:
Or how they all, or each their dates have run
Let poets and historians set these forth,
My obscure lines shall not so dim their worth.

2

But when my wond'ring eyes and envious heart
Great Bartas' sugared lines do but read o'er,
Fool I do grudge the Muses did not part
'Twixt him and me that overfluent store;
A Bartas can do what a Bartas will
But simple I according to my skill.

3

From schoolboy's tongue no rhet'ric we expect,
Nor yet a sweet consort from broken strings,
Nor perfect beauty where's a main defect:
My foolish, broken, blemished Muse so sings,
And this to mend, alas, no art is able,
'Cause nature made it so irreparable.

4

Nor can I, like that fluent sweet tongued Greek,
Who lisped at first, in future times speak plain.
By art he gladly found what he did seek,
A full requital of his striving pain.
Art can do much, but this maxim's most sure:
A weak or wounded brain admits no cure.

5

I am obnoxious to each carping tongue
Who says my hand a needle better fits,
A poet's pen all scorn I should thus wrong,
For such despite they cast on female wits:
If what I do prove well, it won't advance,
They'll say it's stol'n, or else it was by chance.

6

But sure the antique Greeks were far more mild
Else of our sex, why feigned they those nine
And poesy made Calliope's own child;
So 'mongst the rest they placed the arts divine:
But this weak knot they will full soon untie,
The Greeks did nought, but play the fools and lie.

7

Let Greeks be Greeks, and women what they are
Men have precedency and still excel,
It is but vain unjustly to wage war;
Men can do best, and women know it well.
Preeminence in all and each is yours;
Yet grant some small acknowledgement of ours.

8

And oh ye high flown quills that soar the skies,
And ever with your prey still catch your praise,
If e'er you deign these lowly lines your eyes,
Give thyme or parsley wreath, I ask no bays;
This mean and unrefined ore of mine
Will make your glist'ring gold but more to shine.

Childhood

From: The Four Ages of Man

Ah me! conceived in sin and born with sorrow,
A nothing, here today and gone tomorrow,
Whose mean beginning blushing can't reveal,
But night and darkness must with shame conceal.
My mother's breeding sickness I will spare,
Her nine months weary burthen not declare.
To show her bearing pains, I should do wrong,
To tell those pangs which can't be told by tongue:
With tears into the world I did arrive;
My mother still did waste as I did thrive,
Who yet with love and all alacrity,
Spending, was willing to be spent for me.
With wayward cries I did disturb her rest,
Who sought still to appease me with the breast:
With weary arms she danced and "By By" sung,
When wretched I, ingrate, had done the wrong.
When infancy was past, my childishness
Did act all folly that it could express,
My silliness did only take delight
In that which riper age did scorn and slight.
In rattles, baubles, and such toyish stuff,
My then ambitious thoughts were low enough:
My highborn soul so straitly was confin'd,
That its own worth it did not know nor mind:
This little house of flesh did spacious count,
Through ignorance all troubles did surmount;
Yet this advantage had mine ignorance,
Freedom from envy and from arrogance.
How to be rich or great I did not cark,
A baron or a duke ne'er made my mark,
Nor studious was kings' favours how to buy,
With costly presents or base flattery:

No office coveted wherein I might
Make strong myself and turn aside weak right:
No malice bear to this or that great peer,
Nor unto buzzing whisperers gave ear:
I gave no hand nor vote for death or life,
I'd nought to do 'twixt King and people's strife.
No statist I, nor martialist in th' field;
Where e'er I went, mine innocence was shield.
My quarrels not for diadems did rise,
But for an apple, plum, or some such prize:
My strokes did cause no blood, no wounds or scars,
My little wrath did end soon as my wars:
My duel was no challenge nor did seek
My foe should welt'ring in his bowels reek.
I had no suits at law neighbours to vex,
Nor evidence for lands did me perplex.
I feared no storms, nor all the wind that blows,
I had no ships at sea, nor freights to lose.
I feared no drought nor wet, I had no crop,
Nor yet on future things did set my hope.
This was mine innocence, but ah! the seeds
Lay raked up of all the cursed weeds
Which sprouted forth in mine ensuing age,
As he can tell that next comes on the stage:
But yet let me relate before I go
The sins and dangers I am subject to.
Stained from birth with Adam's sinful fact,
Thence I began to sin as soon as act:
A perverse will, a love to what's forbid,
A serpent's sting in pleasing face lay hid:
A lying tongue as soon as it could speak,
And fifth commandment do daily break.
Oft stubborn, peevish, sullen, pout and cry,
Then nought can please, and yet I know not why.
As many are my sins, so dangers too;
For sin brings sorrow, sickness, death, and woe:
And though I miss the tossings of the mind,
Yet griefs in my frail flesh I still do find.
What grippes of wind mine infancy did pain,
What tortures I in breeding teeth sustain?
What crudities my stomach cold hath bred,
Whence vomits, flux, and worms have issued?
What breaches, knocks and falls I daily have,
And some perhaps I carry to my grave;
Sometimes in fire, sometimes in water fall,
Strangely preserved, yet mind it not at all:
At home, abroad my danger's manifold,
That wonder 'tis, my glass till now doth hold.
I've done; unto my elders I give way,
For 'tis but little that a child can say.

In Honour of That High and Mighty Princess Queen Elizabeth of Happy Memory

The Proem

Although, great Queen, thou now in silence lie
Yet thy loud herald Fame doth to the sky
They wondrous worth proclaim in every clime,
And so hath vowed while there is world or time.
So great's thy glory and thine excellence,
The sound thereof rapts every human sense,
That men account it no impiety,
To say thou wert a fleshly deity.
Thousands bring offerings (though out of date)
Thy world of honours to accumulate;
'Mongst hundred hecatombs of roaring verse,
Mine bleating stands before thy royal herse.
Thou never didst nor canst thou now disdain
T' accept the tribute of a loyal brain.
Thy clemency did erst esteem as much
The acclamations of the poor as rich,
Which makes me deem my rudeness is no wrong,
Though I resound thy praises 'mongst the throng.

The Poem

No Phoenix pen, nor Spenser's poetry,
No Speed's nor Camden's learned history,
Eliza's works wars, praise, can e'er compact;
The world's the theatre where she did act.
No memories nor volumes can contain
The 'leven Olympiads of her happy reign.
Who was so good, so just, so learn'd, so wise,
From all the kings on earth she won the prize.
Nor say I more than duly is her due,
Millions will testify that this is true.
She hath wiped off th' aspersion of her sex,
That women wisdom lack to play the rex.
Spain's monarch, says not so, not yet his host;
She taught them better manners, to their cost.
The Salic law, in force now had not been,
If France had ever hoped for such a queen.
But can you, doctors, now this point dispute,
She's argument enough to make you mute.
Since first the Sun did run his ne'er run race,
And earth had, once a year, a new old face,
Since time was time, and man unmanly man,
Come show me such a Phoenix if you can.
Was ever people better ruled than hers?
Was ever land more happy freed from stirs?
Did ever wealth in England more abound?
Her victories in foreign coasts resound;

Ships more invincible than Spain's, her foe,
She wracked, she sacked, she sunk his Armado;
Her stately troops advanced to Lisbon's wall,
Don Anthony in's right there to install.
She frankly helped Frank's brave distressed king;
The states united now her fame do sing.
She their protectrix was; they well do know
Unto our dread virago, what they owe.
Her nobles sacrificed their noble blood,
Nor men nor coin she spared to do them good.
The rude untamed Irish, she did quell,
Before her picture the proud Tyrone fell.
Had ever prince such counsellors as she?
Herself Minerva caused them so to be.
Such captains and such soldiers never seen,
As were the subjects of our Pallas queen.
Her seamen through all straits the world did round;
Terra incognita might know the sound.
Her Drake came laden home with Spanish gold:
Her Essex took Cadiz, their Herculean hold.
But time would fail me, so my tongue would too,
To tell of half she did, or she could do.
Semiramis to her is but obscure,
More infamy than fame she did procure.
She built her glory but on Babel's walls,
World's wonder for a while, but yet it falls.
Fierce Tomris (Cyrus' headsman) Scythians' queen,
Had put her harness off, had she but seen
Our Amazon in th' Camp of Tilbury,
Judging all valour and all majesty
Within that princess to have residence,
And prostrate yielded to her excellence.
Dido, first foundress of proud Carthage walls
(Who living consummates her funerals),
A great Eliza, but compared with ours,
How vanisheth her glory, wealth, and powers.
Profuse, proud Cleopatra, whose wrong name,
Instead of glory, proved her country's shame,
Of her what worth in stories to be seen,
But that she was a rich Egyptian queen.
Zenobya, potent empress of the East,
And of all these without compare the best,
Whom none but great Aurelius could quell;
Yet for our Queen is no fit parallel.
She was a Phoenix queen, so shall she be,
Her ashes not revived, more Phoenix she.

Her personal perfections, who would tell
Must dip his pen in th' Heleconian well,
Which I may not, my pride doth but aspire
To read what others write and so admire.
Now say, have women worth? or have they none?
Or had they some, but with our Queen is't gone?
Nay masculines, you have thus taxed us long,
But she, though dead, will vindicate our wrong.
Let such as say our sex is void of reason,
Know 'tis a slander now but once was treason.
But happy England which had such a queen;
Yea happy, happy, had those days still been.
But happiness lies in a higher sphere,
Then wonder not Eliza moves not here.
Full fraught with honour, riches and with days
She set, she set, like Titan in his rays.
No more shall rise or set so glorious sun
Until the heaven's great revolution;
If then new things their old forms shall retain,
Eliza shall rule Albion once again.

Her Epitaph
Here sleeps the queen, this is the royal bed
Of th' damask rose, sprung from the white and red,
Whose sweet perfume fills the all-filling air.
This rose is withered, once so lovely fair.
On neither tree did grow such rose before,
The greater was our gain, our loss the more.

Another
Here lies the pride of queens, pattern of kings,
So blaze it, Fame, here's feathers for thy wings.
Here lies the envied, yet unparalleled prince,
Whose living virtues speak (though dead long since).
If many worlds, as that fantastic framed,
In every one be her great glory famed.

Before the Birth of One of Her Children

All things within this fading world hath end,
Adversity doth still our joys attend;
No ties so strong, no friends so dear and sweet,
But with death's parting blow is sure to meet.
The sentence past is most irrevocable,
A common thing, yet oh, inevitable.
How soon, my Dear, death may my steps attend,
How soon't may be thy lot to lose thy friend,
We both are ignorant, yet love bids me
These farewell lines to recommend to thee,

That when that knot's untied that made us one,
I may seem thine, who in effect am none.
And if I see not half my days that's due,
What nature would, God grant to yours and you;
The many faults that well you know I have
Let be interred in my oblivious grave;
If any worth or virtue were in me,
Let that live freshly in thy memory
And when thou feel'st no grief, as I no harms,
Yet love thy dead, who long lay in thine arms.
And when thy loss shall be repaid with gains
Look to my little babes, my dear remains.
And if thou love thyself, or loved'st me,
These O protect from step-dame's injury.
And if chance to thine eyes shall bring this verse,
With some sad sighs honour my absent hearse;
And kiss this paper for thy love's dear sake,
Who with salt tears this last farewell did take.

Another   As loving hind that (hartless) wants her deer,
Scuds through the woods and fern with hark'ning ear,
Perplext, in every bush and nook doth pry,
Her dearest deer, might answer ear or eye;
So doth my anxious soul, which now doth miss
A dearer dear (far dearer heart) than this.
Still wait with doubts, and hopes, and failing eye,
His voice to hear or person to descry.
Or as the pensive dove doth all alone
(On withered bough) most uncouthly bemoan
The absence of her love and loving mate,
Whose loss hath made her so unfortunate,
Ev'n thus do I, with many a deep sad groan,
Bewail my turtle true, who now is gone,
His presence and his safe return still woos,
With thousand doleful sighs and mournful coos.
Or as the loving mullet, that true fish,
Her fellow lost, nor joy nor life do wish,
But launches on that shore, there for to die,
Where she her captive husband doth espy.
Mine being gone, I lead a joyless life,
I have a loving peer, yet seem no wife;
But worst of all, to him can't steer my course,
I here, he there, alas, both kept by force.
Return my dear, my joy, my only love,
Unto thy hind, thy mullet, and thy dove,

Who neither joys in pasture, house, nor streams,
The substance gone, O me, these are but dreams.
Together at one tree, oh let us browse,
And like two turtles roost within one house,
And like the mullets in one river glide,
Let's still remain but one, till death divide.
      Thy loving love and dearest dear,
      At home, abroad, and everywhere.

To My Dear and Loving Husband

If ever two were one, then surely we.
If ever man were loved by wife, then thee;
If ever wife was happy in a man,
Compare with me, ye women, if you can.
I prize thy love more than whole mines of gold
Or all the riches that the East doth hold.
My love is such that rivers cannot quench,
Nor ought but love from thee, give recompense.
Thy love is such I can no way repay,
The heavens reward thee manifold, I pray.
Then while we live, in love let's so persevere
That when we live no more, we may live ever.

In reference to her Children, 23 June, 1656

I had eight birds hatcht in one nest,
Four Cocks there were, and Hens the rest,
I nurst them up with pain and care,
Nor cost, nor labour did I spare,
Till at the last they felt their wing,
Mounted the Trees, and learn'd to sing;
Chief of the Brood then took his flight,
To Regions far, and left me quite:
My mournful chirps I after send,
Till he return, or I do end,
Leave not thy nest, thy Dam and Sire,
Fly back and sing amidst this Quire.
My second bird did take her flight,
And with her mate flew out of sight;
Southward they both their course did bend,
And Seasons twain they there did spend.
Till after blown by *Southern* gales,
They *Norward* steer'd with filled sayles.
A prettier bird was no where seen,
Along the Beach among the treen.
I have a third of colour white,
On whom I plac'd no small delight;
Coupled with mate loving and true,
Hath also bid her Dam adieu:

And where *Aurora* first appears,
She now hath percht, to spend her years;
One to the Academy flew
To chat among that learned crew:
Ambition moves still in his breast
That he might chant above the rest,
Striving for more than to do well,
That nightingales he might excell.
My fifth, whose down is yet scarce gone
Is 'mongst the shrubs and bushes flown,
And as his wings increase in strength,
On higher boughs he'l pearch at length.
My other three, still with me nest,
Until: they'r grown, then as the rest,
Or here or there, they'l take their flight,
As is ordain'd, so shall they light.
If birds could weep, then would my tears
Let others know what are my fears
Lest this my brood some harm should catch,
And be surpriz'd for want of watch,
Whilst pecking corn, and void of care
They fall un'wares in Fowlers snare:
Or whilst on trees they sit and sing,
Some untoward boy at them do fling:
Or whilst allur'd with bell and glass,
The net be spread, and caught, alas.
Or least by Lime-twigs they be foyl'd,
Or by some greedy hawks be spoyl'd.
O would my young, ye saw my breast,
And knew what thoughts there sadly rest,
Great was my pain when I you bred,
Great was my care, when I you fed,
Long did I keep you soft and warm,
And with my wings kept off all harm,
My cares are more, and fears than ever,
My throbs such now, as 'fore were never:
Alas my birds, you wisdome want,
Of perils you are ignorant,
Oft times in grass, on trees, in flight,
Sore accidents on you may light.
O to your safety have an eye,
So happy may you live and die:
Mean while my dayes in tunes Ile spend,
Till my weak layes with me shall end.
In shady woods I'le sit and sing,
And things that past, to mind I'le bring.
Once young and pleasant, as are you,
But former toyes (no joyes) adieu.

My age I will not once lament,
But sing, my time so near is spent.
And from the top bough take my flight,
Into a country beyond sight,
Where old ones, instantly grow young,
And there with Seraphims set song:
No seasons cold, nor storms they see;
But spring lasts to eternity,
When each of you shall in your nest
Among your young ones take your rest,
In chirping language, oft them tell,
You had a Dam that lov'd you well,
That did what could be done for young,
And nurst you up till you were strong,
And 'fore she once would let you fly,
She shew'd you joy and misery;
Taught what was good, and what was ill,
What would save life, and what would kill?
Thus gone, amongst you I may live,
And dead, yet speak, and counsel give:
Farewel my birds, farewel adieu,
I happy am, if well with you.

Here Follows Some Verses Upon The Burning of Our House July 10th, 1666. Copied Out of a Loose Paper

In silent night when rest I took
For sorrow near I did not look
I wakened was with thund'ring noise
And piteous shrieks of dreadful voice.
That fearful sound of "Fire!" and "Fire!"
Let no man know is my desire.
I, starting up, the light did spy,
And to my God my heart did cry
To strengthen me in my distress
And not to leave me succorless.
Then, coming out, beheld a space
The flame consume my dwelling place.
And when I could no longer look,
I blest His name that gave and took,
That laid my goods now in the dust.
Yea, so it was, and so 'twas just.
It was His own, it was not mine,
Far be it that I should repine;
He might of all justly bereft
But yet sufficient for us left.
When by the ruins oft I past
My sorrowing eyes aside did cast,
And here and there the places spy
Where oft I sat and long did lie:

Here stood that trunk, and there that chest,
There lay that store I counted best.
My pleasant things in ashes lie,
And them behold no more shall I.
Under thy roof no guest shall sit,
Nor at thy table eat a bit.
No pleasant tale shall e'er be told,
Nor things recounted done of old.
No candle e'er shall shine in thee,
Nor bridegroom's voice e'er heard shall be.
In silence ever shall thou lie,
Adieu, Adieu, all's vanity.
Then straight I 'gin my heart to chide,
And did thy wealth on earth abide?
Didst fix thy hope on mold'ring dust?
The arm of flesh didst make thy trust?
Raise up thy thoughts above the sky
That dunghill mists away may fly.
Thou hast an house on high erect,
Framed by that mighty Architect,
With glory richly furnished,
Stands permanent though this be fled.
It's purchased and paid for too
By Him who hath enough to do.
A price so vast as is unknown
Yet by His gift is made thine own;
There's wealth enough, I need no more,
Farewell, my pelf, farewell my store.
The world no longer let me love,
My hope and treasure lies above.

Katherine Philips (1631-1664)

WHEN THE WOMEN poets of the late seventeenth century looked for a female poet as a model for their own labors, they naturally turned to Katherine Philips, "The Matchless Orinda." She was born Katherine Fowler, the daughter of a London merchant, and though brought up and married to a Puritan, she defied her family and became a firm supporter of Church and King. Katherine's widowed mother took as a second husband a Welshman named Hector Philips, and Katherine married James, Hector's son by his first marriage. The first seven years of Katherine's marriage were childless; when she had a son he died in infancy. Being relatively free from domestic responsibilities, she could devote considerable time to her poetry. Katherine had the additional advantage of being encouraged in her writing by James, who shared many of her intellectual interests. Their home in Cardigan, Wales, became the center for a social and intellectual coterie which called itself the Society of Friendship. Each member adopted a playful pseudonym: Katherine became Orinda and James was Antenor. Among the Philips's friends were the composer Henry Lawes, Bishop Jeremy Taylor, and the poet Henry Vaughan.

Katherine had begun to write poetry when she was quite young. Though much of her verse was circulated privately during her lifetime (as was usual in the seventeenth century) her literary reputation was not publicly made until just after her death. She did publish a translation of Corneille's *Pompey*, which was performed in Dublin. In 1664 there appeared, much to her chagrin, an imperfect edition of her poems. Her own edition came out posthumously in 1667. Her verse was admired by Dryden and Cowley, and their approval helped to confirm her reputation after her death from smallpox at the age of thirty-three.

Philips's career is quite different from those women who had written poetry up to her time. She was gently but not nobly born, and she was at the center, not the periphery, of a literary and intellectual group. She earned her prominence by the strength of her personality as well as by her talents. It is possible that if Anne Bradstreet had stayed in England her life and career might have run along similar lines to those of Katherine Philips. The importance of childbearing in the creative life of a woman writer is shown by a comparison between the two poets. Mrs. Philips died at about the age when Anne Bradstreet, mother of eight, was beginning to produce her mature verse.

Katherine Philips's poetry is always uncluttered and workmanlike. It is witty and—particularly in her poems on friendship—occasionally moving. Yet it suggests a mind that, though widely familiar with the literature of the time, never found a distinctive personal voice. When she takes up a familiar theme, like the pleasures of country life, she does not add much that is new. "A Country Life" has a few nice turns of thought: "Opinion is the rate of things;/from hence our peace doeth flow;/I have a better fate than Kings,/Because I think it so." But compared with roughly contemporary treatments of the subject—Marvell's "The Garden," Cowley's "A Wish," Anne Finch's "A Petition for

Absolute Retreat"—it is clearly inferior in sentiment and expression.

The poems to her friend "Lucasia" (who was probably Anne Owen, Viscountess of Dungannon) are much better, partly because Philips has hit on a theme to which she could add feelings not yet exploited in the poetry of the period. Her political verse has a savage Royalist bite. None of her poetry has much ornament; her Puritan upbringing lurks in it somewhere. It stands on its meanings. When these are conventional pieties about virtue or death her language and imagery do little to redeem them. When the sentiment is personally felt and original the bare style adds to the poem's force.

The poet herself was modest but not retiring. Anne Finch complained that Katherine Philips set a restricting pattern for other women poets in not writing about love between men and women. Perhaps she did not have too much to say on the subject. The headstrong young woman who flouted her Puritan upbringing and Puritan husband may have been, unfashionably, the dominant partner in her marriage. In any case, when a political enemy threatened to publish a Royalist piece by Katherine in order to tarnish James's name she wrote bluntly "To Antenor"

My love and life I must confess are thine,
But not my errors: they are only mine.

Katherine Philips differed from most of her contemporary women poets in that she neither wrote for money nor owed her reputation to a title. Her brief but notable career indicates how far a woman could go without either of these things.

Against Love

Hence Cupid! with your cheating toys,
Your real griefs, and painted joys,
Your pleasure which itself destroys.
Lovers like men in fevers burn and rave,
And only what will injure them do crave.
Men's weakness makes love so severe,
They give him power by their fear,
And make the shackles which they wear.
Who to another does his heart submit,
Makes his own idol, and then worships it.
Him whose heart is all his own,
Peace and liberty does crown,
He apprehends no killing frown.
He feels no raptures which are joys diseased,
And is not much transported, but still pleased.

To Mr. Henry Lawes

Nature, which is the vast creation's soul,
That steady curious agent in the whole,
The art of Heaven, the order of this frame,
Is only number in another name.
For as some king conqu'ring what was his own,
Hath choice of several titles to his crown;
So harmony on this score now, that then,
Yet still is all that takes and governs men.
Beauty is but composure, and we find
Content is but the concord of the mind,
Friendship the unison of well-tuned hearts,
Honour the chorus of the noblest parts,
And all the world on which we can reflect
Music to th'ear, or to the intellect.
If then each man a little world must be,
How many worlds are copied out in thee,
Who art so richly formed, so complete
T'epitomize all that is good and great;
Whose stars this brave advantage did impart,
Thy nature's as harmonious as thy art?
Though dost above the poets' praises live,
Who fetch from thee th'eternity they give.
And as true reason triumphs over sense,
Yet is subjected to intelligence:
So poets on the lower world look down,
But Lawes on them; his height is all his own.
For, like divinity itself, his lyre
Rewards the wit it did at first inspire.
And thus by double right poets allow
His and their laurel should adorn his brow.

Live then, great soul of nature, to assuage
The savage dullness of this sullen age.
Charm us to sense; for though experience fail
And reason too, thy numbers may prevail.
Then, like those ancients, strike, and so command
All nature to obey thy gen'rous hand.
None will resist but such who needs will be
More stupid than a stone, a fish, a tree.
Be it thy care our age to new-create:
What built a world may sure repair a state.

To My Excellent Lucasia, on Our Friendship

I did not live until this time
  Crowned my felicity,
When I could say without a crime,
  I am not thine, but thee.

This carcass breathed, and walked and slept,
  So that the world believed
There was a soul the motions kept;
  But they were all deceived.

For as a watch by art is wound
  To motion, such was mine:
But never had Orinda found
  A soul till she found thine;

Which now inspires, cures, and supplies,
  And guides my darkened breast:
For thou art all that I can prize,
  My joy, my life, my rest.

No bridegroom's nor crown-conqueror's mirth
  To mine compared can be:
They have but pieces of this earth,
  I've all the world in thee.

Then let our flames still light and shine,
  And no false fear control,
As innocent as our design,
  Immortal as our soul.

A Sea-Voyage From Tenby to Bristol, Begun Sept. 5, 1652. Sent From Bristol to Lucasia, Sept. 8, 1652

Hoise up the sail, cried they who understand
No word that carries kindness for the land:
Such sons of clamour, that I wonder not
They love the sea, whom sure some storm begot.
Had he who doubted motion these men seen,
Or heard their tongues, he had convinced been.
For had our bark moved half as fast as they,
We had not need cast anchor by the way.

One of the rest pretending to more wit,
Some small Italian spoke, but murdered it;
For I (thanks to Saburra's letters) knew
How to distinguish 'twixt the false and true.
But t'oppose these as mad a thing would be
As 'tis to contradict a Presbyt'ry.
'Tis Spanish though, (quoth I) e'en what you please:
For him that spoke it, 'tmight be Bread and Cheese.
So softly moves the bark which none controls,
As are the meetings of agreeing souls:
And the moon-beams did on the water play,
As if at midnight 'twould create a day.
The amorous wave that shared in such dispense
Expressed at once delight and reverence.
Such trepidation we in lovers spy
Under th'oppression of a mistress' eye.
But then the wind so high did rise and roar,
Some vowed they'd never trust the traitor more.
Behold the fate that all our glories sweep,
Writ in the dangerous wonders of the deep:
And yet behold man's easy folly more,
How soon we curse what erst we did adore.
Sure he that first himself did thus convey,
Had some strong passion that he would obey.
The bark wrought hard, but found it was in vain
To make its party good against the main,
Tossed and retreated, till at last we see
She must be fast if e'er she should be free.
We gravely anchor cast, and patiently
Lie prisoners to the weather's cruelty.
We had not wind nor tide, nor ought but grief,
Till a kind spring-tide was our first relief.
Then we float merrily, forgetting quite
The sad confinement of the stormy night.
Ere we had lost these thoughts, we ran aground,
And then how vain to be secure we found.
Now they were all surprised. Well, if we must,
Yet none shall say that dust is gone to dust.
But we are off now, and the civil tide
Assisted us the tempests to out-ride.
But what most pleased my mind upon the way,
Was the ship's posture that in harbour lay:
Which to a rocky grove so close were fixed,
That the trees branches with the tackling mixed.
One would have thought it was, as then it stood,
A growing navy, or a floating wood.
But I have done at last, and do confess
My voyage taught me so much tediousness.
In short, the Heav'ns must needs propitious be,
Because Lucasia was concerned in me.

Upon the Double Murther of K(ing) Charles I in Answer to

Libellous Copy of Rhymes by Vavasor Powell

I think not on the State, nor am concerned
Which way soever the great helm is turned:
But as that son, whose father's danger nigh
Did force his native dumbness, and untie
The fettered organs—so this is a cause
That will excuse the breach of Nature's laws.
Silence were now a sin; nay, passion now
Wise men themselves for merit would allow!
What noble eye could see, and careless, pass,
The dying lion kicked by every ass?
Has Charles so broke God's laws he must not have
A quiet crown, nor yet a quiet grave?
Tombs have been sanctuaries, thieves lie there
Secure from all their penalty and fear.
Great Charles his double misery was this:
Unfaithful friends, ignoble enemies.
Had any heathen been this Prince's foe,
He would have wept to see him injured so.
His title was his crime; they'd reason good
To quarrel at the right they had withstood.
"He broke God's Laws, and therefore he must die?"
And what shall then become of thee and I?
Slander must follow treason; but yet, stay!
Take not our reason with our King away.
Though you have seized upon all our defense,
Yet do not sequester our common sense.
"Christ will be King?" but I ne'er understood
His subjects built His Kingdom up with blood,
Except their own; or that He would dispense
With His commands, though for His own defence.
O to what height of horror are they come
Who dare pull down a crown, tear up a tomb!

To Antenor

on a paper of Mine which J. H.
Threatens to Publish to
Prejudice Him

Must then my crimes become thy scandal too?
Why, sure, the devil hath not much to do.
The weakness, of the other charge is clear,
When such a trifle must bring up the rear.
But this is mad design, for who before
Lost his repute upon another's score?
My love and life I must confess are thine,
But not my errors: they are only mine.
And if my faults must be for thine allowed,
It will be hard to dissipate the cloud,
For Eve's rebellion did not Adam blast,
Until himself forbidden fruit did taste.
'Tis possible this magazine of Hell
(Whose name would turn a verse into a spell,

Whose mischief is congenial to his life),
May yet enjoy an honourable wife:
Nor let his ill be reckoned as her blame,
Nor yet my follies blast Antenor's name.
But if those lines a punishment could call
Lasting and great as this dark lanthorn's gall,
Alone I'd court the torments with content,
To testify that thou art innocent.
So if my ink, through malice, proved a stain,
My blood should justly wash it off again.
But since that mint of slander could invent
To make so dull a rhyme his instrument,
Let verse revenge the quarrel! But he's worse
Than wishes, and below a poet's curse;
And more than this wit knows not how to give:
Let him be still himself; and let him live.

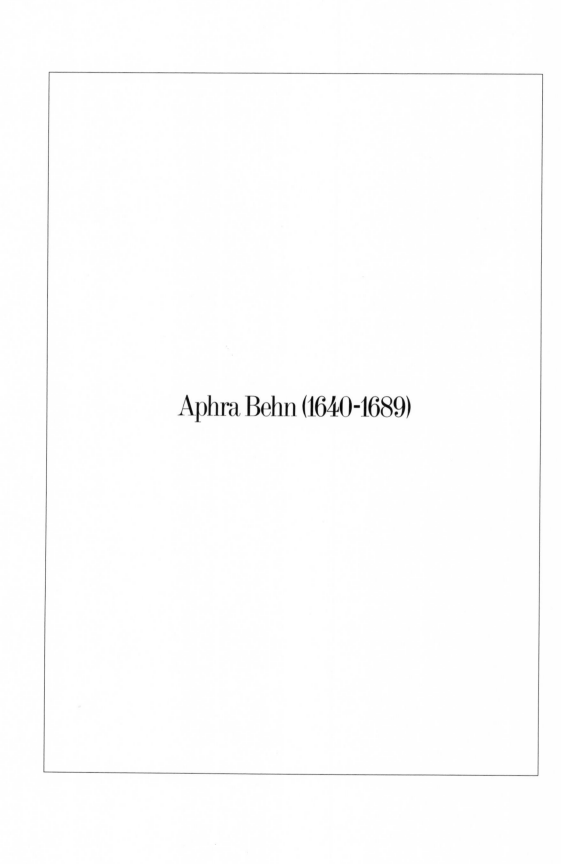

Aphra Behn (1640-1689)

APHRA BEHN was the first professional female author in English history. Yet her personal history, though incompletely recorded, has usually been considered more interesting than her writing. Her birth, childhood and youth remain obscure. Historians trying to reconstruct these early years have had few clues beyond her own testimony, which has since been challenged. The Countess of Winchilsea repeats a rumour that "Mrs. Behn was Daughter to a Barber, who liv'd formerly in Wye, a little market Town (now much decay'd) in Kent." In her novel *Oroonoko* Mrs. Behn testifies vaguely to a grander birth, and her education, manifest in her writings, makes it doubtful that she was brought up the child of a barber. Her residence in Surinam from 1658 to 1663, which she details in *Oroonoko*, and which forms a considerable part of her legend, now seems probable, although it is likely that she accompanied not her own father but some foster-family. Aphra's story, repeated by contemporary biographers, was that her "father" was to have been Lieutenant-General of a group of islands including Surinam. He died on the outward voyage and she, with her family, was stranded there for several years. Aphra somehow returned to England and was married briefly to a Dutch merchant named Behn. Little is known about either of these events. She was back in England for the theater season of 1663–64 and was widowed some time in 1665. The theme of a young woman who is forced to marry an older man runs through her writing, and biographers have conjectured that

her distaste for such unions was based on personal experience.

In 1666 Aphra undertook to spy in the Netherlands for the court of Charles II. Her letters and reports of her difficulties show this mission to have been both unrewarding and unglamorous. Aphra failed to elicit adequate support from her superiors, and she was constantly broke. In order to get herself back to England she had to negotiate a loan, which she was then unable to repay. Only when she had spent some time in debtor's prison did Thomas Killigrew or some other favored courtier pay her debts and secure her release. Spying did not turn her against the crown but it did make her think again about a profession.

Aphra's literary career begins at this point. In choosing to write for the theater she made a decision that George Woodcock, her modern biographer, quite rightly calls revolutionary. *The Forc'd Marriage*, her first play, was written after the style of Beaumont and Fletcher. In spite of some rough edges it was popular with the public. Aphra was well launched. Her plays form the major part of her work. In a period rich in dramatists her work stands up well; although she relied for plots and ideas on earlier works she adapted sources to her own purposes. Between 1670 and her death, fourteen of Mrs. Behn's plays were produced in London, most of them at the Dorset Garden Theatre. In 1684 her *Poems Upon Several Occasions* was published and, in 1688, three volumes of prose fiction. These included *Oroonoko*, which was remarkable for its realistic detail of life in Surinam and its attack on slavery. Ten more novels and another play were published posthumously.

Aphra Behn's major talent was dramatic, but her poetry, the prologues to her plays and the uninhibited amorous songs in them, mark her out as a poet of distinction. She was a fierce Tory throughout her life; her death in 1689 coincided with the end of the Restoration, a period the culture of which she epitomized and enhanced. Her writing in all genres spoke for sexual equality and openness in love—subjects her aristocratic sister poets dared not touch. There is one witty poem about a lesbian attraction and another funny, explicit narrative, told from the woman's point of view, about an impotent lover.

Her lack of title and social respectability set Mrs. Behn apart from her female literary contemporaries. She was more vulnerable to criticism, both of her writing and her personal life than they were; but she had chosen a tough profession for a woman and she was, presumably, toughened by it. Yet her verse, indeed all her work, suggests a love of life, a robust and passionate personality which survived and transcended hardship. It is interesting that almost all the women who wrote in the seventeenth century—we must of course exclude Anne Bradstreet—were Tories by birth or adoption. The wind of change which blew for women was not, it seems, a Puritan or Whig wind, but the bawdy spring breezes of Restoration England. No female author in the English language would be able to write with such sexual license or to find an audience for such writing for another 250 years. Aphra Behn's reputation was in eclipse in these intervening years. Her plays were no more or less obscene than other Restoration drama, but subsequent critics, particularly in the nineteenth century, echoed unquestioningly the contemporary cavil which Aphra says came from her own sex—that *"from a Woman it was unnaturall."* She retorted that such critics must be past passion themselves; and in the epilogue to *Sir Patient Fancy* she challenged the conventional view with characteristic elan:

What has poor Woman done, that she must be
Debar'd from Sense, and sacred Poetry?
Why in this Age has Heaven allow'd you more,
And Women less of Wit than heretofore?
We once were fam'd in story, and could write
Equal to Men; cou'd govern, nay cou'd fight.
We still have passive Valour, and can show,
Wou'd Custom give us leave, the active too,
Since we no Provocation want from you.

On her Loving Two Equally

I.
How strong does my Passion flow,
Divided equally 'twixt two?
Damon had ne'er subdu'd my Heart,
Had not *Alexis* took his part;
Nor cou'd *Alexis* pow'rful prove.
Without my *Damons* Aid, to gain my Love.

II.
When my *Alexis* present is,
Then I for *Damon* sigh and mourn;
But when *Alexis* I do miss,
Damon gains nothing but my Scorn.
But if it chance they both are by,
For both alike I languish, sigh, and die.

III.
Cure then, thou mighty winged God,
This restless Feaver in my Blood;
One Golden-Pointed Dart take back:
But which, O *Cupid*, wilt thou take?
If *Damons*, all my Hopes are crost;
Or that of my *Alexis*, I am lost.

Song in the same Play, by the Wavering Nymph

Pan, grant that I may never prove
So great a *Slave* to fall in love,
And to an Unknown *Deity*
Resign my happy Liberty:
I love to see the Amorous *Swains*
    Unto my Scorn their Hearts resign:
With Pride I see the Meads and Plains
    Throng'd all with *Slaves*, and they all mine:
Whilst I the whining Fools despise,
That pay their Homage to my Eyes.

The Disappointment

I.
One day the Amorous *Lysander*,
By an impatient Passion sway'd,
Surpriz'd fair *Cloris*, that lov'd Maid,
Who could defend her self no longer.
All things did with his Love conspire;
The gilded Planet of the Day,
In his gay Chariot drawn by Fire,
Was now descending to the Sea,
And left no Light to guide the World,
But what from *Cloris* Brighter Eyes was hurld.

51

II.

In a lone Thicket made for Love,
Silent as yielding Maids Consent,
She with a Charming Languishment,
Permits his Force, yet gently strove;
Her Hands his Bosom softly meet,
But not to put him back design'd,
Rather to draw 'em on inclin'd:
Whilst he lay trembling at her Feet,
Resistance 'tis in vain to show;
She wants the pow'r to say—*Ah! What d'ye do?*

III.

Her Bright Eyes sweet, and yet severe,
Where Love and Shame confus'dly strive,
Fresh Vigor to *Lysander* give;
And breathing faintly in his Ear,
She cry'd—*Cease, Cease—your vain Desire,*
Or I'll call out—What would you do?
My Dearer Honour ev'n to You
I cannot, must not give—Retire,
Or take this Life, whose chiefest part
I gave you with the Conquest of my Heart.

IV.

But he as much unus'd to Fear,
As he was capable of Love,
The blessed minutes to improve,
Kisses her Mouth, her Neck, her Hair;
Each Touch her new Desire Alarms,
His burning trembling Hand he prest
Upon her swelling Snowy Brest,
While she lay panting in his Arms.
All her Unguarded Beauties lie
The Spoils and Trophies of the Enemy.

V.

And now without Respect or Fear,
He seeks the Object of his Vows,
(His Love no Modesty allows)
By swift degrees advancing—where
His daring Hand that Altar seiz'd,
Where Gods of Love do sacrifice:
That awful Throne, that Paradice
Where Rage is calm'd, and Anger pleas'd;
That Fountain where Delight still flows,
And gives the Universal World Repose.

VI.

Her Balmy Lips incountring his,
Their Bodies, as their Souls, are joyn'd;
Where both in Transports Unconfin'd
Extend themselves upon the Moss.
Cloris half dead and breathless lay;
Her soft Eyes cast a Humid Light,
Such as divides the Day and Night;
Or falling Stars, whose Fires decay:
And now no signs of Life she shows,
But what in short-breath'd Sighs returns and goes.

VII.

He saw how at her Length she lay;
He saw her rising Bosom bare;
Her loose thin *Robes*, through which appear
A Shape design'd for Love and Play;
Abandon'd by her Pride and Shame.
She does her softest Joys dispence,
Off'ring her Virgin-Innocence
A Victim to Loves Sacred Flame;
While the o'er-Ravish'd Shepherd lies
Unable to perform the Sacrifice.

VIII.

Ready to taste a thousand Joys,
The too transported hapless Swain
Found the vast Pleasure turn'd to Pain;
Pleasure which too much Love destroys:
The willing Garments by he laid,
And Heaven all open'd to his view,
Mad to possess, himself he threw
On the Defenceless Lovely Maid.
But Oh what envying God conspires
To snatch his Power, yet leave him the Desire!

IX.

Nature's Support, (without whose Aid
She can no Humane Being give)
It self wants the Art to live;
Faintness its slack'ned Nerves invade:
In vain th' inraged Youth essay'd
To call its fleeting Vigor back,
No motion 'twill from Motion take;
Excess of Love his Love betray'd:
In vain he Toils, in vain Commands;
The Insensible fell weeping in his Hand.

X.

In this so Amorous Cruel Strife,
Where Love and Fate were too severe,
The poor *Lysander* in despair
Renounc'd his Reason with his Life:
Now all the brisk and active Fire
That should the Nobler Part inflame,
Serv'd to increase his Rage and Shame,
And left no Spark for New Desire:
Not all her Naked Charms cou'd move
Or calm that Rage that had debauch'd his Love.

XI.

Cloris returning from the Trance
Which Love and soft Desire had bred,
Her timerous Hand she gently laid
(Or guided by Design or Chance)
Upon the Fabulous *Priapus*,
That Potent God, as Poets feign;
But never did young *Shepherdess*,
Gath'ring of Fern upon the Plain,
More nimbly draw her Fingers back,
Finding beneath the verdant Leaves a Snake:

XII.

Than *Cloris* her fair Hand withdrew,
Finding that God of her Desires
Disarm'd of all his Awful Fires,
And Cold as Flow'rs bath'd in the Morning Dew.
Who can the *Nymph's* Confusion guess?
The Blood forsook the hinder Place,
And strew'd with Blushes all her Face,
Which both Disdain and Shame exprest:
And from *Lysander's* Arms she fled,
Leaving him fainting on the Gloomy Bed.

XIII.

Like Lightning through the Grove she hies,
Or *Daphne* from the *Delphick God*,
No print upon the grassey Road
She leaves, t' instruct Pursuing Eyes.
The Wind that wanton'd in her Hair,
And with her Ruffled Garments plaid,
Discover'd in the Flying Maid
All that the Gods e'er made, if Fair.
So *Venus*, when her *Love* was slain,
With Fear and Haste flew o'er the Fatal Plain.

XIV.
The *Nymph's* Resentments none but I
Can well Imagine or Condole:
But none can guess *Lysander's* Soul,
But those who sway'd his Destiny.
His silent Griefs swell up to Storms,
And not one God his Fury spares;
He curs'd his Birth, his Fate, his Stars;
But more the *Shepherdess's* Charms,
Whose soft bewitching Influence
Had Damn'd him to the *Hell* of Impotence.

The Willing Mistriss

Amyntas led me to a Grove,
    Where all the Trees did shade us;
The Sun it self, though it had Strove,
    It could not have betray'd us:
The place secur'd from humane Eyes,
    No other fear allows,
    But when the Winds that gently rise,
Doe Kiss the yeilding Boughs.

Down there we satt upon the Moss,
    And did begin to play
A Thousand Amorous Tricks, to pass
    The heat of all the day.
A many Kisses he did give:
    And I return'd the same
Which made me willing to receive
    That which I dare not name.

His Charming Eyes no Aid requir'd
    To tell their softning Tale;
On her that was already fir'd,
    'Twas Easy to prevaile.
He did but Kiss and Clasp me round,
    Whilst those his thoughts Exprest:
And lay'd me gently on the Ground;
    Ah who can guess the rest?

Love Arm'd

Love in Fantastique Triumph satt,
Whilst Bleeding Hearts a round him flow'd,
For whom Fresh paines he did Create,
And strange Tryanick power he show'd;
From thy Bright Eyes he took his fire,
Which round about, in sport he hurl'd;
But 'twas from mine he took desire,
Enough to undo the Amorous World.

From me he took his sighs and tears,
From thee his Pride and Crueltie;
From me his Languishments and Feares,
And every Killing Dart from thee;
Thus thou and I, the God have arm'd,
And sett him up a Deity;
But my poor Heart alone is harm'd,
Whilst thine the Victor is, and free.

Westminster Drollery, 1671

That Beauty I ador'd before,
    I now as much despise:
'Tis Money only makes the Whore:
    She that for love with her Crony lies,
Is chaste: But that's the Whore that kisses for prize.

Let *Jove* with Gold his *Danae* woo,
    It shall be no rule for me:
Nay, 't may be I may do so too,
    When I'me as old as he.
Till then I'le never hire the thing that's free.

If Coin must your affection Imp,
    Pray get some other Friend:
My Pocket ne're shall be my Pimp,
    I never that intend,
Yet can be noble too, if I see they mend.

Since Loving was a Liberal Art,
    How canst thou trade for gain?
The pleasure is on your part,
    'Tis we Men take the pain:
And being so, must Women have the gain?

No, no, I'le never farm your Bed,
    Nor your Smock-Tenant be:
I hate to rent your white and red,
    You shall not let your Love to me:
I court a Mistris, not a Landlady.

A Pox take him that first set up,
    Th' Excise of Flesh and Skin:
And since it will no better be,
    Let's both to kiss begin;
To kiss freely: if not, you may go spin.

To the fair Clarinda, who made Love to me, imagin'd more than Woman

Fair lovely Maid, or if that Title be
Too weak, too Feminine for Nobler thee,
Permit a Name that more Approaches Truth:
And let me call thee, Lovely Charming Youth.
This last will justifie my soft complaint;
While that may serve to lessen my constraint;
And without Blushes I the Youth persue,
When so much beauteous Woman is in view.
Against thy Charms we struggle but in vain
With thy deluding Form thou giv'st us pain,
While the bright Nymph betrays us to the Swain.
In pity to our Sex sure thou wer't sent,
That we might Love, and yet be Innocent:
For sure no Crime with thee we can commit;
Or if we shou'd—thy Form excuses it.
For who, that gathers fairest Flowers believes
A snake lies hid beneath the Fragrant Leaves.

Thou beauteous Wonder of a different kind,
Soft *Cloris* with the dear *Alexis* join'd;
When e'r the Manly part of thee, wou'd plead
Thou tempts us with the Image of the Maid,
While we the noblest Passions do extend
The Love to *Hermes*, *Aphrodite* the Friend.

A thousand Martyrs I have made

A thousand Martyrs I have made,
    All sacrific'd to my desire;
A thousand Beauties have betray'd,
    That languish in resistless Fire.
The untam'd Heart to hand I brought,
And fixt the wild and wandring Thought.

I never vow'd nor sigh'd in vain
    But both, thô false, were well receiv'd.
The Fair are pleas'd to give us pain,
    And what they wish is soon believ'd.
And thô I talk'd of Wounds and Smart,
Loves Pleasures only toucht my Heart.

Alone the Glory and the Spoil
    I always Laughing bore away;
The Triumphs, without Pain or Toil,
    Without the Hell, the Heav'n of Joy.
And while I thus at random rove
Despise the Fools that whine for Love.

Anne Finch,
Countess of Winchilsea (1661-1720)

AMONG STUDENTS of literature, Anne, Countess of Winchilsea, is considered one of the earliest nature poets. In an age characterized by worldly, urban wit, she praised country life and the nightingale's song. Anne Finch was born Anne Kingsmill, daughter of Sir William Kingsmill and Anne Hazlewood. The Kingsmills were old Hampshire gentry. Anne never knew her father; he died either just before or just after her birth in April 1661 and her mother was remarried, in October 1662, to Sir Thomas Ogle. Anne's stepfather was her mother's junior by some six years. The Ogles had a daughter Dorothy, of whom Anne was very fond. By the time Anne was three her mother was dead. She must have spent her childhood in the household of one of her many relatives: both the Kingsmill and Hazlewood connections were large.

Whoever raised Anne gave her a good education and by 1683 she was installed at court as one of six Maids of Honour to Mary of Modena, wife of James II, then Duke of York. Anne was then twenty-two, almost past marriageable age. Witty, beautiful and pure, she was courted strenuously by Colonel Heneage Finch, Captain of Halberdiers and Gentleman of the Bedchamber. They were married on March 14, 1684. Though a childless marriage it was an extremely happy one. Next to his wedding date in his private diary Heneage Finch wrote, some thirty-nine years later, "Most blessed day." Testimony to Anne's domestic contentment abounds in her poems.

Public life was not so uniformly sunny.

The Glorious Revolution was disaster for the Finches. With James in exile the stubborn, principled Finch refused to take the oath to support William. He was removed from office, and the couple lived among their relatives, in what for them must have been genteel poverty, for some years. Some time around 1690 they moved to Eastwell, the seat of the Earl of Winchilsea, a young man in his teens. His unexpected death made Anne's husband the heir. The beautiful house and grounds at Eastwell are the background to much of Anne's poetry.

Anne's reputation as a poet grew with the years. Though she wrote verse when she was single she kept it to herself, knowing that exposure might bring ridicule. ". . . I was not so far abandon'd by my prudence, as out of mistaken vanity, to lett any attempts of mine in Poetry, shew themselves whilst I liv'd in such a publick place as the Court, where every one wou'd have made their remarks upon a Versifying Maid of Honour; and far the greater number with prejudice, if not contempt." She knew and was known by the rising Augustan wits, Pope and Gay. Between Pope and herself there was a certain respect, reflected in verse references, in spite of the outspoken hostility of the Augustans to women of letters. Anne Finch was frequently satirized in contemporary poetry and plays, partly because she was so fortunate in talent and circumstance. She was virtuous and titled, a good poet, militant in defense of her sex, bold in her criticism of male poets and court life. Her husband adored her and admired her work, as did her large circle of family and friends. Still, being a woman and a writer made her open to attack. Towards the end of her life she was a prime butt for anti-"bluestocking" jokes on the stage and in verse. Her collected poems were published in 1713; it is from this edition and two manuscript volumes containing other verse that her work survives. Anne died in 1720. Heneage, who survived her by six years, had long been retired from politics and had settled in the country, happily immersed in antiquarian pursuits.

Wordsworth's admiration contributed to a revived interest in Anne Finch's poems. Some rough parallels in their life histories may in part account for this sympathy. Both were city-bred and came to appreciate natural scenery and country life as a gift to the spirit after a strenuous public existence—Anne after she had been forcibly rusticated from court, and Wordsworth following his disillusionment with the French Revolution. It is a mistake, however, to see Anne merely as a lonely pre-romantic scout, a lost female voice calling from the wilderness, or even as a minor poet out of step with the spirit of the time. She stood in the midst of her age and challenged its mores, its inspiration, and, what may be most important, its view of the role of women. She was not alone. It was a good period for women poets. Her contemporaries—Joan Philips, Anne Killigrew, Mary Lee, Lady Chudleigh—all wrote aggressive and feminist verse. Behind *them* there was already a substantial group of successful women poets—Anne Bradstreet, Margaret Cavendish, Katherine Philips and Aphra Behn. There is a self-confidence in the writing of Anne Finch's generation of woman authors which lapsed somewhat in the mid-eighteenth century. Although Finch never saw it that way, she was the last female poet of

stature to profit from the social changes wrought by the Puritan revolution. A Tory in an age of Whig triumph, she saw perhaps that the new Establishment, whatever its liberal philosophical claims, would do little for women. A whole century elapsed between Mary Astell's plea for women's education in 1694 and Mary Wollstonecraft's demand for more complete emancipation in 1795. Both Astell's and Wollstonecraft's were periods of rapidly increasing affluence. The Countess of Winchilsea notes, with regret and censure, the existence of a large group of leisured women devoted to elaborate dress, social ritual and gossip. It is for this class of women too that Mary Astell begs an equal education. Against the "Time," "Pains," "Care," and "Cost" bestowed on males Mrs. Astell contrasts women's lot:

The latter are restricted, frown'd upon, beat not for *but* from *the Muses; Laughter and Ridicule that never-failing Scare-Crow is set up to drive them from the Tree of Knowledge. But if in spite of all difficulties Nature prevails, and they can't be kept so ignorant as their masters would have them, they are stared upon as Monsters, Censured, Envyd and every way discouraged, or at the best they have the Fate the Proverb assigns them:* Virtue is praised and starved.

The Countess is just as straightforward. She compares women poets to "state-prisoners, pen and ink denied," and notes that "Women are Education's and not Nature's Fools." In her Preface, she explains the constraints very bluntly.

. . . when a Woman meddles with things of this nature,
So strong th' opposing faction still appears,
The hopes to thrive, can ne're outweigh
the fears.

And, I am besides sensible, that Poetry has been of late so explain'd, the laws of itt being putt into familiar languages, that even those of my sex, (if they will be so presumptious as to write) are very accountable for their transgressions against them.

She does not always find the existing tradition of female poetry liberating to her own imagination:

For the subjects, I hope they are att least innofensive; tho' sometimes of Love; for keeping within those limmitts which I have observ'd I know not why itt shou'd be more faulty, to treat of that passion, then of any other violent excursion, or transport of the mind. Tho' I must confess, the great reservedness of Mrs. Philips in this particular, and the prayses I have heard given her upon that account, together with my desire not to give scandal to the most severe, has often discourag'd me from making use of itt. . . .

The Restoration court produced a number of strong-minded women who were quick to criticize men and challenge male ascendence. Mary Lee tells her readers that "Wife and servant are the same,/but only differ in the name . . . Value your selves, and men despise,/You must be proud, if you'll be wise." Anne Killigrew, who served with Anne Kingsmill as a Maid of Honour, was even fiercer in "Upon the Saying that My Verses were Made by Another." She too refers back to Katherine Philips, noting that Orinda's sex did not "at all obstruct her fame,/But higher 'mong the stars it fixed her name." Literary talent was unevenly distributed among these aspiring poets; what they had in common, besides their anger, was a rising collective defense of their eccentric occupation.

With the wit that was the particular donee of the period, they turned this anger on their lords and masters.

Like all poets, the Countess of Winchilsea worked with inherited verse forms—her immediate master was Dryden. Pope's innovations with the couplet were contemporary with her own writing but she was less interested than he in the techniques of versification. She had an ear for easy, colloquial language. Her words call attention to her thoughts and feelings, although there are passages of great elegance in her verse. What emerges as the greatest strength of her work is the creative, judging sensibility, the "I" of the poet. The romantic quality in her poetry is not due solely to her response to nature but to the way in which all things observed, described, commented on, relate back to the speaker. She sets up her own personal philosophy as an alternative to the dominant spirit of the times without adopting an eccentric or egotistical mask. This quality is most apparent and most successful in the *Petition for an Absolute Retreat*, Anne Finch's reworking of a theme already written on by Katherine Philips and others. This achieved personal voice will not be matched again in poetry by a woman until the mid-nineteenth century. It can be found in all her poetry except the Fables, which were unfortunately so popular with eighteenth-century anthologists, and in the plays. About the rest of her work Anne Finch could say, without apology,

My hand delights to trace unusual things,
And deviates from the known and common
                                        way;
Nor will in fading silks compose
Faintly the inimitable rose. . . .

The Introduction

Did I, my lines intend for publick view,
How many censures, wou'd their faults persue,
Some wou'd, because such words they do affect,
Cry they're insipid, empty, uncorrect.
And many, have attain'd, dull and untaught
The name of Witt, only by finding fault.
True judges, might condemn their want of witt,
And all might say, they're by a Woman writt.
Alas! a woman that attempts the pen,
Such an intruder on the rights of men,
Such a presumptuous Creature, is esteem'd,
The fault, can by no vertue be redeem'd.
They tell us, we mistake our sex and way;
Good breeding, fassion, dancing, dressing, play
Are the accomplishments we shou'd desire;
To write, or read, or think, or to enquire
Wou'd cloud our beauty, and exaust our time,
And interrupt the Conquests of our prime;
Whilst the dull mannage, of a servile house
Is held by some, our outmost art, and use.

    Sure 'twas not ever thus, nor are we told
Fables, of Women that excell'd of old;
To whom, by the diffusive hand of Heaven
Some share of witt, and poetry was given.
On that glad day, on which the Ark return'd,
The holy pledge, for which the Land had mourn'd,
The joyfull Tribes, attend itt on the way,
The Levites do the sacred Charge convey,
Whilst various Instruments, before itt play;
Here, holy Virgins in the Concert joyn,
The louder notes, to soften, and refine,
And with alternate verse, compleat the Hymn Devine.
Loe! the yong Poet, after Gods own heart,
By Him inspired, and taught the Muses Art,
Return'd from Conquest, a bright Chorus meets.
That sing his slayn ten thousand in the streets.
In such loud numbers they his acts declare,
Proclaim the wonders, of his early war,
That Saul upon the vast applause does frown,
And feels, itts mighty thunder shake the Crown.
What, can the threat'n'd Judgment now prolong?
Half of the Kingdom is already gone;
The fairest half, whose influence guides the rest,
Have David's Empire, o're their hearts confess't.

    A Woman here, leads fainting Israel on,
She fights, she wins, she tryumphs with a song,
Devout, Majestick, for the subject fitt,
And far above her arms, exalts her witt,
Then, to the peacefull, shady Palm withdraws,
And rules the rescu'd Nation, with her Laws.
How are we fal'n, fal'n by mistaken rules?
And Education's, more than Nature's fools,
Debarr'd from all improve-ments of the mind,
And to be dull, expected and dessigned;

62

And if some one, wou'd Soar above the rest,
With warmer fancy, and ambition press't,
So strong, th' opposing faction still appears,
The hopes to thrive, can ne're outweigh the fears,
Be caution'd then my Muse, and still retir'd;
Nor be dispis'd, aiming to be admir'd;
Conscious of wants, still with contracted wing,
To some few friends, and to thy sorrows sing;
For groves of Lawrell, thou wert never meant;
Be dark enough thy shades, and be thou there content.

The Appology

'Tis true I write and tell me by what Rule
I am alone forbid to play the fool
To follow through the Groves a wand'ring Muse
And fain'd Idea's for my pleasures chuse
Why shou'd it in my Pen be held a fault
Whilst Mira paints her face, to paint a thought
Whilst Lamia to the manly Bumper flys
And borrow'd Spiritts sparkle in her Eyes
Why shou'd itt be in me a thing so vain
To heat with Poetry my colder Brain
But I write ill and there-fore shou'd forbear
Does Flavia cease now at her fortieth year
In ev'ry Place to lett that face be seen
Which all the Town rejected at fifteen
Each Woman has her weaknesse; mind [sic] indeed
Is still to write tho' hoplesse to succeed
Nor to the Men is this so easy found
Ev'n in most Works with which the Witts abound
(So weak are all since our first breach with Heav'n)
Ther's lesse to be Applauded then forgiven.

To The Rt. Hon. The Lady C. Tufton

Upon Addressing to me the first letter that ever she writt at the age of——

To write in Verse has been my pleasing choice
When great Arminda's kindnesse urg'd my voice
Or Madam when in softer Notes I sung
The sweet Serena beautifull and yong
Whil'st euery Muse did chearfully attend
And lent their aid Serena to commend
To speak what in that tender age became
Your blooming Beauty then your cheifest Fame.

On Myselfe

Good Heav'n, I thank thee, since it was design'd
I shou'd be fram'd, but of the weaker kinde,
That yet, my Soul, is rescu'd from the Love
Of all those Trifles, which their Passions move.
Pleasures, and Praise, and Plenty haue with me
But their just value.   If allow'd they be,
Freely, and thankfully as much I tast,
As will not reason, or Religion wast.
If they're deny'd, I on my selfe can Liue,
And slight those aids, unequal chance does give.
When in the Sun, my wings can be display'd,
And in retirement, I can bless the shade.

A Letter to Dafnis
April: 2d 1685

This to the Crown, and blessing of my life,
The much lov'd husband, of a happy wife.
To him, whose constant passion found the art
To win a stubborn, and ungratefull heart;
And to the World, by tend'rest proof discovers
They err, who say that husbands can't be lovers.
With such return of passion, as is due,
Daphnis I love, Daphnis my thoughts persue,
Daphnis, my hopes, my joys, are bounded all in you:
Ev'n I, for Daphnis, and my promise sake,
What I in women censure, undertake.
But this from love, not vanity, proceeds;
You know who writes; and I who 'tis that reads.
Judge not my passion, by my want of skill,
Many love well, though they express itt ill;
And I your censure cou'd with pleasure bear,
Wou'd you but soon return, and speak itt here.

Clarinda's Indifference at
Parting With Her Beauty

Now, age came on, and all the dismal traine
That fright the vitious, and afflicte the vaine.
Departing beauty, now Clarinda spies
Pale in her cheeks, and dying in her eyes;
That youthfull air, that wanders ore the face,
That undescrib'd, that unresisted grace,
Those morning beams, that strongly warm, and shine,
Which men that feel and see, can ne're define,
Now, on the wings of restlesse time, were fled,
And ev'ning shades, began to rise, and spread,
When thus resolv'd, and ready soon to part,
Slighting the short repreives of proffer'd art
She spake—
And what, vain beauty, didst thou 'ere atcheive,
When at thy height, that I thy fall shou'd greive,
When, did'st thou e're successfully persue?
When, did'st thou e're th' appointed foe subdue?
'Tis vain of numbers, of strength to boast,
In an undisciplin'd, unguided Host,
And love, that did thy mighty hopes deride,
Wou'd pay no sacrafice, but to thy pride.
When did'st thou e're a pleasing rule obtain,
A glorious Empire's but a glorious pain,
Thou, art indeed, but vanity's cheife sourse,
But foyle to witt, to want of witt a curse,
For often, by thy gaudy sign's descry'd
A fool, which unobserv'd, had been untry'd,
And when thou doest such empty things adorn,
'Tis but to make them more the publick scorn.
I know thee well, but weak thy reign wou'd be
Did n'one adore, or prize thee more then me.
I see indeed, thy certain ruine neer,
But can't affoard one parting sigh, or tear,
Nor rail at Time, nor quarrell with my glasse,
But unconcern'd, can lett thy glories passe.

The Petition For
An Absolute Retreat

Inscribed to the Right Honble Catharine
Countess of Thanet, mention'd in the Poem
under the Name of Arminda

Give me O indulgent Fate!
Give me yet, before I Dye,
A sweet, but absolute Retreat,
'Mongst Paths so lost, and Trees so high,
That the World may ne'er invade,
Through such Windings and such Shade,
My unshaken Liberty.

   No Intruders thither come!
Who visit, but to be from home;
None who their vain Moments pass,
Only studious of their Glass,
News, that charm to listning Ears;
That false Alarm to Hopes and Fears;
That common Theme for every Fop,
From the Statesman to the Shop,
In those Coverts ne'er be spread,
Of who's Deceas'd, or who's to Wed,
Be no Tidings thither brought
But silent, as a Midnight Thought,
Where the World may ne'er invade,
Be those Windings, and that Shade:

   Courteous Fate! afford me there
A *Table* spread without my Care,
With what the neighb'ring Fields impart,
Whose Cleanliness be all it's Art,
When, of old, the Calf was drest,
(Tho' to make an Angel's Feast)
In the plain, unstudied Sauce
Nor *Treufle*, nor *Morillia* was;
Nor cou'd the mighty Patriarch's Board
One far-fetch'd *Ortolane* afford.
Courteous Fate, then give me there
Only plain, and wholesome Fare.
Fruits indeed (wou'd Heaven bestow)
All, that did in *Eden* grow,
All, but the *Forbidden Tree*,
Wou'd be coveted by me;
Grapes with Juice so crouded up,
As breaking thro' the native Cup;
Figs (yet growing) candy'd o'er,
By the Sun's attracting Pow'r;
Cherries, with the downy Peach,
All within my easie Reach;
Whilst creeping near the humble Ground,
Shou'd the Strawberry be found
Springing wheresoe'er I stray'd,
Thro' those Windings and that Shade.

   For my *Garments;* let them be
What may with the Time agree;
Warm, when *Phœbus* does retire,
And is ill-supply'd by Fire:
But when he renews the Year,
And verdant all the Fields appear;

65

Beauty every thing resumes,
Birds have dropt their Winter-Plumes;
When the Lilly full display'd,
Stands in purer White array'd,
Than that Vest, which heretofore
The Luxurious Monarch wore,
When from *Salem's* Gates he drove,
To the soft Retreat of Love,
Lebanon's all burnish'd House,
And the dear *Egyptian* Spouse.
Cloath me, Fate, tho' not so Gay;
Cloath me light, and fresh as *May:*
In the Fountains let me view
All my Habit cheap and new;
Such as, when sweet *Zephyrs* fly,
With their Motions may comply;
Gently waving, to express
Unaffected Carelesness:
No Perfumes have there a Part,
Borrow'd from the *Chymists* Art;
But such as rise from flow'ry Beds,
Or the falling *Jasmin* Sheds!
'Twas the Odour of the Field,
Esau's rural Coat did yield,
That inspir'd his Father's Pray'r,
For Blessings of the Earth and Air:
Of Gums, or Pouders had it smelt;
The Supplanter, then unfelt,
Easily had been descry'd,
For one that did in Tents abide;
For some beauteous Handmaids Joy,
And his Mother's darling Boy.
Let me then no Fragrance wear,
But what the Winds from Gardens bear,
In such kind, surprizing Gales,
As gather'd from *Fidentia's* Vales,
All the Flowers that in them grew;
Which intermixing, as they flew,
In wreathen Garlands dropt agen,
On *Lucullus*, and his Men;
Who, chear'd by the victorious Sight,
Trebl'd Numbers put to Flight.
Let me, when I must be fine,
In such natural Colours shine;
Wove, and painted by the Sun,
Whose resplendent Rays to shun,
When they do too fiercely beat,
Let me find some close Retreat,
Where they have no Passage made,
Thro' those Windings, and that Shade.

    Give me there (since Heaven has shown
It was not Good to be alone)
A *Partner* suited to my Mind,
Solitary, pleas'd and kind;

Who, partially, may something see
Preferr'd to all the World in me;
Slighting, by my humble Side,
Fame and Splendor, Wealth and Pride.
When but Two the Earth possest,
'Twas their happiest Days, and best;
They by Bus'ness, nor by Wars,
They by no Domestick Cares,
From each other e'er were drawn,
But in some Grove, or flow'ry Lawn,
Spent the Swiftly flying Time,
Spent their own, and Nature's Prime,
In Love; that only Passion given
To perfect Man, whilst Friends with Heaven.
Rage, and Jealousie, and Hate,
Transports of his fallen State,
(When by *Satan's* Wiles betray'd)
Fly those Windings, and that Shade!

   Thus from Crouds, and Noise remov'd,
Let each Moment be improv'd;
Every Object still produce,
Thoughts of Pleasure and of Use:
When some River slides away,
To encrease the boundless Sea;
Think we then, how Time do's haste,
To grow Eternity at last,
By the Willows, on the Banks,
Gather'd into social Ranks,
Playing with the gentle Winds,
Strait the Boughs, and smooth the Rinds,
Moist each Fibre, and each Top,
Wearing a luxurious Crop,
Let the time of Youth be shown,
The time alas! too soon outgrown;
Whilst a lonely stubborn Oak,
Which no Breezes can provoke,
No less Gusts persuade to move,
Than those, which in a Whirlwind drove,
Spoil'd the old Fraternal Feast,
And left alive but one poor Guest;
Rivell'd the distorted Trunk,
Sapless Limbs all bent, and shrunk,
Sadly does the Time presage,
Of our too near approaching Age.
When a helpless Vine is found,
Unsupported on the Ground,
Careless all the Branches spread,
Subject to each haughty Tread,
Bearing neither Leaves, nor Fruit,
Living only in the Root;
Back reflecting let me say,
So the sad *Ardelia* lay;
Blasted by a Storm of Fate,
Felt, thro' all the *British* State;

Fall'n, neglected, lost, forgot,
Dark Oblivion all her Lot;
Faded till *Arminda's* Love,
(Guided by the Pow'rs above)
Warm'd anew her drooping Heart,
And Life diffus'd thro' every Part;
Mixing Words, in wise Discourse,
Of such Weight and wond'rous Force,
As could all her Sorrows charm,
And transitory Ills disarm;
Chearing the delightful Day,
When dispos'd to be more Gay,
With Wit, from an unmeasured Store,
To Woman ne'er allow'd before.
What Nature, or refining Art,
All that Fortune cou'd impart,
Heaven did to *Arminda* send;
Then gave her for *Ardelia's* Friend:
To her Cares the Cordial drop,
Which else had overflow'd the Cup.
So, when once the Son of *Jess*,
Every Anguish did oppress,
Hunted by all kinds of Ills,
Like a *Partridge* on the Hills;
Trains were laid to catch his Life,
Baited with a Royal Wife,
From his House, and Country torn,
Made a Heathen Prince's Scorn;
Fate, to answer all these Harms,
Threw a *Friend* into his Arms.
Friendship still has been design'd,
The Support of Human-kind;
The safe Delight, the useful Bliss,
The next World's Happiness, and this.
Give then, O indulgent Fate!
Give a Friend in that Retreat
(Tho' withdrawn from all the rest)
Still a Clue, to reach my Breast.
Let a Friend be still convey'd
Thro' those Windings, and that Shade!

   Where, may I remain secure,
Waste, in humble Joys and pure,
A Life, that can no Envy yield;
Want of Affluence my Shield.
Thus, had *Crassus* been content,
When from *Marius* Rage he went,
With the Seat that Fortune gave,
The commodious ample Cave,
Form'd, in a divided Rock,
By some mighty Earthquake's Shock,
Into Rooms of every Size,
Fair, as Art cou'd e'er devise,
Leaving, in the marble Roof,
('Gainst all Storms and Tempests proof)

Only Passage for the Light,
To refresh the chearful Sight,
Whilst Three Sharers in his Fate,
On th' Escape with Joy dilate,
Beds of Moss their Bodies bore,
Canopy'd with Ivy o'er;
Rising Springs, that round them play'd
O'er the native Pavement stray'd;
When the Hour arriv'd to Dine,
Various Meats, and sprightly Wine,
On some neighb'ring Cliff they spy'd;
Every Day a-new supply'd
By a Friend's entrusted Care;
Had He still continu'd there,
Made that lonely wond'rous Cave
Both his Palace, and his Grave;
Peace and Rest he might have found,
(Peace and Rest are under Ground)
Nor have been in that Retreat,
Fam'd for a Proverbial Fate;
In pursuit of Wealth been caught,
And punish'd with a golden Draught.
Nor had He, who Crowds cou'd blind,
Whisp'ring with a snowy Hind,
Made 'em think that from above,
(Like the great Impostor's Dove)
Tydings to his Ears she brought,
Rules by which he march'd and fought,
After *Spain* he had o'er-run,
Cities sack'd, and Battles won,
Drove *Rome's* Consuls from the Field,
Made her darling *Pompey* yield,
At a fatal, treacherous Feast,
Felt a Dagger in his Breast;
Had he his once-pleasing Thought
Of Solitude to Practice brought;
Had no wild Ambition sway'd;
In those Islands had he stay'd,
Justly call'd the Seats of Rest,
Truly Fortunate, and Blest,
By the ancient Poets giv'n
As their best discover'd Heav'n.
Let me then, indulgent Fate!
Let me still, in my Retreat,
From all roving Thoughts be freed,
Or Aims, that may Contention breed:
Nor be my Endeavours led
By Goods, that perish with the Dead!
Fitly might the Life of Man
Be indeed esteem'd a Span,
If the present Moment were
Of Delight his only Share;
If no other Joys he knew
Than what round about him grew:
But as those, who Stars wou'd trace
From a subterranean Place,

Through some Engine lift their Eyes
To the outward, glorious Skies;
So th' immortal Spirit may,
When descended to our Clay,
From a rightly govern'd Frame
View the Height, from whence she came;
To her Paradise be caught,
And things unutterable taught.
Give me then, in that Retreat,
Give me, O indulgent Fate!
For all Pleasures left behind,
Contemplations of the Mind.
Let the Fair, the Gay, the Vain
Courtship and Applause obtain;
Let th' Ambitious rule the Earth;
Let the giddy Fool have Mirth;
Give the Epicure his Dish,
Ev'ry one their sev'ral Wish;
Whilst my Transports I employ
On that more extensive Joy,
When all Heaven shall be survey'd
From those Windings and that Shade.

To The Nightingale

Exert thy Voice, sweet Harbinger of Spring!
   This Moment is thy Time to sing,
   This Moment I attend to Praise,
And set my Numbers to thy Layes.
   Free as thine shall be my Song;
   As thy Musick, short, or long.
Poets, wild as thee, were born,
   Pleasing best when unconfin'd,
   When to Please is least design'd,
Soothing but their Cares to rest;
   Cares do still their Thoughts molest,
   And still th' unhappy Poet's Breast,
Like thine, when best he sings, is plac'd against a Thorn.
She begins, Let all be still!
   Muse, thy Promise now fulfill!
Sweet, oh! sweet, still sweeter yet
Can thy Words such Accents fit,
Canst thou Syllables refine,
Melt a Sense that shall retain
Still some Spirit of the Brain,
Till with Sounds like these it join.
   'Twill not be! then change thy Note;
   Let division shake thy Throat.
Hark! Division now she tries;
Yet as far the Muse outflies.
   Cease then, prithee, cease thy Tune;
   Trifler, wilt thou sing till *June?*
Till thy Bus'ness all lies waste,
And the Time of Building's past!
   Thus we Poets that have Speech,
Unlike what thy Forests teach,

> If a fluent Vein be shown
> That's transcendent to our own,
> Criticize, reform, or preach,
> Or censure what we cannot reach.

A Nocturnal Reverie

In such a *Night*, when every louder Wind
Is to its distant Cavern safe confin'd;
And only gentle *Zephyr* fans his Wings,
And lonely *Philomel*, still waking, sings;
Or from some Tree, fam'd for the *Owl's* delight,
She, hollowing clear, directs the Wand'rer right:
In such a *Night,* when passing Clouds give place,
Or thinly vail the Heav'ns mysterious Face;
When in some River, overhung with Green,
The waving Moon and trembling Leaves are seen;
When freshen'd Grass now bears it self upright,
And makes cool Banks to pleasing Rest invite,
Whence springs the *Woodbind*, and the *Bramble*-Rose,
And where the sleepy *Cowslip* shelter'd grows;
Whilst now a paler Hue the *Foxglove* takes,
Yet checquers still with Red the dusky brakes
When scatter'd *Glow-worms*, but in Twilight fine,
Shew trivial Beauties watch their Hour to shine;
Whilst *Salisb'ry* stands the Test of every Light,
In perfect Charms, and perfect Virtue bright:
When Odours, which declin'd repelling Day,
Thro' temp'rate Air uninterrupted stray;
When darken'd Groves their softest Shadows wear,
And falling Waters we distinctly hear;
When thro' the Gloom more venerable shows
Some ancient Fabrick, awful in Repose,
While Sunburnt Hills their swarthy Looks conceal,
And swelling Haycocks thicken up the Vale:
When the loos'd *Horse* now, as his Pasture leads,
Comes slowly grazing thro' th' adjoining Meads,
Whose stealing Pace, and lengthen'd Shade we fear,
Till torn up Forage in his Teeth we hear:
When nibbling *Sheep* at large pursue their Food,
And unmolested Kine rechew the Cud;
When *Curlews* cry beneath the Village-walls,
And to her straggling Brood the *Partridge* calls;
Their shortliv'd Jubilee the Creatures keep,
Which but endures, whilst Tyrant-*Man* do's sleep;
When a sedate Content the Spirit feels,
And no fierce Light disturb, whilst it reveals;
But silent Musings urge the Mind to seek
Something, too high for Syllables to speak;
Till the free Soul to a compos'dness charm'd
Finding the Elements of Rage disarm'd,
O'er all below a solemn Quiet grown,
Joys in th' inferiour World, and thinks it like her Own:
In such a *Night* let Me abroad remain,
Till Morning breaks, and All's confus'd again;
Our Cares, our Toils, our Clamours are renew'd,
Or Pleasures, seldom reach'd, again pursu'd.

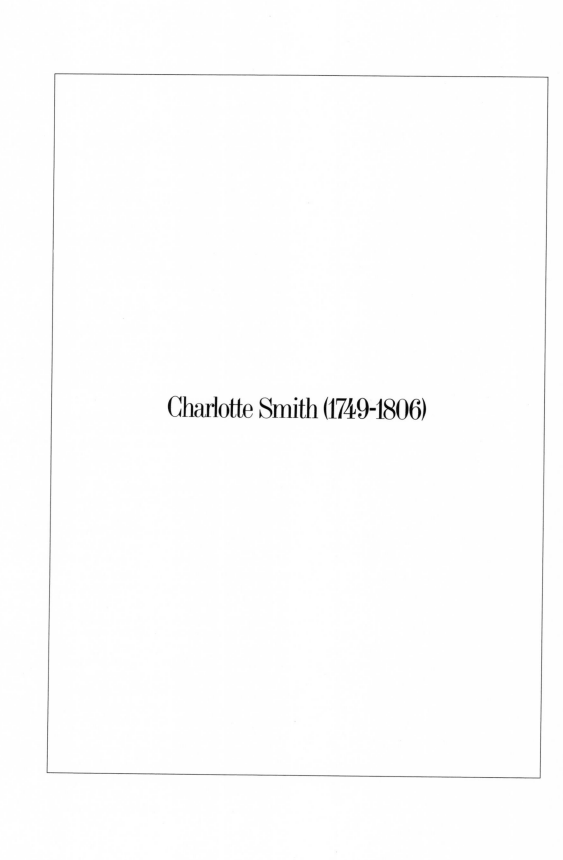

Charlotte Smith (1749-1806)

THE EIGHTEENTH CENTURY gradually brought about a change in the status of women authors: it became more common to find middle-class women who wrote for a living. In England Constantia Grierson edited the Latin classics and Laetitia Pilkington, a friend of Swift, published her memoirs in order to keep herself out of debt. Phillis Wheatley tried, and failed, to support her family by publishing a second book of poems. Female authorship was a chancy thing, but women now turned to it as one of the only respectable professions open to them. Prose fiction and drama brought in more money than poetry.

Like many precocious literary talents Charlotte Smith's first efforts were in verse, but when it became a matter of survival she turned to prose. Charlotte was the daughter of Nicholas Turner, a wealthy Londoner. Her comfortable childhood was spent at Bignor Park in Sussex and the South Coast of England is the landscape for much of her poetry. At sixteen Charlotte married Benjamin Smith, the son of a London merchant. It might have been a good match, but Benjamin's extravagance brought him to bankruptcy and debtor's prison, where the faithful Charlotte stayed with him. Debt was a constant factor in the relationship, as was childbirth. Their tenth child was born in 1785; the year before Charlotte had had her *Elegiac Sonnets and Other Essays* published in the hope of realizing some profit from it. In 1785 she started to write prose fiction and in the next two decades she produced over twenty books.

Charlotte's work reflects the political, philosophical and literary currents which flowed through late Georgian England. She admired Richardson but thought Fielding the master of the novel. Fanny Burney was a strong influence on her prose, Aphra Behn perhaps a more remote one. Like Mrs. Behn, Charlotte introduced descriptions of nature into her stories and two of her novels attack the evils of slavery. Although Anne Radcliffe, the Gothic novelist, was her junior by some years, their periods of heaviest publication coincided in the late 1780's and early 1790's. Charlotte Smith used Gothic devices in a few books, particularly in drawing her backgrounds, but as with Mrs. Radcliffe all supernatural events were given rational explanations. Smith's heroines are educated, virtuous and artistic, but they are considerably sturdier than Mrs. Radcliffe's women, who had those passive qualities which seemed so essential in the stereotypical nineteenth-century heroine. Rousseau was Mrs. Smith's favorite author, though she declined to read *The Confessions*, or anything which seemed to "prove his life contradictory to his principles." A love of nature, an attraction to primitivism, and belief in social democracy run through all her writing. In her novels she criticizes privilege and the British constitution and defends oppressed womanhood. Human and physical "nature" become, in her writing, a lever against unjust and corrupt civilization. In her prose the influence of Rousseau shows most clearly in her social beliefs. *Desmond* includes a plea for female education and autonomy. When, in *Emmeline*, Mrs. Smith allows the victim of a forced marriage to marry her commoner lover, the critic for the *Analytical Review* (July, 1788) was shocked. Yet Mrs. Smith was no revolutionary, sexual or political. Rather, she was infected with the general enthusiasm that the American and French revolutions provoked in Whig England.

In spite of the increasing participation of women in the world of letters, the early Romantic English poets were men. When women were involved in the Romantic movement they were often the relatives of male poets. Yet in the prose genres women were beginning to excel. Virginia Woolf reckons that this was because the novel was a "new" form, created as much by women as by men, and certainly an expanded female audience for fiction helped aspiring women authors. One must reach, however, for a more complex explanation which takes into account the disparity between the philosophy of the Romantic movement and the real situation of the women who were attracted to it. Charlotte Smith, for example, was well born and well educated but she was no more emancipated from domestic responsibility than Anne Bradstreet, who also married at sixteen and raised a large family. Charlotte Smith's initial attraction to literature may have been similar to the "irresistible impulse" that Anne Finch described, but it soon became an economic necessity. In *Beachy Head*, her major poem, Smith calls herself

> *An early worshiper at Nature's shrine,*
> *I loved her rudest scenes—warrens, and*
>   *heaths,*
> *And yellow commons, and birch-shaded*
>   *hollows....*

This predilection for the wild Sussex countryside is part of an idealization of childhood.

> *I once was happy when, while yet a child,*
> *I learned to love these upland solitudes ...*
>   *To my light spirit care was yet*
>   *unknown,*
> *And evil unforseen:—early it came,*
> *And childhood scarcely past, I was*
>   *condemned,*
> *A guiltless exile, silently to sight. . . .*

There is, of course, a connection between these sentiments and Katherine Philips's and Anne Finch's preference for the country. A desire to get out of society was associated from the seventeenth century onward with the artless, unworldly and sensitive women of whom these highly moral ladies approved. In Mrs. Smith's case the nostalgia is biographically rooted. Behind it lies a deep urge to return to childhood and perhaps even a pre-sexual state, not merely a fancy to retreat from the responsibilities and social inanities of town life. Rousseau's primitivism and "nature" as an ideal environment had a sexually determined meaning for Mrs. Smith that it could not have for Wordsworth, Coleridge or Keats. The intellectual influences on her work were the same as those which worked upon all the novelists and poets of the nineties; her novels are linked in plot, device and attitudes with those of most of her contemporaries and particularly those who, like William Godwin and Bage, were ardent Republicans. The novel presented a social situation in which women's lack of freedom could be demonstrated through plot, and desired changes in social attitudes indicated by the manipulation of characters and the working out of their fates. The author's individual stake in such reforms was less obvious than in poetry where the poet's identification with the "speaker" is closer, particularly as personal lyric poetry came back into fashion with the

Romantics. The female poet, contemplating nature along with her contemporaries, saw the freedom of wild nature in contrast to, rather than in harmony with, her own possibilities.

This predicament is especially clear in Charlotte Smith's poetry, but the problem is not confined to her. A highly ambivalent attitude toward nature characterizes the work of most of the late Romantic women poets. In *Beachy Head* there is a central definition of the romantic conception of nature and its relation to reason:

> And they who reason, with abhorrence see
> Man, for such gaudes and baubles, violate
> The sacred freedom of his fellow man—
> Erroneous estimate! As Heaven's pure air,
> Fresh as it blows on this aerial height,
> Or sound of seas upon the stony strand,
> Or inland, the gay harmony of birds,
> And winds that wander in the leafy woods;
> Are to the unadulterate taste more worth
> Than the elaborate harmony, brought out
> from fretted stop, or modulated airs
> Of vocal science.—

Yet even so optimistic a statement leads inexorably to contemplation of the mutability of happiness and to a belief in death as the only release. One must strongly resist the notion that there is anything biological in women's attraction to the gloomier tracks of romantic feeling. "Melancholy," Anne Finch's "inveterate foe," was on the increase as a theme a century after she wrote of it, and it was socially, not sexually, determined. When, in *Beachy Head*, Charlotte Smith envies the peasant girl, it is because she is free of middle-class female anxiety which produced depression.

Charlotte Smith's fresh emphasis on nature in her sonnets and longer poems was taken up by dozens of inferior women poets in the century to follow. The *Elegiac Sonnets* ran through eleven editions by 1851. Nature, and all it had came to stand for in the popular imagination, was also an approved subject for nice girls to write verses on. Women's novels moved away from pure gothic melodrama and towards ever greater psychological and social realism. Poetry, on the other hand, had come to be almost wholly identified with the representation of feeling. It soon became masked in a collection of sentimental attitudes about death, nature, childhood and love which it would be caricature to call Romantic. Until the two great mid-century Romantics, Elizabeth Barrett Browning and Emily Dickinson, women poets after Charlotte Smith were unable to come at the raw experience of the frustrated female ego head on. Charlotte Smith almost succeeds in this. She grew up and was educated in a pre-industrial world which had not yet refined its methods of social control. For women social control meant the normative modes of behavior and feeling now called Victorian. In the 1790's it was beginning to operate on women who, like Charlotte Smith's heroines and their creator, were increasingly beautiful, bright, educated, potentially rebellious, and—her favorite word—in despair.

From: **Beachy Head**

On thy stupendous summit, rock sublime!
That o'er the channel rear'd, half way at sea
The mariner at early morning hails,
I would recline; while Fancy should go forth,
And represent the strange and awful hour
Of vast concussion; when the Omnipotent
Stretch'd forth his arm, and rent the solid hills,
Bidding the impetuous main flood rush between
The rifted shores, and from the continent
Eternally divided this green isle.
Imperial lord of the high southern coast!
From thy projecting head-land I would mark
Far in the east the shades of night disperse,
Melting and thinned, as from the dark blue wave
Emerging, brilliant rays of arrowy light
Dart from the horizon; when the glorious sun
Just lifts above it his resplendent orb.
Advances now, with feathery silver touched,
The rippling tide of flood; glisten the sands,
While, inmates of the chalky clefts that scar
Thy sides precipitous, with shrill harsh cry,
Their white wings glancing in the level beam,
The terns, and gulls, and tarrocks, seek their food,
And thy rough hollows echo to the voice
Of the gray choughs, and ever restless daws,
With clamour, not unlike the chiding hounds,
While the lone shepherd, and his baying dog,
Drive to thy turfy crest his bleating flock.

The high meridian of the day is past,
And Ocean now, reflecting the calm Heaven,
Is of cerulean hue; and murmurs low
The tide of ebb, upon the level sands.
The sloop, her angular canvas shifting still,
Catches the light and variable airs
That but a little crisp the summer sea,
Dimpling its tranquil surface.

                      Afar off,
And just emerging from the arch immense
Where seem to part the elements, a fleet
Of fishing vessels stretch their lesser sails;
While more remote, and like a dubious spot
Just hanging in the horizon, laden deep,
The ship of commerce richly freighted, makes
Her slower progress, on her distant voyage,
Bound to the orient climates, where the sun
Matures the spice within its odorous shell,
And, rivalling the gray worm's filmy toil,
Bursts from its pod the vegetable down;
Which in long turban'd wreaths, from torrid heat
Defends the brows of Asia's countless casts.
There the Earth hides within her glowing breast
The beamy adamant, and the round pearl

Enchased in rugged covering; which the slave,
With perilous and breathless toil, tears off
From the rough sea-rock, deep beneath the waves.
These are the toys of Nature; and her sport
Of little estimate in Reason's eye:
And they who reason, with abhorrence see
Man, for such gaudes and baubles, violate
The sacred freedom of his fellow man—
Erroneous estimate! As Heaven's pure air,
Fresh as it blows on this aërial height,
Or sound of seas upon the stony strand,
Or inland, the gay harmony of birds,
And winds that wander in the leafy woods;
Are to the unadulterate taste more worth
Than the elaborate harmony, brought out
From fretted stop, or modulated airs
Of vocal science.—So the brightest gems,
Glancing resplendent on the regal crown,
Or trembling in the high born beauty's ear,
Are poor and paltry, to the lovely light
Of the fair star, that as the day declines,
Attendant on her queen, the crescent moon,
Bathes her bright tresses in the eastern wave.
For now the sun is verging to the sea,
And as he westward sinks, the floating clouds
Suspended, move upon the evening gale,
And gathering round his orb, as if to shade
The insufferable brightness, they resign
Their gauzy whiteness; and more warm'd, assume
All hues of purple. There, transparent gold
Mingles with ruby tints, and sapphire gleams,
And colours, such as Nature through her works
Shews only in the ethereal canopy.
Thither aspiring Fancy fondly soars,
Wandering sublime thro' visionary vales,
Where bright pavilions rise, and trophies, fann'd
By airs celestial; and adorn'd with wreaths
Of flowers that bloom amid elysian bowers.
Now bright, and brighter still the colours glow,
Till half the lustrous orb within the flood
Seems to retire: the flood reflecting still
Its splendor, and in mimic glory drest;
Till the last ray shot upward, fires the clouds
With blazing crimson; then in paler light,
Long lines of tenderer radiance, lingering yield
To partial darkness; and on the opposing side
The early moon distinctly rising, throws
Her pearly brilliance on the trembling tide.

       *   *   *

Ah! who *is* happy? Happiness! a word
That like false fire, from marsh effluvia born,
Misleads the wanderer, destin'd to contend
In the world's wilderness, with want or woe—

Yet *they* are happy, who have never ask'd
What good or evil means. The boy
That on the river's margin gaily plays,
Has heard that Death is there—He knows not Death,
And therefore fears it not; and venturing in
He gains a bullrush, or a minnow—then,
At certain peril, for a worthless prize,
A crow's, or raven's nest, he climbs the boll
Of some tall pine; and of his prowess proud,
Is for a moment happy. Are *your* cares,
Ye who despise him, never worse applied?
The village girl is happy, who sets forth
To distant fair, gay in her Sunday suit,
With cherry colour'd knots, and flourish'd shawl,
And bonnet newly purchas'd. So is he
Her little brother, who his mimic drum
Beats, till he drowns her rural lovers' oaths
Of constant faith, and still increasing love;
Ah! yet a while, and half those oaths believ'd,
Her happiness is vanish'd; and the boy
While yet a stripling, finds the sound he lov'd
Has led him on, till he has given up
His freedom, and his happiness together.
I once was happy, when while yet a child,
I learn'd to love these upland solitudes,
And, when elastic as the mountain air,
To my light spirit, care was yet unknown
And evil unforeseen:—Early it came,
And childhood scarcely passed, I was condemned,
A guiltless exile, silently to sigh,
While Memory, with faithful pencil, drew
The contrast; and regretting, I compar'd
With the polluted smoky atmosphere
And dark and stifling streets, the southern hills
That to the setting Sun, their graceful heads
Rearing, o'erlook the frith, where Vecta breaks
With her white rocks, the strong impetuous tide,
When western winds the vast Atlantic urge
To thunder on the coast—Haunts of my youth!
Scenes of fond day dreams, I behold ye yet!
Where 'twas so pleasant by thy northern slopes
To climb the winding sheep-path, aided oft
By scatter'd thorns: whose spiny branches bore
Small woolly tufts, spoils of the vagrant lamb
There seeking shelter from the noon-day sun;
And pleasant, seated on the short soft turf,
To look beneath upon the hollow way
While heavily upward mov'd the labouring wain,
And stalking slowly by, the sturdy hind
To ease his panting team, stopp'd with a stone
The grating wheel.

               Advancing higher still
The prospect widens, and the village church

But little, o'er the lowly roofs around
Rears its gray belfry, and its simple vane;
Those lowly roofs of thatch are half conceal'd
By the rude arms of trees, lovely in spring,
When on each bough, the rosy-tinctur'd bloom
Sits thick, and promises autumnal plenty.
For even those orchards round the Norman farms,
Which, as their owners mark the promis'd fruit,
Console them for the vineyards of the south,
Surpass not these.

                        Where woods of ash, and beech,
And partial copses, fringe the green hill foot,
The upland shepherd rears his modest home,
There wanders by, a little nameless stream
That from the hill wells forth, bright now and clear,
Or after rain with chalky mixture gray,
But still refreshing in its shallow course,
The cottage garden; most for use design'd,
Yet not of beauty destitute. The vine
Mantles the little casement; yet the briar
Drops fragrant dew among the July flowers;
And pansies rayed, and freak'd and mottled pinks
Grow among balm, and rosemary and rue:
There honeysuckles flaunt, and roses blow
Almost uncultured: Some with dark green leaves
Contrast their flowers of pure unsullied white;
Others, like velvet robes of regal state
Of richest crimson, while in thorny moss
Enshrined and cradled, the most lovely, wear
The hues of youthful beauty's glowing cheek. —
With fond regret I recollect e'en now
In Spring and Summer, what delight I felt
Among these cottage gardens, and how much
Such artless nosegays, knotted with a rush
By village housewife or her ruddy maid,
Were welcome to me; soon and simply pleas'd.

An early worshipper at Nature's shrine,
I loved her rudest scenes—warrens, and heaths,
And yellow commons, and birch-shaded hollows,
And hedge rows, bordering unfrequented lanes
Bowered with wild roses, and the clasping woodbine
Where purple tassels of the tangling vetch
With bittersweet, and bryony inweave,
And the dew fills the silver bindweed's cups—
I loved to trace the brooks whose humid banks
Nourish the harebell, and the freckled pagil;
And stroll among o'ershadowing woods of beech,
Lending in Summer, from the heats of noon
A whispering shade; while haply there reclines
Some pensive lover of uncultur'd flowers,
Who, from the tumps with bright green mosses clad,
Plucks the wood sorrel, with its light thin leaves,

Heart-shaped, and triply folded; and its root
Creeping like beaded coral; or who there
Gathers, the copse's pride, anémones,
With rays like golden studs on ivory laid
Most delicate: but touch'd with purple clouds,
Fit crown for April's fair but changeful brow.

Ah! hills so early loved! in fancy still
I breathe your pure keen air; and still behold
Those widely spreading views, mocking alike
The Poet and the Painter's utmost art.
The visionary, nursing dreams like these,
Is not indeed unhappy. Summer woods
Wave over him, and whisper as they wave,
Some future blessings he may yet enjoy.
And as above him sail the silver clouds,
He follows them in thought to distant climes,
Where, far from the cold policy of this,
Dividing him from her he fondly loves,
He, in some island of the southern sea,
May haply build his cane-constructed bower
Beneath the bread-fruit, or aspiring palm,
With long green foliage rippling in the gale.
Oh! let him cherish his ideal bliss—
For what is life, when Hope has ceas'd to strew
Her fragile flowers along its thorny way?
And sad and gloomy are his days, who lives
Of Hope abandon'd!

                    Just beneath the rock
Where Beachy overpeers the channel wave,
Within a cavern mined by wintry tides
Dwelt one, who long disgusted with the world
And all its ways, appear'd to suffer life
Rather than live; the soul-reviving gale,
Fanning the bean-field, or the thymy heath,
Had not for many summers breathed on him;
And nothing mark'd to him the season's change,
Save that more gently rose the placid sea,
And that the birds which winter on the coast
Gave place to other migrants; save that the fog,
Hovering no more above the beetling cliffs
Betray'd not then the little careless sheep
On the brink grazing, while their headlong fall
Near the lone Hermit's flint-surrounded home,
Claim'd unavailing pity; for his heart
Was feelingly alive to all that breath'd;
And outraged as he was, in sanguine youth,
By human crimes, he still acutely felt
For human misery.

                    Wandering on the beach,
He learn'd to augur from the clouds of heaven,
And from the changing colours of the sea,
And sullen murmurs of the hollow cliffs,

Or the dark porpoises, that near the shore
Gambol'd and sported on the level brine
When tempests were approaching: then at night
He listen'd to the wind; and as it drove
The billows with o'erwhelming vehemence
He, starting from his rugged couch, went forth
And hazarding a life, too valueless,
He waded thro' the waves, with plank or pole
Towards where the mariner in conflict dread
Was buffeting for life the roaring surge;
And now just seen, now lost in foaming gulphs,
The dismal gleaming of the clouded moon
Shew'd the dire peril. Often he had snatch'd
From the wild billows, some unhappy man
Who liv'd to bless the hermit of the rocks.
But if his generous cares were all in vain,
And with slow swell the tide of morning bore
Some blue swol'n cor'se to land; the pale recluse
Dug in the chalk a sepulchre—above
Where the dank sea-wrack mark'd the utmost tide,
And with his prayers perform'd the obsequies
For the poor helpless stranger.

       One dark night
The equinoctial wind blew south by west,
Fierce on the shore;—the bellowing cliffs were shook
Even to their stony base, and fragments fell
Flashing and thundering on the angry flood.
At day-break, anxious for the lonely man,
His cave the mountain shepherds visited,
Tho'sand and banks of weeds had choak'd their way—
He was not in it; but his drowned cor'se
By the waves wafted, near his former home
Receiv'd the rites of burial. Those who read
Chisel'd within the rock, these mournful lines,
Memorials of his sufferings, did not grieve,
That dying in the cause of charity
His spirit, from its earthly bondage freed,
Had to some better region fled for ever.

**He may be envied,
who with tranquil breast**

He may be envied, who with tranquil breaſt
 Can wander in the wild and woodland ſcene,
When Summer's glowing hands have newly dreſt
 The ſhadowy foreſts, and the copſes green;
Who, unpurſued by care, can paſs his hours
 Where briony and woodbine fringe the trees,
 On thymy banks repoſing, while the bees
Murmur "their fairy tunes in praiſe of flowers;"
Or on the rock with ivy clad, and fern
 That overhangs the ozier-whiſpering bed
Of ſome clear current, bid his wiſhes turn
 From this bad world; and by calm reaſon led,
Knows, in refined retirement, to poſſeſs
By friendſhip hallow'd—rural happineſs!

Mute is thy wild harp, now, O Bard sublime!

To the shade of Burns

Mute is thy wild harp, now, O Bard sublime!
  Who, amid Scotia's mountain solitude,
Great Nature taught to "build the lofty rhyme,"
  And even beneath the daily pressure, rude,
  Of labouring Poverty, thy generous blood,
  Fired with the love of freedom—Not subdued
Wert thou by thy low fortune: But a time
Like this we live in, when the abject chime
Of echoing Parasite is best approved,
  Was not for thee—Indignantly is fled
Thy noble Spirit; and no longer moved
  By all the ills o'er which thine heart has bled,
Associate, worthy of the illustrious dead,
Enjoys with them "the Liberty it loved."

Press'd by the Moon, mute arbitress of tides

Written in the church-yard at Middleton in Sussex.

Press'd by the Moon, mute arbitress of tides,
  While the loud equinox its power combines,
  The sea no more its swelling surge confines,
But o'er the shrinking land sublimely rides.
The wild blast, rising from the Western cave,
  Drives the huge billows from their heaving bed;
  Tears from their grassy tombs the village dead,
And breaks the silent sabbath of the grave!
With shells and sea-weed mingled, on the shore
  Lo! their bones whiten in the frequent wave;
  But vain to them the winds and waters rave;
They hear the warring elements no more:
While I am doom'd—by life's long storm opprest,
To gaze with envy on their gloomy rest.

Thirty-Eight

Addressed to Mrs. H——y.

In early youth's unclouded scene,
The brilliant morning of eighteen,
With health and sprightly joy elate
  We gazed on life's enchanting spring,
  Nor thought how quickly time would bring
The mournful period——Thirty-eight.

Then the starch maid, or matron sage,
Already of that sober age,
We view'd with mingled scorn and hate;
  In whole sharp words, or sharper face,
  With thoughtless mirth we loved to trace
The sad effects of——Thirty-eight.

Till saddening, sickening at the view,
We learn'd to dread what Time might do;
And then preferr'd a prayer to Fate
  To end our days ere that arrived;
  When (power and pleasure long survived)
We met neglect and——Thirty-eight.

But Time, in fpite of wifhes flies,
And Fate our fimple prayer denies,
And bids us Death's own hour await:
    The auburn locks are mix'd with grey,
    The tranfient rofes fade away,
But Reafon comes at——Thirty-eight.

Her voice the anguifh contradicts
That dying vanity inflicts;
Her hand new pleafures can create,
    For us fhe opens to the view
    Profpects lefs bright—but far more true,
And bids us fmile at——Thirty-eight.

No more fhall *Scandal's* breath deftroy
The focial converfe we enjoy
With bard or critic tête à tête;—
    O'er Youth's bright blooms her blights fhall pour,
    But fpare the improving friendly hour
That Science gives to——Thirty-eight.

Stripp'd of their gaudy hues by Truth,
We view the glitt'ring toys of youth,
And blufh to think how poor the bait
    For which to public fcenes we ran
    And fcorn'd of fober Senfe the plan
Which gives content at——Thirty-eight.

Tho' Time's inexorable fway
Has torn the myrtle bands away,
For other wreaths 'tis not too late,
    The amaranth's purple glow furvives,
    And ftill Minerva's olive lives
On the calm brow of——Thirty-eight.

With eye more fteady we engage
To contemplate approaching age,
And life more juftly eftimate;
    With firmer fouls, and ftronger powers,
    With reafon, faith, and friendfhip ours,
    We'll not regret the ftealing hours
That lead from Thirty——even to Forty-eight.

Phillis Wheatley (c.1753-1784)

IT IS DIFFICULT to understand the forces that led Anne Bradstreet to spend her first years in the wilderness writing verse. We need an even greater imaginative stretch to comprehend the "intrinsic ardor" that led black Phillis Wheatley to write poetry in a world where to be black, female and a slave was to be under the weight of a triple oppression. Phillis was born somewhere on the west coast of Africa. She endured the middle passage and was bought in 1761 by John Wheatley, a Boston tailor, to serve as a domestic in a comfortable household which already had several slaves. Phillis must have shown extraordinary qualities, for Susannah Wheatley, John's wife, quickly decided that she was not to be brought up as a slave, but educated as a daughter. In sixteen months from the time of her purchase she was fluent enough in English to read the Bible. The Wheatleys had acquired a child prodigy in the frail black girl, and they had the sense and kindness to encourage her talents.

With the help of Mrs. Wheatley's daughter Mary (herself a clever, well-educated woman) Phillis was provided with a classical education which would not have disgraced a Harvard undergraduate of the day. In her correspondence with Obour Tanner, a black woman friend who lived in Rhode Island, she speaks mostly about God, health and family. It must have been a relief to Phillis to be able to write to another woman who, like herself, was literate and black.

Like so many of the poets in this collection, Phillis turned to verse early. Her first published poem, "To the University of Cambridge," was written when she was fourteen. This poem is a blank verse injunction to the students of Harvard to accept God and turn their back on "the sable monster." Devout and unexceptional in sentiment as the poem is, there is yet something impish and tough in its conception. For a young black girl to lecture the future governors of the colony on piety required a courage that few adolescent girls in revolutionary America could summon. The poem represents blackness as evil, Africa as a satanic place and the speaker as a convert to light and Christianity. When she revised the poem for publication some years later, Phillis altered this racist attitude as much as she could. She had by then made some black friends and had come to think better of her race. Her initial view of color was probably that held by her owners and was typical of the time; what is amazing is that she struggled against it.

'Twas mercy brought me from my Pagan
land,
Taught my benighted soul to understand
That there's a God, that there's a Saviour
too:
Once I redemption neither sought nore knew.
Some view our sable race with scornful eye.
"Their colour is a diabolic die."
Remember Christians, Negroes, *black as*
Cain,
May be refin'd and join the angelic train.

How much more authentic a voice of blackness this is than Blake's invented ebony infant who cries "And I am black, but O! my soul is white." To the conventional idea in the first four lines that her being sold into slavery saved her for Christ, Phillis adds in the last four lines, an insistence that the reader see the situation from her point of view.

By the time she was seventeen Phillis was a talked-about phenomenon, not only in Boston but throughout the western world. The intellectual capacity of blacks was a favorite topic among Enlightenment gentlemen and ladies, and Phillis became a piece of vital evidence in arguments about "nature versus nurture." Thomas Jefferson uncharitably attributed her inspiration to religion, and would not consider her writing as poetry. Voltaire, among others, disagreed. In 1774 he wrote that "there is right now a Negress who writes excellent verse in English." Her sex was almost as much remarked on as her color. Benjamin Rush, an eminent Philadelphia physician, ardent abolitionist and revolutionary, spoke of her in the 1770's as a girl "whose singular genius and accomplishments are such as not only do honor to her sex but to human nature." His comment on her singularity underscores both the extent of her achievement and the extent to which she was regarded, by her admirers as well as by her detractors, as a sort of freak. Phillis was only too aware of her curious status. When she visited white households in Boston she herself asked to dine at a separate table: whether from pride or humility it is hard to know. Of no specimen of the human race were lower expectations made than of a black woman brought up in bondage. Ministers, merchants and scholars from the Boston area met and spoke with her in order to produce a testimonial that she was not a fake. The emergence of an independent talent in such a situation must be considered little short of miraculous. In fact, the scanty evidence we have suggests that Phillis never passively received the education her owners provided but constantly pressed them for more knowledge.

In 1772 she thought of producing a book. John Wheatley sent her manuscript to Archibald Bell in London, and he in turn showed it to the anti-slavery Countess of Huntingdon, whom Phillis admired. Another black poet and slave, as well as artist, Scipio Moorehead, provided a frontispiece portrait. Partly as a cure for her poor health Phillis sailed to London for the publication of the book and met the reformers of the day. Benjamin Franklin, in England on America's business, waited on "the black poetess." She was interested in politics and eagerly embraced the patriotic cause, as did most of Boston. The trip broadened her horizons and the deference she received impressed her, but she returned early to Boston because Susannah Wheatley was ill. At home Phillis industriously promoted her book, *Poems on Various Subjects Religious and Moral*, which would go through seven editions in the following thirty years.

Susannah Wheatley died when Phillis was only twenty-one, and her death marks the beginning of a decline in Phillis's fortune. She continued to write, notably an adulatory address to Washington, to which the flattered general sent a fulsome reply. In 1778 Phillis took a big step: she married a free black man of some education, John Peters. The marriage soon caused a rift with the Wheatleys; some biographical evidence suggests that John, who was proud but unsuccessful in life, did not allow himself to be included in the affectionate condescension bestowed on Phillis by her foster family. The Peters' were poor; at one time John was jailed for debt and Phillis scrubbed to support her family. She bore three children; two died in infancy, the last when a little older. Through these last sad struggling years she continued to write, but without her white patrons she lost her precarious interest with the white community, which was, in any case, preoccupied by the war. Although the poems were ready, she could not find a publisher for a new book. The manuscript of her last poems was lost; John Peters advertised for it in vain after her death. Phillis died, aged thirty-one, in December 1784.

The poems we have show a considerable talent and vigor of expression. We do not know, and may doubt that Phillis ever got any expert criticism of her verse. This was an undistinguished period in American poetry, so perhaps there were few persons who could have advised her. That she should write at all was phenomenon enough for most acquaintances and friends. She could never be regarded as an ordinary aspiring writer. The poems betray a depth of feeling and strength of character surprising in such a young woman. There is no hint in Phillis's letters to Obour or in her verse that she herself felt the frustration of her particular situation; her nature was such that rebellious feelings were worked out through religion or through strong political sympathy for her race and country.

The opening up of education to women, the rise of a strong lobby for the rights of blacks, and the general liberal heat engendered during the revolutionary period in America helped to bring Phillis into the public eye. One might add that John and Susannah Wheatley were themselves part of a new enlightened middle class which did not assume the inferiority of either women or blacks. Phillis, in marrying John Peters and choosing to become a wife and mother as well as a poet, chose real life instead of life-long performance for the white gentry. Such a restricting role was tolerable in her adolescence. A talented young girl of any color would receive and accept a certain amount of patronizing admiration as a matter of course. That it was *not* tolerable for Phillis, after she was grown and her closest emotional tie to the Wheatley household had been broken by Susannah's death, is made manifest by her marriage. It is even more remarkable, and admirable, that she continued to write in her reduced circumstances. Her whole life and the choices she made in it were indeed an "honor to her sex" and to "human nature."

To the University of Cambridge, in New-England

While an intrinsic ardor prompts to write,
The muses promise to assist my pen;
'Twas not long since I left my native shore
The land of errors, and *Egyptian* gloom:
Father of mercy, 'twas thy gracious hand
Brought me in safety from those dark abodes.

Students, to you 'tis giv'n to scan the heights
Above, to traverse the ethereal space,
And mark the systems of revolving worlds.
Still more, ye sons of science ye receive
The blissful news by messengers from heav'n,
How *Jesus'* blood for your redemption flows.
See him with hands out-stretcht upon the cross;
Immense compassion in his bosom glows;
He hears revilers, nor resents their scorn:
What matchless mercy in the Son of God!
When the whole human race by sin had fall'n,
He deign'd to die that they might rise again,
And share with him in the sublimest skies,
Life without death, and glory without end.

Improve your privileges while they stay,
Ye pupils, and each hour redeem, that bears
Or good or bad report of you to heav'n.
Let sin, that baneful evil to the soul,
By you be shunn'd, nor once remit your guard;
Suppress the deadly serpent in its egg.
Ye blooming plants of human race devine,
An *Ethiop* tells you 'tis your greatest foe;
Its transient sweetness turns to endless pain,
And in immense perdition sinks the soul.

On Being Brought From Africa to America

'Twas mercy brought me from my *Pagan* land,
Taught my benighted soul to understand
That there's a God, that there's a *Saviour* too:
Once I redemption neither sought nor knew.
Some view the sable race with scornful eye,
"Their colour is a diabolic die."
Remember, *Christians, Negroes*, black as *Cain*,
May be refin'd, and join th' angelic strain.

To The Right Honourable William, Earl of Dartmouth, His Majesty's Principal Secretary of State for North America, & C.

Hail, happy day, when, smiling like the morn,
Fair *Freedom* rose *New-England* to adorn:
The northern clime beneath her genial ray,
Dartmouth, congratulates thy blissful sway:
Elate with hope her race no longer mourns,
Each soul expands, each grateful bosom burns,
While in thine hand with pleasure we behold
The silken reins, and *Freedom's* charms unfold.
Long lost to realms beneath the northern skies
She shines supreme, while hated *faction* dies:
Soon as appear'd the *Goddess* long desir'd,

Sick at the view, she lanquish'd and expir'd;
Thus from the splendors of the morning light
The owl in sadness seeks the caves of night.

No more, *America*, in mournful strain
Of wrongs, and grievance unredress'd complain,
No longer shalt thou dread the iron chain,
Which wanton *Tyranny* with lawless hand
Had made, and with it meant t' enslave the land.

Should you, my lord, while you peruse my song,
Wonder from whence my love of *Freedom* sprung,
Whence flow these wishes for the common good,
By feeling hearts alone best understood,
I, young in life, by seeming cruel fate
Was snatch'd from *Afric's* fancy'd happy seat:
What pangs excruciating must molest,
What sorrows labour in my parent's breast?
Steel'd was that soul and by no misery mov'd
That from a father seiz'd his babe belov'd:
Such, such my case. And can I then but pray
Others may never feel tyrannic sway?

For favours past, great Sir, our thanks are due,
And thee we ask thy favours to renew,
Since in thy pow'r, as in thy will before,
To sooth the griefs, which thou did'st once deplore.
May heav'nly grace the sacred sanction give
To all thy works, and thou for ever live
Not only on the wings of fleeting *Fame*,
Though praise immortal crowns the patriot's name,
But to conduct to heav'ns refulgent fane,
May fiery courses sweep th' ethereal plain,
And bear thee upwards to that blest abode,
Where, like the prophet, thou shalt find thy God.

To His Excellency, General Washington

Celestial choir, enthron'd in realms of light,
Columbia's scenes of glorious toils I write.
While freedom's cause her anxious breast alarms,
She flashes dreadful in refulgent arms.
See mother earth her offspring's fate bemoan,
And nations gaze at scenes before unknown;
See the bright beams of heaven's revolving light
Involved in sorrows and the veil of night!

The goddess comes, she moves divinely fair,
Olive and laurel binds her golden hair:
Wherever shines this native of the skies,
Unnumber'd charms and recent graces rise.

Muse! bow propitious while my pen relates
How pour her armies through a thousand gates,
As when Eolus heaven's fair face deforms,
Enwrapp'd in tempest and a night of storms;

Astonish'd ocean feels the wild uproar,
The refluent surges beat the sounding shore;
Or thick as leaves in Autumn's golden reign,
Such, and so many, moves the warrior's train.
In bright array they seek the work of war,
Where high unfurl'd the ensign waves in air.
Shall I to Washington their praise recite?
Enough thou know'st them in the fields of fight.
Thee, first in peace and honours,—we demand
The grace and glory of thy martial band.
Fam'd for thy valour, for thy virtues more,
Hear every tongue thy guardian aid implore!

One century scarce perform'd its destined round,
When Gallic powers Columbia's fury found;
And so may you, whoever dares disgrace
The land of freedom's heaven-defended race!
Fix'd are the eyes of nations on the scales,
For in their hopes Columbia's arm prevails.
Anon Britannia droops the pensive head,
While round increase the rising hills of dead.
Ah! cruel blindness to Columbia's state!
Lament thy thirst of boundless power too late.

Proceed, great chief, with virtue on thy side,
Thy ev'ry action let the goddess guide.
A crown, a mansion, and a throne that shine,
With gold unfading, Washington! be thine.

Liberty and Peace

Lo freedom comes. Th' prescient muse foretold,
All eyes th' accomplish'd prophecy behold:
Her port describ'd, "She moves divinely fair,
Olive and laurel bind her golden hair."
She, the bright progeny of Heaven, descends,
And every grace her sovereign step attends;
For now kind Heaven, indulgent to our prayer,
In smiling peace resolves the din of war.
Fix'd in Columbia her illustrious line,
And bids in thee her future council shine.
To every realm her portals open'd wide,
Receives from each the full commercial tide.
Each art and science now with rising charms,
Th' expanding heart with emulation warns.
E'en great Britannia sees with dread surprise,
And from the dazzling splendors turns her eyes.
Britain, whose navies swept th' Atlantic o'er,
And thunder sent to every distant shore;
E'en thou, in manners cruel as thou art,
The sword resign'd, resume the friendly part.
For Gallia's power espous'd Columbia's cause,
And new-born Rome shall give Britannia laws,
Nor unremember'd in the grateful strain,
Shall princely Louis' friendly deeds remain;

The generous prince th' impending vengeance eyes,
Sees the fierce wrong and to the rescue flies.
Perish that thirst of boundless power, that drew
On Albion's head the curse to tyrants due.
But thou appeas'd submit to Heaven's decree,
That bids this realm of freedom rival thee.
Now sheathe the sword that bade the brave atone
With guiltless blood for madness not their own.
Sent from th' enjoyment of their native shore,
Ill-fated—never to behold her more.
From every kingdom on Europe's coast
Throng'd various troops, their glory, strength, and boast.
With heart-felt pity fair Hibernia saw
Columbia menac'd by the Tyrant's law:
On hostile fields fraternal arms engage,
And mutual deaths, all dealt with mutual rage:
The muse's ear hears mother earth deplore
Her ample surface smoke with kindred gore:
The hostile field destroys the social ties,
And everlasting slumber seals their eyes.
Columbia mourns, the haughty foes deride,
Her treasures plunder'd and her towns destroy'd:
Witness how Charlestown's curling smokes arise,
In sable columns to the clouded skies.
The ample dome, high-wrought with curious toil,
In one sad hour the savage troops despoil.
Descending peace the power of war confounds;
From every tongue celestial peace resounds:
As from the east th' illustrious king of day,
With rising radiance drives the shades away,
So freedom comes array'd with charms divine,
And in her train commerce and plenty shine.
Britannia owns her independent reign,
Hibernia, Scotia and the realms of Spain;
And great Germania's ample coast admires
The generous spirit that Columbia fires.
Auspicious Heaven shall fill with fav'ring gales,
Where e'er Columbia spreads her swelling sails:
To every realm shall peace her charms display,
And heavenly freedom spread her golden ray.

Felicia Hemans (1793-1835)

FELICIA HEMANS was perhaps the most famous female poet of her generation. She is remembered today for one or two patriotic lyrics which, deservedly, still survive in anthologies. Unlike most of the other poets in this collection, a reinspection of her complete works does not turn up many new gems. She is included here because her life and art illustrate the social, psychological and aesthetic problems faced by the increasing numbers of women authors in the nineteenth century. The constraints on Mrs. Hemans were imposed to some extent by literary critics who were chiefly interested in defining, through her verse and that of other women, a limited, passive role for women as persons and poets. Mrs. Hemans, however, met her judges halfway: she internalized and identified with the emerging Victorian stereotype of the pure, long-suffering female.

The symbolic representation of these attributes in verse is complex. *Records of Women*, Felicia Hemans's most important book, attempts a series of semi-historical poems, narrative in form, which present peasant girls, heroic women of title, female artists, Joan of Arc and Indian maidens—all virtuous, all embedded in tragic situations which usually end in death. Barrett Browning transformed her melodramatic material by allowing her women to be violent and amoral; in Hemans the treatment is uniformly sentimental and morally unexceptionable. Yet rolled up in any of Hemans's poems on these themes is a set of contradictory attitudes about the role of women. In her prologue to the "Indian Woman's Death-Song," Hemans tells of "An Indian woman, driven to despair by her husband's desertion of her for another wife, entered a canoe with her children, and rowed it down the Mississippi towards a cataract . . ." In this poem the wife instructs the river: "Roll, dark foaming stream, on to the better shore!" and, Hiawatha-like, she heads towards oblivion. The suicide is excused, of course, since the woman concerned is a pagan. Though she herself is a child of nature, like her civilized sisters she is at the mercy of man, and her feelings are as sensitive as those of the most genteel English wife. Women, it is suggested, have a unity of experience and a fineness of feeling that transcend culture and class. "Natural" society is just as brutal to women as civilized society, and self-destruction is the only recourse. Even in savage culture, self-wounding is the appropriate, if tragic, act of the female victim. The analysis of women's situation is substantially correct. It is the poetic treatment of the event, and the way in which Hemans's sentiment lends a sort of approved normative morality to it, that betrays the extent to which the poet as well as her women protagonists turned their anger inward.

Hemans's personal history was as pathetic if not as dramatic as that of her heroines. She was born Felicia Dorothea Browne in Liverpool on September 25, 1793. Her father was a successful Irish merchant and her mother, an educated woman, was the daughter of the Consul for the Austrian and Tuscan governments. Felicia was the fifth of seven children. Precocious and beautiful, she was encouraged intellectually by her family and given a fairly broad education by her mother. Her photographic memory helped her to memorize verse and learn languages easily, and she read Shakespeare at six. (As an adult she could read at least five languages and she drew well enough to illustrate her own books.) When she was seven her father's business failed and the family moved to Wales, where Felicia spent most of her life. In 1807, when she was fourteen, her first volume of poems was published. While still in her teens she fell in love with Captain Hemans, a poor but handsome and well-educated officer. In 1812 Felicia published another book of poems, *The Domestic Affections*, and in that summer married Hemans. She bore him five sons in quick succession. Sometime in this period Felicia's father emigrated to Quebec in search of a new career and the family went to live at Bronwylfa with Felicia's mother. Captain Hemans, for reasons unknown, also decided to desert his family. In 1818 he went to Italy and never saw his wife again. The official explanation given by the family was that his health had been shattered by the war, but some deeper marital disturbance lay at the root of the separation.

Felicia now turned to writing as a means of support. *The Restoration of Works of Art to Italy* and *Modern Greece* appeared in quick succession, followed by two plays, one of which, *The Vespers of Palermo*, was unsuccessfully produced in London. Three books of poems were collected and published in the 1820's: *Lays of Many Lands* (1824), *Records of Woman* (1828) and *Songs of the Affections* (1830). Mrs. Hemans's mother, to whom she was deeply attached, died in 1827 and the following year her own health failed. By this time she had a considerable following. She was offered the editorship of a Boston periodical. She knew Scott, visited Wordsworth, and was a friend and/or correspondent of other literary women. Felicia left Wales in 1828 so that her son might be educated in a town. After a brief, unhappy residence in Liverpool she moved to Dublin, where she spent her last few years. Her already precarious health was further undermined by her own neglect, and she died after a series of weakening illnesses in 1834.

William Rossetti, who introduces a late nineteenth-century edition of Felicia Hemans's work in the Moxon Popular Poets series, comments that "She had a keen dislike to any sort of coarseness in conversation or in books, and would often tear out peccant pages from volumes in her possession." This description gives rise to an irresistibly comic image: Mrs. Hermans in the act of bowdlerizing her own library. However, it is a key to her inability to make her talent work for her. She was attracted to subjects that were in their essence "coarse," but was forbidden by her upbringing and instincts, as well as by the prejudices of the day, from treating them fully. Unlike Mrs. Browning, she had to make a living from her verse; she had therefore to write quickly, often without revising, and on topics which had already caught the popular taste.

As William Rossetti pointed out, there was a gift "and culture added to the gift." But the poetry, he says, fails "perhaps through a cloying flow of right-minded perceptions of moral and material beauty than through any other defect." Rossetti is caught in an interesting bind when he tries to criticize Hemans's poetry. He recognizes that its flaws are partly culturally imposed but cannot resist ascribing it to female nature. The trouble with Mrs. Hemans's verse, he says, is that it is "female" poetry, and has "the monotone of mere sex."

The operative approving word in contemporary criticism of Mrs. Hemans's poetry was that it was "feminine," a term which embraced, indeed, corseted, all those qualities of which William Rossetti disapproved. Mrs. Hemans attempted a broad range of subjects— she liked history and occasionally tackled biblical themes. She could spot a good story, but the poems almost always emerge as "balmy" rather than "bracing." The bitter, feminine but pre-feminist consciousness is disguised by proper sentiments. The emotions of loss and feelings of betrayal are invested in plots which were foreign to her own experience, and expressed in a stilted language which rarely sustains itself through a whole poem.

Records of Woman is by far her most personal book and the one with the most promising idea behind it. She is best in her public, patriotic poems. A piece like "The Stately Homes of England" is not afflicted with the kind of emotional impediments that mar her other work. For all her faults, Mrs. Hemans ought to be read at length before trying any of the great women poets of the nineteenth century. Her unsuccessful effort to find an individual poetic voice helps us to appreciate the triumphs of Mrs. Browning, Emily Dickinson, Christina Rossetti, Alice Meynell, Emma Lazarus. Her career converts some of her sentiment into fact. We may say of her, as she said of one of her many heroines, that "She met the tempest, meekly brave,/Then turn'd o'erwearied to the grave."

Indian Woman's Death-Song

(An Indian woman, driven to despair by her husband's desertion of her for another wife, entered a canoe with her children, and rowed it down the Mississippi towards a cataract. Her voice was heard from the shore singing a mournful death-song, until overpowered by the sound of the waters in which she perished. The tale is related in Long's "Expedition to the Source of St. Peter's River.")

"Non, je ne puis vivre avec un coeur brisé. If faut que je retrouve la joie, et que je m'unisse aux esprits libres de l'air."
Bride of Messina—Translated by Madame De Stael.

"Let not my child be a girl, for very sad is the life of a woman." The Prairie.

Down a broad river of the western wilds,
Piercing thick forest-glooms, a light canoe
Swept with the current: fearful was the speed
Of the frail bark, as by a tempest's wing
Borne leaf-like on to where the mist of spray
Rose with the cataract's thunder. Yet within,
Proudly, and dauntlessly, and all alone,
Save that a babe lay sleeping at her breast,
A woman stood! Upon her Indian brow
Sat a strange gladness, and her dark hair waved
As if triumphantly. She pressed her child,
In its bright slumber, to her beating heart,
And lifted her sweet voice, that rose awhile
Above the sound of waters, high and clear,
Wafting a wild proud strain—a song of death.

"Roll swiftly to the spirit's land, thou mighty stream and free!
Father of ancient waters, roll! and bear our lives with thee!
The weary bird that storms have tossed would seek the sunshine's calm,
And the deer that hath the arrow's hurt flies to the woods of balm.

"Roll on!—my warrior's eye hath looked upon another's face,
And mine hath faded from his soul, as fades a moonbeam's trace:
My shadow comes not o'er his path, my whisper to his dream,
He flings away the broken reed. Roll swifter yet, thou stream!

"The voice that spoke of other days is hushed within *his* breast,
But *mine* its lonely music haunts, and will not let me rest;
It sings a low and mornful song of gladness that is gone—
I cannot live without that light. Father of waves! roll on!

"Will he not miss the bounding step that met him from the chase?
The heart of love that made his home an ever-sunny place?
The hand that spread the hunter's board, and decked his couch of yore?—
He will not! Roll, dark foaming stream, on to the better shore!

"Some blessed fount amidst the woods of that bright land must flow,
Whose waters from my soul may lave the memory of this woe;
Some gentle wind must whisper there, whose breath may waft away
The burden of the heavy night, the sadness of the day.

"And thou, my babe! though born, like me, for woman's weary lot,
Smile!—to that wasting of the heart, my own! I leave thee not;
Too bright a thing art *thou* to pine in aching love away—
Thy mother bears thee far, young fawn! from sorrow and decay.

"She bears thee to the glorious bowers where none are heard to weep,
And where the unkind one hath no power again to trouble sleep;
And where the soul shall find its youth, as wakening from a dream:
One moment, and that realm is ours. On, on, dark rolling stream!"

The Memorial Pillar

(*On the road-side, between Penrith and Appleby, stands a small pillar, with this inscription:—"This pillar was erected in the year 1656, by Ann, Countess-Dowager of Pembroke, for a memorial of her last parting, in this place, with her good and pious mother, Margaret, Countess-Dowager of Cumberland, on the 2d April 1616."*

*"Hast thou through Eden's wild-wood vales, pursued
   Each mountain scene magnificently rude,
Nor with attention's lifted eye revered
   That modest stone, by pious Pembroke reared,
Which still records, beyond the pencil's power,
   The silent sorrows of a parting hour?"*

ROGERS.

Mother and child! whose blending tears
   Have sanctified the place,
Where, to the love of many years
   Was given one last embrace—
Oh! ye have shrined a spell of power
Deep in your record of that hour!

A spell to waken solemn thought—
   A still, small under tone,
That calls back days of childhood, fraught
   With many a treasure gone;
And smites, perchance, the hidden source,
Though long untroubled—of remorse.

For who, that gazes on the stone
   Which marks your parting spot,
Who but a mother's love hath known—
   The *one* love changing not?
Alas! and haply learned its worth
First with the sound of "Earth to earth!"

But thou, high-hearted daughter! thou,
   O'er whose bright honoured head
Blessings and tears of holiest flow
   E'en here were fondly shed—
Thou from the passion of thy grief,
In its full burst, couldst draw relief.

For, oh! though painful be the excess,
   The might wherewith it swells,
In nature's fount no bitterness
   Of nature's mingling dwells;
And thou hadst not, by wrong or pride,
Poisoned the free and healthful tide.

But didst thou meet the face no more
   Which thy young heart first knew?
And all—was all in this world o'er
   With ties thus close and true?
It was! On earth no other eye
Could give thee back thine infancy.

No other voice could pierce the maze
  Where, deep within thy breast,
The sounds and dreams of other days
  With memory lay at rest;
No other smile to thee could bring
A gladdening, like the breath of spring.

Yet, while thy place of weeping still
  Its lone memorial keeps,
While on thy name, midst wood and hill,
  The quiet sunshine sleeps,
And touches, in each graven line,
Of reverential thought a sign;

Can I, while yet these tokens wear
  The impress of the dead,
Think of the love embodied there
  As of a vision fled?
A perished thing, the joy and flower
And glory of one earthly hour?

Not so!—I will not bow me so
  To thoughts that breathe despair!
A loftier faith we need below,
  Life's farewell words to bear.
Mother and child!—your tears are past—
Surely your hearts have met at last.

Properzia Rossi

(Properzia Rossi (1491?–1530) was a female sculptor of Bologna. She is said to have died of unrequited love for a Roman knight.)

"Tell me no more, no more
Of my soul's lofty gifts! Are they not vain
To quench its haunting thirst for happiness?
Have I not loved, and striven, and failed to bind
One true heart unto me, whereon my own
Might find a resting-place, a home for all
Its burden of affections? I depart,
Unknown, though Fame goes with me; I must leave
The earth unknown. Yet it may be that death
Shall give my name a power to win such tears
As would have made life precious."

I
One dream of passion and of beauty more!
And in its bright fulfilment let me pour
My soul away! Let earth retain a trace
Of that which lit my being, though its race
Might have been loftier far. Yet one more dream!
From my deep spirit one victorious gleam

98

Ere I depart! For thee alone, for thee!
May this last work, this farewell triumph be—
Thou, loved so vainly! I would leave enshrined
Something immortal of my heart and mind,
That yet may speak to thee when I am gone,
Shaking thine inmost bosom with a tone
Of lost affection,—something that may prove
What she hath been, whose melancholy love
On thee was lavished; silent pang and tear,
And fervent song that gushed when none were near,
And dream by night, and weary thought by day,
Stealing the brightness from her life away—
While thou—Awake! not yet within me die!
Under the burden and the agony
Of this vain tenderness—my spirit, wake!
Even for thy sorrowful affection's sake,
Live! in thy work breathe out!—that he may yet,
Feeling sad mastery there, perchance regret
Thine unrequited gift.

II
                    It comes! the power
Within me born flows back—my fruitless dower
That could not win me love. Yet once again
I greet it proudly, with its rushing train
Of glorious images: they throng—they press—
A sudden joy lights up my loneliness—
I shall not perish all!

                    The bright work grows
Beneath my hand, unfolded as a rose,
Leaf after leaf, to beauty; line by line.
I fix my thought, heart, soul, to burn, to shine,
Through the pale marble's veins. It grows!—and now
I give my own life's history to thy brow,
Forsaken Ariadne!—thou shalt wear
My form, my lineaments; but oh! more fair,
Touched into lovelier being by the glow
   Which in me dwells, as by the summer light
All things are glorified. From thee my woe
   Shall yet look beautiful to meet his sight,
When I am passed away. Thou art the mould,
Wherein I pour the fervent thoughts, the untold,
The self-consuming! Speak to him of me,
Thou, the deserted by the lonely sea,
With the soft sadness of thine earnest eye—
Speak to him, lorn one! deeply, mournfully,
Of all my love and grief! Oh! could I throw
Into thy frame a voice—a sweet, and low,
And thrilling voice of song! when he came nigh,

To send the passion of its melody
Through his pierced bosom—on its tones to bear
My life's deep feeling, as the southern air
Wafts the faint myrtle's breath—to rise, to swell,
To sink away in accents of farewell,
Winning but one, *one* gush of tears, whose flow
Surely my parted spirit yet might know,
If love be strong as death!

III
           Now fair thou art,
Thou form, whose life is of my burning heart!
Yet all the vision that within me wrought,
  I cannot make thee. Oh! I might have given
Birth to creations of far nobler thought;
  I might have kindled, with the fire of heaven,
Things not of such as die! But I have been
Too much alone! A heart whereon to lean,
With all these deep affections that o'erflow
My aching soul, and find no shore below;
An eye to be my star; a voice to bring
Hope o'er my path like sounds that breathe of spring:
These are denied me—dreamt of still in vain.
Therefore my brief aspirings from the chain
Are ever but as some wild fitful song,
Rising triumphantly, to die ere long
In dirge-like echoes.

IV
           Yet the world will see
Little of this, my parting work! in thee.
   Thou shalt have fame! Oh, mockery! give the reed
From storms a shelter—give the drooping vine
Something round which its tendrils may entwine—
  Give the parched flower a rain-drop, and the meed
Of love's kind words to woman! Worthless fame!
That in *his* bosom wins not for my name
The abiding place it asked! Yet how my heart,
In its own fairy world of song and art,
Once beat for praise! Are those high longings o'er?
That which I have been can I be no more?
Never! oh, never more! though still thy sky
Be blue as then, my glorious Italy!
And though the music, whose rich breathings fill
Thin air with soul, be wandering past me still;
And though the mantle of thy sunlight streams
Unchanged on forms, instinct with poet-dreams.
Never! oh, never more! Where'er I move,
The shadow of this broken-hearted love
Is on me and around! Too well *they* know

Whose life is all within, too soon and well,
When there the blight hath settled! But I go
  Under the silent wings of peace to dwell;
From the slow wasting, from the lonely pain,
The inward burning of those words—*"in vain,"*
  Seared on the heart—I go. 'Twill soon be past!
Sunshine and song, and bright Italian heaven,
  And thou, oh! thou, on whom my spirit cast
Unvalued wealth—who knowest not what was given
In that devotedness—the sad, and deep,
And unrepaid—farewell! If I could weep
Once, only once, beloved one! on thy breast,
Pouring my heart forth ere I sink to rest!
But that were happiness!—and unto me
Earth's gift is *fame*. Yet I was formed to be
So richly blessed! With thee to watch the sky,
Speaking not, feeling but that thou wert nigh;
With thee to listen, while the tones of song
Swept even as part of our sweet air along—
To listen silently; with thee to gaze
On forms, the deified of olden days—
This had been joy enough; and hour by hour,
From its glad well-springs drinking life and power,
How had my spirit soared, and made its fame
  A glory for thy brow! Dreams, dreams!—the fire
Burns faint within me. Yet I leave my name—
  As a deep thrill may linger on the lyre
When its full chords are hushed—awhile to live,
And one day haply in thy heart revive
Sad thoughts of me. I leave it, with a sound,
A spell o'er memory, mournfully profound;
I leave it, on my country's air to dwell—
Say proudly yet—" *'Twas hers who loved me well!"*

The Landing of The Pilgrim Fathers in New England

"Look now abroad! Another race has fill'd
* Those populous borders—wide the wood recedes,*
And towns shoot up, and fertile realms are till'd;
* The land is full of harvests and green meads."*   BRYANT.

The breaking waves dash'd high
  On a stern and rock-bound coast,
And the woods against a stormy sky
  Their giant branches toss'd;

And the heavy night hung dark
  The hills and waters o'er,
When a band of exiles moor'd their bark
  On the wild New England shore.

Not as the conqueror comes,
    They, the true-hearted, came;
Not with the roll of the stirring drums,
    And the trumpet that sings of fame;

Not as the flying come,
    In silence and in fear;—
They shook the depths of the desert gloom
    With their hymns of lofty cheer.

Amidst the storm they sang,
    And the stars heard and the sea;
And the sounding aisles of the dim woods rang
    To the anthem of the free!

The ocean eagle soar'd
    From his nest by the white wave's foam;
And the rocking pines of the forest roar'd—
    This was their welcome home!

There were men with hoary hair
    Amidst that pilgrim band;—
Why had *they* come to wither there,
    Away from their childhood's land?

There was woman's fearless eye,
    Lit by her deep love's truth;
There was manhood's brow serenely high,
    And the fiery heart of youth.

What sought they thus afar?—
    Bright jewels of the mine?
The wealth of seas, the spoils of war?—
    They sought a faith's pure shrine!

Ay, call it holy ground,
    The soil where first they trode.
They have left unstain'd what there they found—
    Freedom to worship God.

The Homes of England

"Where's the coward that would not dare
To fight for such a land?"   MARMION.

The stately homes of England!
    How beautiful they stand,
Amidst their tall ancestral trees,
    O'er all the pleasant land!
The deer across their greensward bound,
    Through shade and sunny gleam;
And the swan glides past them with the sound
    Of some rejoicing stream.

The merry homes of England!
  Around their hearths by night,
What gladsome looks of household love
  Meet in the ruddy light!
There woman's voice flows forth in song,
  Or childhood's tale is told,
Or lips move tunefully along
  Some glorious page of old.

The blessed homes of England!
  How softly on their bowers
Is laid the holy quietness
  That breathes from Sabbath hours!
Solemn, yet sweet, the church-bell's chime
  Floats through their woods at morn;
All other sounds, in that still time,
  Of breeze and leaf are born.

The cottage homes of England!
  By thousands on her plains,
They are smiling o'er the silvery brooks,
  And round the hamlet fanes.
Through glowing orchards forth they peep,
  Each from its nook of leaves;
And fearless there the lowly sleep,
  As the bird beneath their eaves.

The free, fair homes of England!
  Long, long, in hut and hall,
May hearts of native proof be rear'd
  To guard each hallow'd wall!
And green for ever be the groves,
  And bright the flowery sod,
Where first the child's glad spirit loves
  Its country and its God!

Elizabeth Barrett Browning (1806-1861)

THE ROMANCE surrounding Elizabeth Barrett's life and the continuing popularity of her love poems, *Sonnets from the Portuguese*, are, ironically, the surviving legacy of one of England's great Victorian poets, who was a serious candidate for Poet Laureate on Wordsworth's death in 1850. The most important poems of her maturity were political and feminist, and she was preoccupied with the liberation of Italy, anti-slavery and the role of women. It is in the context of these concerns that her justly famous love poems to Browning ought to be read—side by side with *Casa Guidi Windows* (1851), *Aurora Leigh* (1856), *Poems Before Congress* (1860), and *Last Poems* (1862). Unfortunately, these poems are rarely read today. Elizabeth's personal history provided the public with a story as compelling as *Jane Eyre* or *Wuthering Heights*. The legend of the invalid lady in ringlets, rescued from the tyranny of a super-Victorian parent by a dashing young lover, was the raw material for nineteenth-century melodrama, and it survived the real figure of the poet-crusader for unpopular causes. The legend's durability has conspired with critical prejudice to insult both Mrs. Browning's life and art. As a result, the highly unorthodox ways in which Elizabeth viewed her marriage and her role in it are lost or perverted.

Edward Moulton Barrett, Elizabeth's father, owed his considerable fortune to family plantations in Jamaica. Elizabeth always shrank from the family connection with slavery, but it surfaces when she says that her autocratic father treated his children as "chattels." His eldest daughter was born at Coxhoe Hall, Durham on March 6, 1806; ten more children would follow. Mary Barrett, the weak mother, was not a personal model for her precocious daughter. Elizabeth describes her with sympathy, pity and telling distance as "one of those women who can never resist, but in submitting and bowing themselves, make a mark, a plait, within—a sign of suffering." In *Aurora Leigh* she elaborates her attitude on nineteenth-century models of femininity:

> By the way,
> The works of women are symbolical,
> We sew, sew, prick our fingers, dull our sight.
> Producing what? A pair of slippers, sir,
> To put on when you're weary—or a stool
> To stumble over and vex you . . . "curse
>   that stool!"
> Or else at best, a cushion, where you lean
> And sleep, and dream of something we are not
> But would be for your sake.

Of her father, who has become a popular caricature of the arbitrary parent with "all those patriarchal ideas of governing grown-up children," she wrote with bitter perception on the eve of her escape from his prison. "The evil is in the system—" she told Browning, "and he simply takes it to be his duty to rule . . . like the Kings of Christendom, by divine right." In her own marriage Elizabeth was not only the elder by some years but was, by common agreement, the center of its concerns. She was also, in that genuine democracy of intellect and feeling that existed between herself and Browning, the dominant personality. After her experience of her parents' lives she could not have tolerated a different arrangement.

In *Aurora Leigh* the heroine, a poet, rejects her cousin Romney as a suitor because he has patronized her person and her art. She marries him years later after she has made herself into a successful independent poet and person. His cold obsession with theoretical radicalism has ruined himself and others and left him, like Rochester in *Jane Eyre*, blind and homeless. Elizabeth's politics seem to have been built on an acceptance of Edward Barrett's liberal persuasion and a fierce rejection of his personal coldness and loveless rule. Her childhood was happy; she was given a good classical education and allowed a limited intercourse with minds better than her father's. She worshipped the Romantic poets and most modern writers were available to her: she remembered reading Paine, Hume and Mary Wollstonecraft. Her views in the 'forties and 'fifties were typical of these pious second-generation romantics. She espoused a fervid Christian democratic nationalism which depended on the spiritual reform of nations and individuals and shrank from the sort of social revolution favored by the left. This vision also includes her feminism.

The plot of *Aurora Leigh* is as complicated and implausible as that of most Victorian novels. The important events of the poems are Aurora's growth through her own efforts and the parallel transformation of her rival and friend Marian Erle. Marian begins as one of Romney's good works and moves from being his adoring tool to full independent womanhood, as the loving mother of a son got on her through rape. Marian is rescued from poverty by Aurora and is able to reject Romney's offer of marriage as protection or reparation. Contemporary critics disliked the poem, emphasizing its "unfeminine" feminist theme and the vagueness of its political sentiments. The real politics of the poem, however, are sexual: Mrs. Browning rejects male political formulations as well as male clichés about women's talents and personality. Unlike the more conventional fantasies worked out in the Brontes' novels, Mrs. Browning's best and most ambitious work was not essentially about the trials of virtue and the vicissitudes of love. Next to the achievements of Aurora and Marian the resolution of the love story seems incidental.

Mrs. Browning's insistence on women's ability to initiate action runs through the poems and letters of her Italian years. In *The Runaway Slave at Pilgrim's Point* (1850) she anticipates, by two years, the theme of Mrs. Stowe's *Uncle Tom's Cabin*. The poem's plot is more savage than any episode in that book: the speaker, a woman slave who is raped by her white master, kills her white baby lest he, too, claim his "master-right." She defies the "white men . . . not gods indeed,/Nor able to make Christs again/Do good with bleeding." All the poems of the late 'forties and 'fifties have an energy and personal commitment to their ideas which are clearly the product of Mrs. Browning's emancipation from Victorian England. Her political passions for Napoleon III and Cavour are perfectly compatible with her general nationalist bias. (Even her interest in spiritualism was common among intellectuals. She lived in a time when the pseudo-sciences were barely distinguished from their more respectable relations, and phrenology was a serious study in distinguished circles). Yet the critics were hard on her poetry in the last six years of her life; they disliked *Aurora Leigh* and rejected her more blatantly political poems as doctrinaire and uninspired. This last judgment has lingered today, for the prejudice against political poetry by women remains. Yet these poems are as strong as her love sonnets and, rhetorically, far more inventive.

Mrs. Browning's life and career were a source of inspiration to other women thinkers and writers straining against the stereotypes of the age. She was a personal friend to many of her activist contemporaries—Harriet Martineau, Harriet Beecher Stowe, Margaret Fuller and George Sand—and was interested in the work of all women authors, though severe in her critical judgments of them. Her own experience revealed to her the nexus between woman's passivity and the repressive politics of the time. She expresses this knowledge eloquently in her poetry and letters and sums it up in an outburst to a woman friend on Mrs. Stowe's *Uncle Tom's Cabin*:

Her book is quite a sign of the times, and has otherwise and intrinsically considerable power. For myself, I rejoice in the success, both as a woman and a human being. Oh, and is it possible that you think a woman has no business with questions like the question of slavery? Then she had better use a pen no more. She had better subside into slavery and concubinage herself, I think, as in the times of old, shut herself up with the Penelopes in the "women's apartment," and take no rank among thinkers and speakers.

Grief I tell you, hopeless grief is passionless;
That only men incredulous of despair,
Half-taught in anguish, through the midnight air
Beat upward to God's throne in loud access
Of shrieking and reproach. Full desertness,
In souls as countries, lieth silent-bare
Under the blanching, vertical eye-glare
Of the absolute Heavens. Deep-hearted man, express
Grief for thy Dead in silence like to death—
Most like a monumental statue set
In everlasting watch and moveless woe
Till itself crumble to the dust beneath.
Touch it; the marble eyelids are not wet:
If it could weep, it could arise and go.

Adequacy Now, by the verdure on thy thousand hills,
Beloved England, doth the earth appear
Quite good enough for men to overbear
The will of God in, with rebellious wills!
We cannot say the morning-sun fulfils
Ingloriously its course, nor that the clear
Strong stars without significance insphere
Our habitation: we, meantime, our ills
Heap up against this good and lift a cry
Against this work-day world, this ill-spread feast,
As if ourselves were better certainly
Than what we come to. Maker and High Priest,
I ask thee not my joys to multiply,—
Only to make me worthier of the least.

To George Sand

A recognition True genius, but true woman! dost deny
The woman's nature with a manly scorn,
And break away the gauds and armlets worn
By weaker women in captivity?
Ah, vain denial! that revolted cry
Is sobbed in by a woman's voice forlorn,—
Thy woman's hair, my sister, all unshorn
Floats back dishevelled strength in agony,
Disproving thy man's name: and while before
The world thou burnest in a poet-fire,
We see thy woman-heart beat evermore
Through the large flame. Beat purer, heart, and higher,
Till God unsex thee on the heavenly shore
Where unincarnate spirits purely aspire!

The Runaway Slave at Pilgrim's Point

I

I stand on the mark beside the shore
  Of the first white pilgrim's bended knee,
Where exile turned to ancestor,
  And God was thanked for liberty.
I have run through the night, my skin is as dark,
I bend my knee down on this mark:
  I look on the sky and the sea.

II

O pilgrim-souls, I speak to you!
  I see you come proud and slow
From the land of the spirits pale as dew
  And round me and round me ye go.
O pilgrims, I have gasped and run
All night long from the whips of one
  Who in your names works sin and woe!

III

And thus I thought that I would come
  And kneel here where ye knelt before,
And feel your souls around me hum
  In undertone to the ocean's roar;
And lift my black face, my black hand,
Here, in your names, to curse this land
  Ye blessed in freedom's, evermore.

IV

I am black, I am black,
  And yet God made me, they say:
But if He did so, smiling back
  He must have cast his work away
Under the feet of his white creatures,
With a look of scorn, that the dusky features
  Might be trodden again to clay.

V

And yet He has made dark things
  To be glad and merry as light:
There's a little dark bird sits and sings,
  There's a dark stream ripples out of
        sight,
And the dark frogs chant in the safe morass,
And the sweetest stars are made to pass
  O'er the face of the darkest night.

VI

But *we* who are dark, we are dark!
  Ah God, we have no stars!
About our souls in care and cark
  Our blackness shuts like prison-bars:
The poor souls crouch so far behind
That never a comfort can they find
  By reaching through the prison-bars.

VII

Indeed we live beneath the sky,
  That great smooth Hand of God stretched out
On all his children fatherly,
  To save them from the dread and doubt
Which would be if, from this low place,
All opened straight up to his face
  Into the grand eternity.

VIII

And still God's sunshine and his frost,
    They make us hot, they make us cold,
As if we were not black and lost;
    And the beasts and birds, in wood and fold,
Do fear and take us for very men:
Could the whip-poor-will or the cat of the glen
    Look into my eyes and be bold?

IX

I am black, I am black!
    But, once, I laughed in girlish glee,
For one of my color stood in the track
    Where the drivers drove, and looked at me,
And tender and full was the look he gave—
Could a slave look *so* at another slave?—
    I look at the sky and the sea.

X

And from that hour our spirits grew
    As free as if unsold, unbought:
Oh, strong enough, since we were two,
    To conquer the world, we thought.
The drivers drove us day by day;
We did not mind, we went one way,
    And no better a freedom sought.

XI

In the sunny ground between the canes,
    He said "I love you" as he passed;
When the shingle-roof rang sharp with the rains,
    I heard how he vowed it fast:
While others shook he smiled in the hut,
As he carved me a bowl of the cocoa-nut
    Through the roar of the hurricanes.

XII

I sang his name instead of a song,
    Over and over I sang his name,
Upward and downward I drew it along
    My various notes,—the same, the same!
I sang it low, that the slave-girls near
Might never guess, from aught they could hear,
    It was only a name—a name.

XIII

I look on the sky and the sea.
    We were two to love and two to pray:
Yes, two, O God, who cried to Thee,
    Though nothing didst Thou say!
Coldly Thou sat'st behind the sun:
And now I cry who am but one,
    Thou wilt not speak to-day.

XIV

We were black, we were black,
   We had no claim to love and bliss,
What marvel if each went to wrack?
   They wrung my cold hands out of his,
They dragged him—where? I crawled to touch
His blood's mark in the dust . . . not much,
   Ye pilgrim-souls, though plain as *this!*

XV

Wrong, followed by a deeper wrong!
   Mere grief's too good for such as I:
So the white men brought the shame ere long
   To strangle the sob of my agony.
They would not leave me for my dull
Wet eyes!—it was too merciful
   To let me weep pure tears and die.

XVI

I am black, I am black!
   I wore a child upon my breast,
An amulet that hung too slack,
   And, in my unrest, could not rest:
Thus we went moaning, child and mother,
One to another, one to another,
   Until all ended for the best.

XVII

For hark! I will tell you low, low,
   I am black, you see,—
And the babe who lay on my bosom so,
   Was far too white, too white for me;
As white as the ladies who scorned to pray
Beside me at church but yesterday,
   Though my tears had washed a place for
      my knee.

XVIII

My own, own child! I could not bear
   To look in his face, it was so white;
I covered him up with a kerchief there,
   I covered his face in close and tight:
And he moaned and struggled, as well
      might be,
For the white child wanted his liberty—
   Ha, ha! he wanted the master-right.

XIX

He moaned and beat with his head and feet,
   His little feet that never grew;
He struck them out, as it was meet,
   Against my heart to break it through:
I might have sung and made him mild,
But I dared not sing to the white-faced child
   The only song I knew.

XX

I pulled the kerchief very close:
  He could not see the sun, I swear,
More, then, alive, than now he does
  From between the roots of the mango
        . . . where?
I know where. Close! A child and mother
Do wrong to look at one another
  When one is black and one is fair.

XXI

Why, in that single glance I had
  Of my child's face, . . . I tell you all,
I saw a look that made me mad!
  The *master's* look, that used to fall
On my soul like a lash . . . or worse!
And so, to save it from my curse,
  I twisted it round in my shawl.

XXII

And he moaned and trembled from foot to head,
  He shivered from head to foot;
Till after a time, he lay instead
  Too suddenly still and mute.
I felt, beside, a stiffening cold:
I dared to lift up just a fold,
  As in lifting a leaf of the mango-fruit.

XXIII

But *my* fruit . . . ha, ha!—there, had been
  (I laugh to think on't at this hour!)
Your fine white angels (who have seen
  Nearest the secret of God's power)
And plucked my fruit to make them wine,
And sucked the soul of that child of mine
  As the humming-bird sucks the soul of
        the flower.

XXIV

Ha, ha, the trick of the angels white!
  They freed the white child's spirit so.
I said not a word, but day and night
  I carried the body to and fro,
And it lay on my heart like a stone, as chill.
—The sun may shine out as much as he will:
  I am cold, though it happened a month ago.

XXV

From the white man's house, and the
        black man's hut,
  I carried the little body on:
The forest's arms did round us shut,
  And silence through the trees did run:
They asked no question as I went,
They stood too high for astonishment,
  They could see God sit on his throne.

XXVI

My little body, kerchiefed fast,
  I bore it on through the forest, on;
And when I felt it was tired at last,
  I scooped a hole beneath the moon:
Through the forest-tops the angels far,
With a white sharp finger from every star,
    Did point and mock at what was done.

XXVII

Yet when it was all done aright,—
  Earth, 'twixt me and my baby, strewed,—
All, changed to black earth,—nothing white,—
  A dark child in the dark!—ensued
Some comfort, and my heart grew young;
I sate down smiling there and sung
    The song I learnt in my maidenhood.

XXVIII

And thus we two were reconciled,
  The white child and black mother, thus;
For as I sang it soft and wild,
  The same song, more melodious,
Rose from the grave whereon I sate:
It was the dead child singing that,
    To join the souls of both of us.

XXIX

I look on the sea and the sky.
  Where the pilgrims' ships first anchored lay
The free sun rideth gloriously,
  But the pilgrim-ghosts have slid away
Through the earliest streaks of the morn:
My face is black, but it glares with a scorn
    Which they dare not meet by day.

XXX

Ha!—in her stead, their hunter sons!
  Ha, ha! they are on me—they hunt in a ring!
Keep off! I brave you all at once,
  I throw off your eyes like snakes that sting!
You have killed the black eagle at nest, I think:
Did you ever stand still in your triumph,
      and shrink
    From the stroke of her wounded wing?

XXXI

(Man, drop that stone you dared to lift!—)
  I wish you who stand there five abreast,
Each, for his own wife's joy and gift,
  A little corpse as safely at rest
As mine in the mangoes! Yes, but *she*
May keep live babies on her knee,
    And sing the song she likes the best.

XXXII

I am not mad: I am black.
  I see you staring in my face—
I know you staring, shrinking back,
  Ye are born of the Washington-race,
And this land is the free America,
And this mark on my wrist—(I prove what I say)
  Ropes tied me up here to the flogging-place.

XXXIII

You think I shrieked then? Not a sound.
  I hung, as a gourd hangs in the sun;
I only cursed them all around
  As softly as I might have done
My very own child: from these sands
Up to the mountains, lift your hands,
  O slaves, and end what I begun!

XXXIV

Whips, curses; these must answer those!
  For in this UNION you have set
Two kinds of men in adverse rows,
  Each loathing each; and all forget
The seven wounds in Christ's body fair,
While HE sees gaping everywhere
  Our countless wounds that pay no debt.

XXXV

Our wounds are different. Your white men
  Are, after all, not gods indeed,
Nor able to make Christs again
  Do good with bleeding.   We who bleed
(Stand off!) we help not in our loss!
We are too heavy for our cross,
  And fall and crush you and your seed.

XXXVI

I fall, I swoon! I look at the sky.
  The clouds are breaking on my brain;
I am floated along, as if I should die
  Of liberty's exquisite pain.
In the name of the white child waiting for me
In the death-dark where we may kiss and agree,
White men, I leave you all curse-free
  In my broken heart's disdain!

Hiram Powers' "Greek Slave"

*The American sculptor Hiram Powers and
his family were among the few intimate
friends of the Brownings during their first
years in Florence.*

They say Ideal beauty cannot enter
The house of anguish. On the threshold stands
An alien Image with enshackled hands,
Called the Greek Slave! as if the artist meant her
(That passionless perfection which he lent her,
Shadowed not darkened where the sill expands)
To so confront man's crimes in different lands
With man's ideal sense. Pierce to the centre,

Art's fiery finger, and break up ere long
The serfdom of this world. Appeal, fair stone,
From God's pure heights of beauty against man's wrong!
Catch up in thy divine face, not alone
East griefs but west, and strike and shame the strong,
By thunders of white silence, overthrown.

From: **Sonnets from the Portuguese**

XXII

When our two souls stand up erect and strong,
Face to face, silent, drawing nigh and nigher,
Until the lengthening wings break into fire
At either curved point,—what bitter wrong
Can the earth do to us, that we should not long
Be here contented? Think. In mounting higher,
The angels would press on us and aspire
To drop some golden orb of perfect song
Into our deep, dear silence. Let us stay
Rather on earth, Belovèd,—where the unfit
Contrarious moods of men recoil away
And isolate pure spirits, and permit
A place to stand and love in for a day,
With darkness and the death-hour rounding it.

A Curse For A Nation

Prologue

I heard an angel speak last night,
        And he said "Write!
Write a Nation's curse for me,
And send it over the Western Sea."

I faltered, taking up the word:
        "Not so, my lord!
If curses must be, choose another
To send thy curse against my brother.

"For I am bound by gratitude,
        By love and blood,
To brothers of mine across the sea,
Who stretch out kindly hands to me."

"Therefore," the voice said, "shalt thou write
        My curse to-night.
From the summits of love a curse is driven,
As lightning is from the tops of heaven."

"Not so," I answered. "Evermore
        My heart is sore
For my own land's sins: for little feet
Of children bleeding along the street:

"For parked-up honors that gainsay
        The right of way:
For almsgiving through a door that is
Not open enough for two friends to kiss:

115

"For love of freedom which abates
        Beyond the Straits:
For patriot virtue starved to vice on
Self-praise, self-interest, and suspicion:

"For an oligarchic parliament,
        And bribes well-meant.
What curse to another land assign,
When heavy-souled for the sins of mine?"

"Therefore," the voice said, "shalt thou write
        My curse to-night.
Because thou hast strength to see and hate
A foul thing done *within* thy gate."

"Not so," I answered once again.
        "To curse, choose men.
For I, a woman, have only known
How the heart melts and the tears run down."

"Therefore," the voice said, "shalt thou write
        My curse to-night.
Some women weep and curse, I say
(And no one marvels), night and day.

"And thou shalt take their part to-night,
        Weep and write.
A curse from the depths of womanhood
Is very salt, and bitter, and good."

So thus I wrote, and mourned indeed,
        What all may read.
And thus, as was enjoined on me,
I send it over the Western Sea.

The Curse

I
Because ye have broken your own chain
        With the strain
Of brave men climbing a Nation's height,
Yet thence bear down with brand and thong
On souls of others,—for this wrong
        This is the curse.   Write.

Because yourselves are standing straight
        In the state
Of Freedom's foremost acolyte,
Yet keep calm footing all the time
On writhing bond-slaves,—for this crime
        This is the curse.   Write.

Because ye prosper in God's name,
        With a claim
To honor in the old world's sight,
Yet do the fiend's work perfectly
In strangling martyrs,—for this lie
        This is the curse.   Write.

116

II

Ye shall watch while kings conspire
Round the people's smouldering fire,
   And, warm for your part,
Shall never dare—O shame!
To utter the thought into flame
   Which burns at your heart.
          This is the curse.   Write.

Ye shall watch while nations strive
With the bloodhounds, die or survive,
   Drop faint from their jaws,
Or throttle them backward to death;
And only under your breath
   Shall favour the cause.
          This is the curse.   Write.

Ye shall watch while strong men draw
The nets of feudal law
   To strangle the weak;
And, counting the sin for a sin,
Your soul shall be sadder within
   Than the word ye shall speak.
          This is the curse.   Write.

When good men are praying erect
That Christ may avenge his elect
   And deliver the earth,
The prayer in your ears, said low,
Shall sound like the tramp of a foe
   That's driving you forth.
          This is the curse.   Write.

When wise men give you their praise,
They shall pause in the heat of the phrase,
   As if carried too far.
When ye boast your own charters kept true,
Ye shall blush; for the thing which ye do
   Derides what ye are.
          This is the curse.   Write.

When fools cast taunts at your gate,
Your scorn ye shall somewhat abate
   As ye look o'er the wall;
For your conscience, tradition, and name
Explode with a deadlier blame
   Than the worst of them all.
          This is the curse.   Write.

Go, wherever ill deeds shall be done,
Go, plant your flag in the sun
   Beside the ill-doers!
And recoil from clenching the curse
Of God's witnessing Universe
   With a curse of yours.
          THIS is the curse.   Write.

A Song For The Ragged Schools of London

I am listening here in Rome.
  "England's strong," say many speakers,
"If she winks, the Czar must come,
  Prow and topsail, to the breakers."

"England's rich in coal and oak,"
  Adds a Roman, getting moody;
"If she shakes a travelling cloak,
  Down our Appian roll the scudi."

"England's righteous," they rejoin:
  "Who shall grudge her exaltations,
When her wealth of golden coin
  Works the welfare of the nations?"

I am listening here in Rome.
  Over Alps a voice is sweeping—
"England's cruel, save us some
  Of these victims in her keeping!"

As the cry beneath the wheel
  Of an old triumphant Roman
Cleft the people's shouts like steel,
  While the show was spoilt for no man,

Comes that voice.   Let others shout,
  Other poets praise my land here:
I am sadly sitting out.
  Praying, "God forgive her grandeur."

Shall we boast of empire, where
  Time with ruin sits commissioned?
In God's liberal blue air
  Peter's dome itself looks wizened;

And the mountains, in disdain,
  Gather back their lights of opal
From the dumb despondent plain
  Heaped with jawbones of a people.

Lordly English, think it o'er,
  Cæsar's doing is all undone!
You have cannons on your shore,
  And free Parliaments in London;

Princes' parks, and merchants' homes,
  Tents for soldiers, ships for seamen,—
Ay, but ruins worse than Rome's
  In your pauper men and women.

Women leering through the gas
  (Just such bosoms used to nurse you),
Men, turned wolves by famine—pass!
  Those can speak themselves, and curse you.

But these others—children small,
   Spilt like blots about the city,
Quay, and street, and palace-wall—
   Take them up into your pity!

Ragged children with bare feet,
   Whom the angels in white raiment
Know the names of, to repeat
   When they come on you for payment.

Ragged children, hungry-eyed,
   Huddled up out of the coldness
On your doorsteps, side by side,
   Till your footman damns their boldness.

In the alleys, in the squares,
   Begging, lying little rebels;
In the noisy thoroughfares,
   Struggling on with piteous trebles.

Patient children—think what pain
   Makes a young child patient—ponder!
Wronged too commonly to strain
   After right, or wish, or wonder.

Wicked children, with peaked chins,
   And old foreheads! there are many
With no pleasures except sins,
   Gambling with a stolen penny.

Sickly children, that whine low
   To themselves and not their mothers,
From mere habit,—never so
   Hoping help or care from others.

Healthy children, with those blue
   English eyes, fresh from their Maker,
Fierce and ravenous, staring through
   At the brown loaves of the baker.

I am listening here in Rome,
   And the Romans are confessing,
"English children pass in bloom
   All the prettiest made for blessing.

"*Angli angeli!*" (resumed
   From the mediæval story)
"Such rose angelhoods, emplumed
   In such ringlets of pure glory!"

Can we smooth down the bright hair,
   O my sisters, calm, unthrilled in
Our heart's pulses? Can we bear
   The sweet looks of our own children,

While those others, lean and small,
　　Scurf and mildew of the city,
Spot our streets, convict us all
　　Till we take them into pity?

"Is it our fault?" you reply,
　　"When, throughout civilization,
Every nation's empery
　　Is asserted by starvation?

"All these mouths we cannot feed,
　　And we cannot clothe these bodies."
Well, if man's so hard indeed,
　　Let them learn at least what God is!

Little outcasts from life's fold,
　　The grave's hope they may be joined in,
By Christ's covenant consoled
　　For our social contract's grinding.

If no better can be done,
　　Let us do but this,—endeavor
That the sun behind the sun
　　Shine upon them while they shiver!

On the dismal London flags,
　　Through the cruel social juggle,
Put a thought beneath their rags
　　To ennoble the heart's struggle.

O my sisters, not so much
　　Are we asked for—not a blossom
From our children's nosegay, such
　　As we gave it from our bosom,—

Not the milk left in their cup,
　　Not the lamp while they are sleeping,
Not the little cloak hung up
　　While the coat's in daily keeping,—

But a place in RAGGED SCHOOLS,
　　Where the outcasts may to-morrow
Learn by gentle words and rules
　　Just the uses of their sorrow.

O my sisters! children small,
　　Blue-eyed, wailing through the city—
Our own babes cry in them all:
　　Let us take them into pity.

Mother and Poet

Turin, after News from Gaeta, 1861

The mother was Laura Savio of Turin, poet and patriot, whose two sons were killed at Ancona and Gaeta.

I

Dead! One of them shot by the sea in the east,
    And one of them shot in the west by the sea.
Dead! both my boys! When you sit at the feast
    And are wanting a great song for Italy free,
        Let none look at *me!*

II

Yet I was a poetess only last year,
    And good at my art, for a woman, men said;
But *this* woman, *this*, who is agonized here,
    —The east sea and west sea rhyme on in her head
        For ever instead.

III

What art can a woman be good at? Oh, vain!
    What art *is* she good at, but hurting her breast
With the milk-teeth of babes, and a smile at the pain?
    Ah boys, how you hurt! you were strong as you pressed,
        And I proud, by that test.

IV

What art's for a woman? To hold on her knees
    Both darlings! to feel all their arms round her throat,
Cling, strangle a little! to sew by degrees
    And 'broider the long-clothes and neat little coat;
        To dream and to doat.

V

To teach them . . . It stings there! *I* made them indeed
    Speak plain the word *country*. *I* taught them, no doubt,
That a country's a thing men should die for at need.
    I prated of liberty, rights, and about
        The tyrant cast out.

VI

And when their eyes flashed . . . O my beautiful eyes! . . .
    I exulted; nay, let them go forth at the wheels
Of the guns, and denied not. But then the surprise
    When one sits quite alone! Then one weeps, then one kneels!
        God, how the house feels!

VII

At first, happy news came, in gay letters moiled
    With my kisses,—of camp-life and glory, and how
They both loved me; and, soon coming home to be spoiled
    In return would fan off every fly from my brow
        With their green laurel-bough.

VIII

Then was triumph at Turin: "Ancona was free!"
    And some one came out of the cheers in the street,
With a face pale as stone, to say something to me.
    My Guido was dead! I fell down at his feet,
        While they cheered in the street.

IX

I bore it; friends soothed me; my grief looked sublime
  As the ransom of Italy.   One boy remained
To be leant on and walked with, recalling the time
   When the first grew immortal, while both of us strained
    To the height he had gained.

X

And letters still came, shorter, sadder, more strong,
  Writ now but in one hand, "I was not to faint,—
One loved me for two—would be with me ere long:
  And *Viva l' Italia!*—*he* died for, our saint,
   Who forbids our complaint."

XI

My Nanni would add, "he was safe, and aware
  Of a presence that turned off the balls,—was imprest
It was Guido himself, who knew what I could bear,
  And how 't was impossible, quite dispossessed
   To live on for the rest."

XII

On which, without pause, up the telegraph line
  Swept smoothly the next news from Gaeta:—*Shot.*
Tell his mother. Ah, ah, "his," "their" mother,—not "mine,"
  No voice says "*My* mother" again to me.   What!
   You think Guido forgot?

XIII

Are souls straight so happy that, dizzy with Heaven,
  They drop earth's affections, conceive not of woe?
I think not.   Themselves were too lately forgiven
  Through THAT Love and Sorrow which reconciled so
   The Above and Below.

XIV

O Christ of the five wounds, who look'dst through the dark
  To the face of thy mother! consider, I pray,
How we common mothers stand desolate, mark,
  Whose sons, not being Christs, die with eyes turned away,
   And no last word to say!

XV

Both boys dead? but that's out of nature.   We all
  Have been patriots, yet each house must always keep one.
'Twere imbecile, hewing out roads to a wall;
  And, when Italy's made, for what end is it done
   If we have not a son?

XVI

Ah, ah, ah! when Gaeta's taken, what then?
  When the fair wicked queen sits no more at her sport
Of the fire-balls of death crashing souls out of men?
  When the guns of Cavalli with final retort
   Have cut the game short?

XVII

When Venice and Rome keep their new jubilee,
   When your flag takes all heaven for its white, green, and red,
When *you* have your country from mountain to sea,
   When King Victor has Italy's crown on his head,
     (And *I* have my Dead)—

XVIII

What then? Do not mock me. Ah, ring your bells low,
   And burn your lights faintly! *My* country is *there*,
Above the star pricked by the last peak of snow:
   My Italy's THERE, with my brave civic Pair,
     To disfranchise despair!

XIX

Forgive me. Some women bear children in strength,
   And bite back the cry of their pain in self-scorn;
But the birth-pangs of nations will wring us at length
   Into wail such as this—and we sit on forlorn
     When the man-child is born.

XX

Dead! One of them shot by the sea in the east,
   And one of them shot in the west by the sea.
Both! both my boys! If in keeping the feast
   You want a great song for your Italy free,
     Let none look at *me!*

Christina Rossetti (1830-1894)

CHRISTINA ROSSETTI'S reputation has suffered, like Elizabeth Barrett's, from the selective attention of her admirers. Her lyrics on love and death are always represented in anthologies, but because of her role in the Pre-Raphaelite movement (founded by her brother, artist and poet Dante Gabriel Rossetti) her poetry has generally been considered by modern critics solely in relation to that loosely defined "school." In her own day she and Elizabeth Barrett Browning were generally considered the two leading woman poets in England.

Christina Rossetti was born in London on December 5, 1830, the youngest of four children of an Italian political refugee poet and his half-Italian wife. The Rossettis were a happy and democratic family. The parents encouraged the intellectual and artistic leanings of their children, male and female. Christina, like Elizabeth Barrett Browning, spent much of her girlhood as a semi-invalid, suffering from inadequately diagnosed ailments. Christina also started writing verse in her teens, and the protected life she was to live acted to extend her girlhood. Much of her poetry, though technically skillful and inventive, seems the intellectual product of adolescent piety and sentimental dolor. This pleasantly vague emotional melancholy, expressed with an adult control of language, is part of the attraction of her verse.

Although her parents lived amicably in a mixed Catholic and Anglican household, Christina and her much-loved sister Maria embraced Anglicanism with a fanatic intensity. Christina refused two suitors ostensibly because they could not meet her doctrinal standards, and Maria eventually became an Anglican nun. Against the theme of self-abnegating love of God and doomed unhappy love of men in Christina's poems, runs the theme of warm, abiding relationships between women. Christina's day-to-day life was lived largely with women. After her mother's death in 1886 she nursed her two old aunts until their deaths. She herself died in August 1894.

Goblin Market, the title poem of her first volume, published in 1861, is the story of two sisters who are tempted by the magic sensuous fruit of the brotherhood of goblins. Today the sexual allegory in *Goblin Market* seems transparent, but it is doubtful that Christina, who denied that the poem had symbolic meaning, understood its subversive message. Those who buy and eat the fruit sold at Goblin Market are seized with a "passionate" craving for more. The goblins only sell once to each maiden; their victims pine and die for the forbidden fruit. To save Laura who has succumbed, Lizzie allows the little men to assault her, literally squashing the fruit on her face. Without swallowing the juice she runs home and lets Laura kiss and lick it off her. The curse is lifted, and both sisters live to marry and bear children whom they warn and entertain with the cautionary tale. The happy ending provides a conventional justification for Lizzie's daring but also seems to obscure the live emotion of the poem—a vividly expressed revulsion against the tempting lure of male sensuality. Lizzie is physically attacked by the goblin men when she refuses to eat the fruit in their presence; Laura is saved by sucking the juice from her sister's flesh. During the years before and after the writing of *Goblin Market*, Christina had ample opportunity to see the unhappy results of sexual infatuation in the stormy love affair and marriage of Dante Gabriel and Lizzie Siddal, which ended in Lizzie's suicide in 1862, and Dante Gabriel's physical and emotional decline.

The publication of her second book made Christina's reputation as a poet, but she was always awkward in literary society and therefore avoided it. In most of her poems she accepts her isolation from love and society, which was in large part self-imposed, and equally accepts what one contemporary critic called "the burden of womanhood." Because of this acceptance, male critics usually preferred her to Mrs. Browning. Few cared to extract an undertext in *Goblin Market*. Few pursued the more profound alienation and bitterness in another long poem, *An Old-World Thicket*, where she speaks of her "rebellious soul" which "vainly shakes, and cannot shake the gate." Christina's attitude toward women's position was ambivalent to the end. In a late sonnet, "Let women fear to teach and bear to learn," she sees the snake's treachery and Eve's temptation of Adam as the cause both of the "process" by which the world must burn and of the romantic love which redeems it. Yet these poems do "burn" with a steady and barely sublimated anger at women's position. This anger, never argued or analyzed but conjured up by symbolic language, has greater density and strength than the thinner, sadder emotions of the more familiar lyrics.

The contradictions in Christina Rossetti's attitude to women's role is in a sonnet *A Soul* which echoes, perhaps consciously, Elizabeth Barrett Browning's "Grief."

She stands as pale as Parían statues stand;
Like Cleopatra when she turned at bay,
And felt her strength above the Roman sway,
And felt the aspic writhing in her hand.
Her face is steadfast toward the shadowy
     land,
For dim beyond it looms the land of day:
Her feet are steadfast, all the arduous way
That foot-track doth not waver on the sand.
She stands there like a beacon through the
     night,
A pale clear beacon where the storm-drift is—
She stands alone, a wonder deathly-white:
She stands there patient nerved with inner
     might,
Indomitable in her feebleness,
Her face and will athirst against the light.

Goblin Market

Morning and evening
Maids heard the goblins cry:
"Come buy our orchard fruits,
Come buy, come buy:
Apples and quinces,
Lemons and oranges,
Plump unpecked cherries,
Melons and raspberries,
Bloom-down-cheeked peaches,
Swart-headed mulberries,
Wild free-born cranberries,
Pine-apples, blackberries,
Apricots, strawberries;—
All ripe together
In summer weather,—
Morns that pass by,
Fair eves that fly;
Come buy, come buy:
Our grapes fresh from the vine,
Pomegranates full and fine,
Dates and sharp bullaces,
Rare pears and greengages,
Damsons and bilberries,
Taste them and try:
Currants and gooseberries,
Bright-fire-like barberries,
Figs to fill your mouth,
Citrons from the South,
Sweet to tongue and sound to eye;
Come buy, come buy."

Evening by evening
Among the brookside rushes
Laura bowed her head to hear,
Lizzie veiled her blushes:
Crouching close together
In the cooling weather,
With clasping arms and cautioning lips,
With tingling cheeks and finger-tips.
"Lie close," Laura said,
Pricking up her golden head:
"We must not look at goblin men,
We must not buy their fruits:
Who knows upon what soil they fed
Their hungry thirsty roots?"
"Come buy," call the goblins
Hobbling down the glen.
"O," cried Lizzie, "Laura, Laura,
You should not peep at goblin men."

Lizzie covered up her eyes,
Covered close lest they should look;
Laura reared her glossy head,
And whispered like the restless brook:
"Look, Lizzie, look, Lizzie,
Down the glen tramp little men.
One hauls a basket,
One bears a plate,
One lugs a golden dish
Of many pounds' weight.
How fair the vine must grow
Whose grapes are so luscious;
How warm the wind must blow
Through those fruit bushes."
"No," said Lizzie, "no, no, no;
Their offers should not charm us,
Their evil gifts would harm us."
She thrust a dimpled finger
In each ear, shut eyes and ran:
Curious Laura chose to linger
Wondering at each merchant man.
One had a cat's face,
One whisked a tail,
One tramped at a rat's pace,
One crawled like a snail,
One like a wombat prowled obtuse and furry,
One like a ratel tumbled hurry-scurry.
She heard a voice like of doves
Cooing all together:
They sounded kind and full of loves
In the pleasant weather.

Laura stretched her gleaming neck
Like a rush-imbedded swan,
Like a lily from the beck,
Like a moonlit poplar branch,
Like a vessel at the launch
When its last restraint is gone.

Backwards up the mossy glen
Turned and trooped the goblin men,
With their shrill repeated cry,
"Come buy, come buy."
When they reached where Laura was
They stood stock still upon the moss,
Leering at each other,
Brother with queer brother;
Signalling each other,
Brother with sly brother.
One set his basket down,
One reared his plate;
One began to weave a crown
Of tendrils, leaves, and rough nuts brown
(Men sell not such in any town);

One heaved the golden weight
Of dish and fruit to offer her:
"Come buy, come buy," was still their cry.
Laura stared but did not stir,
Longed but had no money:
The whisk-tailed merchant bade her taste
In tones as smooth as honey,
The cat-faced purr'd,
The rat-paced spoke a word
Of welcome, and the snail-paced even was heard;
One parrot-voiced and jolly
Cried "Pretty Goblin" still for "Pretty Polly";—
One whistled like a bird.

But sweet-tooth Laura spoke in haste:
"Good folk, I have no coin;
To take were to purloin:
I have no copper in my purse,
I have no silver either,
And all my gold is on the furze
That shakes the windy weather
Above the rusty heather."
"You have much gold upon your head,"
They answered altogether:
"Buy from us with a golden curl."
She clipped a precious golden lock,
She dropped a tear more rare than pearl,
Then sucked their fruit globes fair or red:
Sweeter than honey from the rock,
Stronger than man-rejoicing wine,
Clearer than water flowed that juice;
She never tasted such before,
How should it cloy with length of use?
She sucked and sucked and sucked the more
Fruits which that unknown orchard bore;
She sucked until her lips were sore;
Then flung the emptied rinds away,
But gathered up one kernel stone,
And knew not was it night or day
As she turned home alone.

Lizzie met her at the gate
Full of wise upbraidings:
"Dear, you should not stay so late,
Twilight is not good for maidens;
Should not loiter in the glen
In the haunts of goblin men.
Do you not remember Jeanie,
How she met them in the moonlight,
Took their gifts both choice and many,
Ate their fruits and wore their flowers
Plucked from bowers
Where summer ripens at all hours?

But ever in the noonlight
She pined and pined away;
Sought them by night and day,
Found them no more, but dwindled and grew gray;
Then fell with the first snow,
While to this day no grass will grow
Where she lies low:
I planted daisies there a year ago
That never blow.
You should not loiter so."
"Nay, hush," said Laura:
"Nay, hush, my sister:
I ate and ate my fill;
Yet my mouth waters still;
To-morrow night I will
Buy more,"—and kissed her.
"Have done with sorrow;
I'll bring you plums to-morrow
Fresh on their mother twigs,
Cherries worth getting;
You cannot think what figs
My teeth have met in,
What melons icy-cold
Piled on a dish of gold
Too huge for me to hold,
What peaches with a velvet nap,
Pellucid grapes without one seed:
Odorous indeed be the mead
Whereon they grow, and pure the wave they drink,
With lilies at the brink,
And sugar-sweet their sap."

Golden head by golden head,
Like two pigeons in one nest
Folded in each other's wings,
They lay down in their curtained bed:
Like two blossoms on one stem,
Like two flakes of new-fallen snow,
Like two wands of ivory
Tipped with gold for awful kings.
Moon and stars gazed in at them,
Wind sang to them lullaby,
Lumbering owls forbore to fly,
Not a bat flapped to and fro
Round their rest:
Cheek to cheek and breast to breast
Locked together in one nest.

Early in the morning
When the first cock crowed his warning,
Neat like bees, as sweet and busy,
Laura rose with Lizzie:
Fetched in honey, milked the cows,
Aired and set to rights the house,

Kneaded cakes of whitest wheat,
Cakes for dainty mouths to eat,
Next churned butter, whipped up cream,
Fed their poultry, sat and sewed;
Talked as modest maidens should:
Lizzie with an open heart,
Laura in an absent dream,
One content, one sick in part;
One warbling for the mere bright day's delight,
One longing for the night.

At length slow evening came:
They went with pitchers to the reedy brook;
Lizzie most placid in her look,
Laura most like a leaping flame.
They drew the gurgling water from its deep;
Lizzie plucked purple and rich golden flags,
Then turning homeward said: "The sunset flushes
Those furthest loftiest crags;
Come, Laura, not another maiden lags,
No wilful squirrel wags,
The beasts and birds are fast asleep."
But Laura loitered still among the rushes
And said the bank was steep.

And said the hour was early still,
The dew not fallen, the wind not chill:
Listening ever, but not catching
The customary cry,
"Come buy, come buy,"
With its iterated jingle
Of sugar-baited words:
Not for all her watching
Once discerning even one goblin
Racing, whisking, tumbling, hobbling;
Let alone the herds
That used to tramp along the glen,
In groups or single,
Of brisk fruit-merchant men.

Till Lizzie urged: "O Laura, come;
I hear the fruit-call, but I dare no look:
You should not loiter longer at this brook:
Come with me home.
The stars rise, the moon bends her arc,
Each glow-worm winks her spark,
Let us get home before the night grows dark;
For clouds may gather
Though this is summer weather,
Put out the lights and drench us through;
Then if we lost our way what should we do?"

Laura turned cold as stone
To find her sister heard that cry alone,

That goblin cry,
"Come buy our fruits, come buy."
Must she then buy no more such dainty fruit?
Must she no more such succous pasture find,
Gone deaf and blind?
Her tree of life drooped from the root:
She said not one word in her heart's sore ache;
But peering thro' the dimness, naught discerning,
Trudged home, her pitcher dripping all the way;
So crept to bed, and lay
Silent till Lizzie slept;
Then sat up in a passionate yearning,
And gnashed her teeth for balked desire, and wept
As if her heart would break.

Day after day, night after night,
Laura kept watch in vain,
In sullen silence of exceeding pain.
She never caught again the goblin cry:
"Come buy, come buy";—
She never spied the goblin men
Hawking their fruits along the glen:
But when the noon waxed bright
Her hair grew thin and gray;
She dwindled, as the fair full moon doth turn
To swift decay and burn
Her fire away.

One day remembering her kernel-stone
She set it by a wall that faced the south;
Dewed it with tears, hoped for a root,
Watched for a waxing shoot,
But there came none;
It never saw the sun,
It never felt the tickling moisture run:
While with sunk eyes and faded mouth
She dreamed of melons, as a traveller sees
False waves in desert drouth
With shade of leaf-crowned trees,
And burns the thirstier in the sandful breeze.

She no more swept the house,
Tended the fowls or cows,
Fetched honey, kneaded cakes of wheat,
Brought water from the brook:
But sat down listless in the chimney-nook
And would not eat.

Tender Lizzie could not bear
To watch her sister's cankerous care,
Yet not to share.
She night and morning
Caught the goblins' cry:
"Come buy our orchard fruits,
Come buy, come buy."

Beside the brook, along the glen,
She heard the tramp of goblin men,
The voice and stir
Poor Laura could not hear;
Longed to buy fruit to comfort her,
But feared to pay too dear.
She thought of Jeanie in her grave,
Who should have been a bride;
But who for joys brides hope to have
Fell sick and died
In her gay prime,
In earliest winter-time,
With the glazing rime,
With the first snow-fall of crisp winter-time.

   Till Laura, dwindling,
Seemed knocking at Death's door:
Then Lizzie weighed no more
Better and worse,
But put a silver penny in her purse,
Kissed Laura, crossed the heath with clumps of furze
At twilight, halted by the brook;
And for the first time in her life
Began to listen and look.

   Laughed every goblin
When they spied her peeping:
Came towards her hobbling,
Flying, running, leaping,
Puffing and blowing,
Chuckling, clapping, crowing,
Clucking and gobbling,
Mopping and mowing,
Full of airs and graces,
Pulling wry faces,
Demure grimaces,
Cat-like and rat-like,
Ratel and wombat-like,
Snail-paced in a hurry,
Parrot-voiced and whistler,
Helter-skelter, hurry-skurry,
Chattering like magpies,
Fluttering like pigeons,
Gliding like fishes,—
Hugged her and kissed her;
Squeezed and caressed her;
Stretched up their dishes,
Panniers and plates:
''Look at our apples
Russet and dun,
Bob at our cherries,
Bite at our peaches,
Citrons and dates,

Grapes for the asking,
Pears red with basking
Out in the sun,
Plums on their twigs;
Pluck them and suck them,
Pomegranates, figs."

    "Good folk," said Lizzie,
Mindful of Jeanie,
"Give me much and many";—
Held out her apron,
Tossed them her penny.
"Nay, take a seat with us,
Honor and eat with us,"
They answered grinning:
"Our feast is but beginning.
Night yet is early,
Warm and dew-pearly,
Wakeful and starry:
Such fruits as these
No man can carry;
Half their bloom would fly,
Half their dew would dry,
Half their flavor would pass by.
Sit down and feast with us,
Be welcome guest with us,
Cheer you and rest with us."
"Thank you," said Lizzie; "but one waits
At home alone for me:
So, without further parleying,
If you will not sell me any
Of your fruits though much and many,
Give me back my silver penny
I tossed you for a fee."
They began to scratch their pates,
No longer wagging, purring,
But visibly demurring,
Grunting and snarling.
One called her proud,
Cross-grained, uncivil;
Their tones waxed loud,
Their looks were evil.
Lashing their tails
They trod and hustled her,
Elbowed and jostled her,
Clawed with their nails,
Barking, mewing, hissing, mocking,
Tore her gown and soiled her stocking,
Twitched her hair out by the roots,
Stamped upon her tender feet,
Held her hands and squeezed their fruits
Against her mouth to make her eat.

White and golden Lizzie stood,
Like a lily in a flood, —
Like a rock of blue-veined stone
Lashed by tides obstreperously, —
Like a beacon left alone
In a hoary roaring sea,
Sending up a golden fire, —
Like a fruit-crowned orange-tree
White with blossoms honey-sweet
Sore beset by wasp and bee, —
Like a royal virgin town
Topped with gilded dome and spire
Close beleaguered by a fleet
Mad to tug her standard down.

One may lead a horse to water,
Twenty cannot make him drink.
Though the goblins cuffed and caught her,
Coaxed and fought her,
Bullied and besought her,
Scratched her, pinched her black as ink,
Kicked and knocked her,
Mauled and mocked her,
Lizzie uttered not a word;
Would not open lip from lip
Lest they should cram a mouthful in;
But laughed in heart to feel the drip
Of juice that syrupped all her face,
And lodged in dimples of her chin,
And streaked her neck which quaked like curd.
At last the evil people,
Worn out by her resistance,
Flung back her penny, kicked their fruit
Along whichever road they took,
Not leaving root or stone or shoot.
Some writhed into the ground,
Some dived into the brook
With ring and ripple,
Some scudded on the gale without a sound,
Some vanished in the distance.

In a smart, ache, tingle,
Lizzie went her way;
Knew not was it night or day;
Sprang up the bank, tore through the furze,
Threaded copse and dingle,
And heard her penny jingle
Bouncing in her purse, —
Its bounce was music to her ear.
She ran and ran
As if she feared some goblin man
Dogged her with gibe or curse
Or something worse:

But not one goblin skurried after,
Nor was she pricked by fear;
The kind heart made her windy-paced
That urged her home quite out of breath with haste
And inward laughter.

She cried "Laura," up the garden,
"Did you miss me?
Come and kiss me.
Never mind my bruises,
Hug me, kiss me, suck my juices
Squeezed from goblin fruits for you,
Goblin pulp and goblin dew.
Eat me, drink me, love me;
Laura, make much of me:
For your sake I have braved the glen
And had to do with goblin merchant men."

Laura started from her chair,
Flung her arms up in the air,
Clutched her hair:
"Lizzie, Lizzie, have you tasted
For my sake the fruit forbidden?
Must your light like mine be hidden,
Your young life like mine be wasted,
Undone in mine undoing
And ruined in my ruin,
Thirsty, cankered, goblin-ridden?"
She clung about her sister,
Kissed and kissed and kissed her:
Tears once again
Refreshed her shrunken eyes,
Dropping like rain
After long sultry drouth;
Shaking with aguish fear, and pain,
She kissed and kissed her with a hungry mouth.

Her lips began to scorch,
That juice was wormwood to her tongue,
She loathed the feast:
Writhing as one possessed she leaped and sung,
Rent all her robe, and wrung
Her hands in lamentable haste,
And beat her breast.
Her locks streamed like the torch
Borne by a racer at full speed,
Or like the mane of horses in their flight,
Or like an eagle when she stems the light
Straight toward the sun,
Or like a caged thing freed,
Or like a flying flag when armies run.

Swift fire spread through her veins, knocked at her heart,
Met the fire smouldering there

And overbore its lesser flame;
She gorged on bitterness without a name:
Ah! fool, to choose such part
Of soul-consuming care!
Sense failed in the mortal strife:
Like the watch-tower of a town
Which an earthquake shatters down,
Like a lightning-stricken mast,
Like a wind-uprooted tree
Spun about,
Like a foam-topped water-spout
Cast down headlong in the sea,
She fell at last;
Pleasure past and anguish past,
Is it death or is it life?

    Life out of death.
That night long Lizzie watched by her,
Counted her pulse's flagging stir,
Felt for her breath,
Held water to her lips, and cooled her face
With tears and fanning leaves:
But when the first birds chirped about their eaves,
And early reapers plodded to the place
Of golden sheaves,
And dew-wet grass
Bowed in the morning winds so brisk to pass,
And new buds with new day
Opened of cup-like lilies on the stream,
Laura awoke as from a dream,
Laughed in the innocent old way,
Hugged Lizzie but not twice or thrice;
Her gleaming locks showed not one thread of gray,
Her breath was sweet as May,
And light danced in her eyes.

    Days, weeks, months, years
Afterwards, when both were wives
With children of their own;
Their mother-hearts beset with fears,
Their lives bound up in tender lives;
Laura would call the little ones
And tell them of her early prime,
Those pleasant days long gone
Of not-returning time:
Would talk about the haunted glen,
The wicked, quaint fruit-merchant men,
Their fruits like honey to the throat,
But poison in the blood;
(Men sell not such in any town;)
Would tell them how her sister stood
In deadly peril to do her good,
And win the fiery antidote:
Then joining hands to little hands

Would bid them cling together,
"For there is no friend like a sister,
In calm or stormy weather,
To cheer one on the tedious way,
To fetch one if one goes astray,
To lift one if one totters down,
To strengthen whilst one stands."

From Sunset To Star Rise

Go from me, summer friends, and tarry not:
    I am no summer friend, but wintry cold,
    A silly sheep benighted from the fold,
A sluggard with a thorn-choked garden plot.
Take counsel, sever from my lot your lot,
    Dwell in your pleasant places, hoard your gold;
    Lest you with me should shiver on the wold,
Athirst and hungering on a barren spot.
For I have hedged me with a thorny hedge,
    I live alone, I look to die alone:
Yet sometimes when a wind sighs through the sedge,
    Ghosts of my buried years and friends come back,
My heart goes sighing after swallows flown
    On sometime summer's unreturning track.

A Dirge

Why were you born when the snow was falling?
You should have come to the cuckoo's calling,
Or when grapes are green in the cluster,
Or, at least, when lithe swallows muster
    For their far off flying
    From summer dying.

Why did you die when the lambs were cropping?
You should have died at the apples' dropping,
When the grasshopper comes to trouble,
And the wheat-fields are sodden stubble,
    And all winds go sighing
    For sweet things dying.

Remember

Remember me when I am gone away,
    Gone far away into the silent land;
    When you can no more hold me by the hand,
Nor I half turn to go yet turning stay.
Remember me when no more, day by day,
    You tell me of our future that you planned:
    Only remember me; you understand
It will be late to counsel then or pray.
Yet if you should forget me for a while
    And afterwards remember, do not grieve:
    For if the darkness and corruption leave
    A vestige of the thoughts that once I had,
Better by far you should forget and smile
    Than that you should remember and be sad.

On The Wing

Once in a dream (for once I dreamed of you)
    We stood together in an open field;
    Above our heads two swift-winged pigeons wheeled,
Sporting at ease and courting full in view.
When loftier still a broadening darkness flew,
    Down-swooping, and a ravenous hawk revealed;
    Too weak to fight, too fond to fly, they yield;
So farewell life and love and pleasures new.
Then, as their plumes fell fluttering to the ground,
    Their snow-white plumage flecked with crimson drops,
      I wept, and thought I turned towards you to weep:
    But you were gone; while rustling hedgerow tops
Bent in a wind which bore to me a sound
    Of far-off piteous bleat of lambs and sheep.

An Old-World Thicket

    . . . *"Una selva oscura."*—DANTE.

Awake or sleeping (for I know not which)
    I was or was not mazed within a wood
    Where every mother-bird brought up her brood
      Safe in some leafy niche
Of oak or ash, of cypress or of beech,

Of silvery aspen trembling delicately,
    Of plane or warmer-tinted sycamore,
    Of elm that dies in secret from the core,
      Of ivy weak and free,
Of pines, of all green lofty things that be.

Such birds they seemed as challenged each desire;
    Like spots of azure heaven upon the wing,
    Like downy emeralds that alight and sing,
      Like actual coals on fire,
Like anything they seemed, and everything.

Such mirth they made, such warblings and such chat
    With tongue of music in a well-turned beak,
    They seemed to speak more wisdom than we speak,
      To make our music flat
And all our subtlest reasonings wild or weak.

Their meat was nought but flowers like butterflies,
    With berries coral-colored or like gold;
    Their drink was only dew, which blossoms hold
      Deep where the honey lies;
Their wings and tails were lit by sparkling eyes.

The shade wherein they revelled was a shade
    That danced and twinkled to the unseen sun;
    Branches and leaves cast shadows one by one,
      And all their shadows swayed
To breaths of air that rustled and that played.

A sound of waters neither rose nor sank,
　　And spread a sense of freshness through the air;
　　It seemed not here or there, but everywhere,
　　　As if the whole earth drank,
Root fathom deep and strawberry on its bank.

But I who saw such things as I have said,
　　Was overdone with utter weariness;
　　And walked in care, as one whom fears oppress
　　　Because above his head
Death hangs, or damage, or the dearth of bread.

Each sore defeat of my defeated life
　　Faced and outfaced me in that bitter hour;
　　And turned to yearning palsy all my power,
　　　And all my peace to strife,
Self stabbing self with keen lack-pity knife.

Sweetness of beauty moved me to despair,
　　Stung me to anger by its mere content,
　　Made me all lonely on that way I went,
　　　Piled care upon my care,
Brimmed full my cup, and stripped me empty and bare.

For all that was but showed what all was not,
　　But gave clear proof of what might never be;
　　Making more destitute my poverty,
　　　And yet more blank my lot,
And me much sadder by its jubilee.

Therefore I sat me down: for wherefore walk?
　　And closed mine eyes: for wherefore see or hear?
　　Alas, I had no shutter to mine ear,
　　　And could not shun the talk
Of all rejoicing creatures far or near.

Without my will I hearkened and I heard
　　(Asleep or waking, for I know not which),
　　Till note by note the music changed its pitch;
　　　Bird ceased to answer bird,
And every wind sighed softly if it stirred.

The drip of widening waters seemed to weep,
　　All fountains sobbed and gurgled as they sprang,
Somewhere a cataract cried out in its leap
　　　Sheer down a headlong steep;
　　High over all cloud-thunders gave a clang.

Such universal sound of lamentation
　　I heard and felt, fain not to feel or hear;
　　Nought else there seemed but anguish far and near;
　　　Nought else but all creation
Moaning and groaning wrung by pain or fear,

Shuddering in the misery of its doom:
   My heart then rose a rebel against light,
    Scouring all earth and heaven and depth and height
      Ingathering wrath and gloom,
Ingathering wrath to wrath and night to night.

Ah me, the bitterness of such revolt,
   All impotent, all hateful, and all hate,
That kicks and breaks itself against the bolt
      Of an imprisoning fate,
   And vainly shakes, and cannot shake the gate.

Agony to agony, deep called to deep,
   Out of the deep I called of my desire;
   My strength was weakness and my heart was fire;
    Mine eyes that would not weep
Or sleep, scaled height and depth, and could not sleep;

The eyes, I mean, of my rebellious soul,
   For still my bodily eyes were closed and dark:
   A random thing I seemed without a mark,
    Racing without a goal,
   Adrift upon life's sea without an ark.

More leaden than the actual self of lead
   Outer and inner darkness weighed on me.
   The tide of anger ebbed. Then fierce and free
    Surged full above my head
   The moaning tide of helpless misery.

Why should I breathe, whose breath was but a sigh?
   Why should I live, who drew such painful breath?
Oh weary work, the unanswerable why!—
    Yet I, why should I die,
   Who had no hope in life, no hope in death?

Grasses and mosses and the fallen leaf
   Make peaceful bed for an indefinite term;
   But underneath the grass there gnaws a worm—
    Haply, there gnaws a grief—
Both, haply always; not, as now, so brief.

The pleasure I remember, it is past;
   The pain I feel is passing, passing by;
   Thus all the world is passing, and thus I:
    All things that cannot last
   Have grown familiar, and are born to die.

And being familiar, have so long been borne
   That habit trains us not to break but bend:
Mourning grows natural to us who mourn
    In foresight of an end,
   But that which ends not who shall brave or mend?

Surely the ripe fruits tremble on their bough,
    They cling and linger trembling till they drop:
I, trembling, cling to dying life; for how
        Face the perpetual Now?
    Birthless and deathless, void of start or stop,

Void of repentance, void of hope and fear,
    Of possibility, alternative,
    Of all that ever made us bear to live
        From night to morning here,
    Of promise even which has no gift to give.

The wood, and every creature of the wood,
    Seemed mourning with me in an undertone;
    Soft scattered chirpings and a windy moan,
        Trees rustling where they stood
And shivered, showed compassion for my mood.

Rage to despair; and now despair had turned
    Back to self-pity and mere weariness,
With yearnings like a smouldering fire that burned,
        And might grow more or less,
    And might die out or wax to white excess.

Without, within me, music seemed to be;
    Something not music, yet most musical,
Silence and sound in heavenly harmony;
        At length a pattering fall
    Of feet, a bell, and bleatings, broke through all.

Then I looked up. The wood lay in a glow
    From golden sunset and from ruddy sky;
    The sun had stooped to earth though once so high;
        Had stooped to earth, in slow
Warm dying loveliness brought near and low.

Each water-drop made answer to the light,
    Lit up a spark and showed the sun his face;
    Soft purple shadows paved the grassy space
        And crept from height to height,
    From height to loftier height crept up apace.

While opposite the sun a gazing moon
    Put on his glory for her coronet,
Kindling her luminous coldness to its noon,
        As his great splendor set;
    One only star made up her train as yet.

Each twig was tipped with gold, each leaf was edged
    And veined with gold from the gold-flooded west,
Each mother-bird, and mate-bird, and unfledged
        Nestling, and curious nest,
    Displayed a gilded moss or beak or breast.

And filing peacefully between the trees,
    Having the moon behind them, and the sun
Full in their meek mild faces, walked at ease
        A homeward flock, at peace
        With one another and with every one.

A patriarchal ram with tinkling bell
    Led all his kin; sometimes one browsing sheep
    Hung back a moment, or one lamb would leap
        And frolic in a dell;
Yet still they kept together, journeying well,

And bleating, one or other, many or few,
    Journeying together toward the sunlit west;
    Mild face by face, and woolly breast by breast,
        Patient, sun-brightened too,
        Still journeying toward the sunset and their rest.

Emily Dickinson (1830-1886)

AMERICA PRODUCED two great romantic poets in the nineteenth century. Emily Dickinson was one, Walt Whitman the other. Although both were eccentric and innovative figures in their own time, they have come to be seen as "representative" American poets.

Perhaps their popular images conform to a sexual stereotype of the male and female poet of the last century. Whitman is the epic, national bard, a bluff public figure and overt rebel. Dickinson appears as the lyric metaphysician, the spinster recluse whose defense of the female heart and spirit against cold Massachusetts orthodoxy was a quintessentially private affair. Her poetry, published posthumously, was quickly recognized by critics as a major event in American letters. More, probably, has been written about her work in the last seventy years than about any other woman who wrote poetry in English. Much of this criticism is sensitive and illuminating, yet her genius is such that no reading has defined her. Central meanings and themes in her poetry are still to be uncovered as society retrospectively gives women a proper place in the history of sensibility. Dickinson herself recognized that her poems conveyed a message too radical for her society: she saw her life and her words as a "loaded gun" waiting to be fired.

Emily Dickinson was the middle child of a successful Massachusetts lawyer, Edward Dickinson, whose rigorous authority she outwardly accepted. She was devoted to him. Her childhood and youth can be seen perhaps as a more provincial version of Mrs. Browning's or Christina Rossetti's. Emily was educated well by American standards of the time. She attended Amherst Academy and Mt. Holyoke Seminary, although she never finished the course. She had a brother and sister to whom she was strongly attached. All her family were Congregational church members, but Emily never experienced conversion or formally joined the church. Her comments about her mother are startlingly similar to those of Barrett Browning. Both mothers were passive, domestic, and not very close to their daughters. Dickinson wrote that "I never had a mother. I suppose a mother is one to whom you hurry when you are troubled." This gentle and compliant figure outlived Emily's father and was nursed by her two unmarried daughters through a long illness.

Dickinson was influenced by two men outside the immediate family circle. One was Benjamin Newton, a law student of her father's, who died young. The other, perhaps more important figure, was the Reverend Charles Wadsworth, a happily-married and by most accounts conventional man with a reputation as a charismatic preacher, whom Emily knew in her late twenties. Newton was the first contemporary to talk about ideas with her, but Wadsworth elicited a more profound response. Although there is no evidence that he shared her feelings, Dickinson's love poems of the 60's seem to be about an impossible—but reciprocal—passion. There may have been other men in later years toward whom she felt more than friendship, but her passions were one-sided, and she saw very few people. Nevertheless, it is clear from her poems that she conceived of heterosexual love as a whole experience, physical and spiritual—her imaginative appreciation of the event is profound.

Frail health, mental and physical, and her father's dislike of having his two daughters away from home, confirmed Emily's reclusive tendencies. She began deliberately to indulge in certain eccentricities. Sometime in the 1860's she began to dress all in white; by 1870 she saw almost no one but her immediate family. Her friendships were conducted through an extensive correspondence. In 1862 she had sent her verses for comment to Thomas Wentworth Higginson, editor, abolitionist and ardent feminist. She did not meet him until 1870.

By her own wish, almost no poems were published in her lifetime. The editions brought out in the 1890's, soon after Dickinson's death, were emended to provide the smoother meter, phrasing and rhyme demanded by contemporary taste. It was not until 1914, when Dickinson's niece brought out an edition of her aunt's verse, that the poems began to appear as they were written. In 1955 Thomas Johnson gave the public a variorum edition which comes as close as possible to the poet's own text and punctuation.

In her copy of Elizabeth Barrett Browning's *Aurora Leigh*, Emily Dickinson had underlined the bitter feminist passage beginning "By the way,/The works of women are symbolical" and ending "This hurts most, this—that after all, we are paid/The worth of our work perhaps." Of all Emily Dickinson's comments in praise of the "Anglo-Florentine" (whose framed portrait hung on her wall), these swift underlinings are the most eloquent. They make a bridge of sensibility between Barrett Browning, the recluse rescued by love and singled out for fame,

and her sister poet who lived largely in self-imposed seclusion. Emily Dickinson's admiration for the elder poet "Not on Record—bubbled other,/Flute—or Woman—/So divine—" suggests the extent of Barrett Browning's influence on aspiring women writers. In Emily Dickinson's case the influence was somewhat indirect, but in several poems she picks up images from Barrett Browning's verse. More important, a significant number of Dickinson's poems deal with the subject of the first part of *Aurora Leigh*: society's attempt to stifle or destroy the female imagination. This theme emerges very strongly if Dickinson's poems are read through in the complete edition. It tends to become blurred when her work is selected or anthologized. Critics have traditionally preferred the poetry in which this particular anger is either absent or universalized into a general statement.

Almost all the poems of the rich creative period in the early 1860's reflect Dickinson's preoccupation with the restrictions placed on women and with the internalization of these restrictions. "I can wade Grief—/Whole Pools of it—/I'm used to that—/But the least push of Joy/Breaks up my feet—" echoes Barrett Browning's more general comment in "Curse for a Nation" that "women weep and curse . . . (And no one marvels) night and day."

In a series of minor poems written in the early 1860's, Dickinson treats the subject of childhood directly.

They shut me up in Prose
As when a little Girl
They put me in the Closet—
Because they liked me "still"

She connects the suffocation of the imagination with the suppression of a more general spirit. Even more angrily she wrote,

It would have starved a Gnat—
To live so small as I—
And yet I was a living Child
With Food's necessity

Upon me—like a claw—
I could no more remove
Than I could coax a Leech away—
Or make a Dragon move—

These explicitly "social" poems provide a gloss and an historical context for more abstract statements about the starvation of the soul, as in the better-known "I had been hungry, all the Years—," which concludes "That Hunger—was a way/Of Persons outside Windows—/The Entering —takes away—".

In another mood she extends forgiveness.

'Tis true—They shut me in the Cold
But then—Themselves were warm
And could not know the feeling 'twas—
Forget it—Lord—of Them. . . .

And in an even lighter vein she makes a joke of the prohibitions imposed on little girls:

Over the fence—
Strawberries—grow—
Over the fence—
I could Climb—if I tried I know—
Berries are nice!

But—if I stain my Apron—
God would certainly scold!
Oh dear,—I guess if He were a Boy—
He'd—climb—if he could!

Imprisonment, suffocation, starvation, bloodsucking, burning (the Dragon) and most of all, freezing—this is how Emily Dickinson imaged the oppressions of a nineteenth-century girlhood. These poems are interspersed with the more popular ones about adult love, pain and death. Even the most innocent of these quoted poems (there are many more) relate to the mature experience. Strawberries, after all, would stain her "apron" red; this poem is written at about the same time as "Wild Nights," which deals with open sexual longing.

The love poems contain the same antagonism toward the constraints of conventional morality. Many are implicitly or explicitly blasphemous. She says of her lover that he "saturated Sight—/And I had no more eyes/For sordid excellence/ As Paradise." The whole meaning of sordidness is transformed in this poem in which life is ". . . over there behind the shelf/The Sexton keeps the Key to—/ Putting up/Our Life—His Porcelain—/ Like a Cup." The collusive ideology of church and home not only keeps life on a back shelf, but is especially indifferent to the odd cup "Discarded of the Housewife/Quaint—or Broke—".

A love affair that defies social and religious conventions can exist only in the imagination.

So We must meet apart—
You there—I—here—
With just the Door ajar
That Oceans are—and Prayer—
And that White Sustenance—
Despair. . . .

But the moments of abnegation are more than matched by the moments of challenge. In "Wild Nights" the poet and her lover are "Rowing in Eden" in a world where consummated passion does not lead to the Fall.

These love lyrics, like the poetry of Christina Rossetti, have a special concentration and poignancy because they are projected images of physically unrealized passion. However, the psychic cost of all that a fully human woman must suppress is anatomized in a series of poems about pain. In these poems the death of the heart and the imagination are always related as they are in "Me From Myself . . .", a curiously intense and reflexive poem about the divided self.

Dickinson never allowed herself to subjugate consciousness. As Richard Chase and others suggest, the cost of maintaining the mutual monarchy of the heart and the intellect may have been her strategic withdrawal from the world.

Nature is a constant source of analogy in Emily Dickinson's poetry, although she generally does not maintain that frustrated relationship between self and nature which is so common in women poets of the period.

Like Barrett Browning, Dickinson wrote very directly of women's struggle to develop an independent sense of themselves. In a very moving poem she rejects her infant baptism, where she was

> Crowned—Crowing—on my Father's
> breast—
> A half unconscious Queen—
> But this time—Adequate—Erect,
> With Will to choose, or to reject,
> And I choose, just a Crown—

Whether as bird or queen—two common roles for the speaker—the poet concentrates on the ability to fly and to choose, in spite of the constraints imposed by sex and genteel society.

A large number of Dickinson's poems are written in the first person. Critics tend to prefer either those poems which avoid this too-personal and troubling "I" or those in which the "I" is safely encased in a more general metaphor, as in "Because I could not stop for Death—". These poems are, perhaps, more accessible to a male readership. But there are plenty of fine poems in which the poet is clearly trying to keep her meanings in specific relation to the female experience.

Yet even Dickinson's most discerning and sympathetic male critics tend to see her sex, and its cultural influence on her life, as a limitation on her art. Richard Chase wrote in 1951, "if feminine vanity, fear, and Puritan fastidiousness were indeed strong elements of her character and strong forces in confirming her reclusive ways, her life had nevertheless the effect of a strong rhetorical statement of dissent." Chase regards this dissent as essentially private as compared with the radicalism of her male contemporaries Hawthorne and Melville, and thus as less interesting and valuable. Her revolt, remarks Chase, was "entirely personal." While readers and critics of different political persuasions may differ about the value of "personal" or "public" dissent in a work of art, what Chase's distinction suggests is the habit of mind which automatically sees a revolt against cultural tyranny over sexual roles and female "feelings" as less political than attacks on other sorts of injustice. "Personal" in this context becomes a code word for self-concerned. Chase's assessment of Emily Dickinson as one of the great poets and true dissenters of her time ought to be reasserted today, without any sexual qualifications.

67   Success is counted sweetest
By those who ne'er succeed.
To comprehend a nectar
Requires sorest need.

Not one of all the purple Host
Who took the Flag today
Can tell the definition
So clear of Victory

As he defeated—dying—
On whose forbidden ear
The distant strains of triumph
Burst agonized and clear!

214   I taste a liquor never brewed—
From Tankards scooped in Pearl—
Not all the Vats upon the Rhine
Yield such an Alcohol!

Inebriate of Air—am I—
And Debauchee of Dew—
Reeling—thro endless summer days—
From inns of Molten Blue—

When "Landlords" turn the drunken Bee
Out of the Foxglove's door—
When Butterflies—renounce their "drams"—
I shall but drink the more!

Till Seraphs swing their snowy Hats—
And Saints—to windows run—
To see the little Tippler
Leaning against the—Sun—

249   Wild Nights—Wild Nights!
Were I with thee
Wild Nights should be
Our luxury!

Futile—the Winds—
To a Heart in port—
Done with the Compass—
Done with the Chart!

Rowing in Eden—
Ah, the Sea!
Might I but moor—Tonight—
In Thee!

251   Over the fence—
     Strawberries—grow—
     Over the fence—
     I could climb—if I tried, I know—
     Berries are nice!

     But—if I stained my Apron—
     God would certainly scold!
     Oh, dear,—I guess if He were a Boy—
     He'd—climb—if He could!

254   "Hope" is the thing with feathers—
     That perches in the soul—
     And sings the tune without the words—
     And never stops—at all—

     And sweetest—in the Gale—is heard—
     And sore must be the storm—
     That could abash the little Bird
     That kept so many warm—

     I've heard it in the chillest land—
     And on the strangest Sea—
     Yet, never, in Extremity,
     It asked a crumb—of Me.

258   There's a certain Slant of light,
     Winter Afternoons—
     That oppresses, like the Heft
     Of Cathedral Tunes—

     Heavenly Hurt, it gives us—
     We can find no scar,
     But internal difference,
     Where the Meanings, are—

     None may teach it—Any—
     'Tis the Seal Despair—
     An imperial affliction
     Sent us of the Air—

     When it comes, the Landscape listens—
     Shadows—hold their breath—
     When it goes, 'tis like the Distance
     On the look of Death—

288   I'm Nobody! Who are you?
     Are you—Nobody—Too?
     Then there's a pair of us?
     Don't tell! they'd advertise—you know!

How dreary—to be—Somebody!
How public—like a Frog—
To tell one's name—the livelong June—
To an admiring Bog!

303   The Soul selects her own Society—
Then—shuts the Door—
To her divine Majority—
Present no more—

Unmoved—she notes the Chariots—pausing—
At her low Gate—
Unmoved—an Emperor be kneeling
Upon her Mat—

I've known her—from an ample nation—
Choose One—
Then—close the Valves of her attention—
Like Stone—

312   Her—"last Poems"—
Poets—ended—
Silver—perished—with her Tongue—
Not on Record—bubbled other,
Flute—or Woman—
So divine—
Not unto its Summer—Morning
Robin—uttered Half the Tune—
Gushed too free for the Adoring—
From the Anglo-Florentine—
Late—the Praise—
'Tis dull—conferring
On the Head too High to Crown—
Diadem—or Ducal Showing—
Be its Grave—sufficient sign—
Nought—that We—No Poet's Kinsman—
Suffocate—with easy woe—
What, and if, Ourself a Bridegroom—
Put Her down—in Italy?

341   After great pain, a formal feeling comes—
The Nerves sit ceremonious, like Tombs—
The stiff Heart questions was it He, that bore,
And Yesterday, or Centuries before?

The Fleet, mechanical, go round—
Of Ground, or Air, or Ought—
A Wooden way
Regardless grown,
A Quartz contentment, like a stone—

This is the Hour of Lead—
Remembered, if outlived,
As Freezing persons, recollect the Snow—
First—Chill—then Stupor—then the letting go—

151

449   I died for Beauty—but was scarce
Adjusted in the Tomb
When One who died for Truth, was lain
In an adjoining Room—

He questioned softly "Why I failed"?
"For Beauty", I replied—
"And I—for Truth—Themself are One—
We Brethren, are", He said—

And so, as Kinsmen, met a Night—
We talked between the Rooms—
Until the Moss had reached our lips—
And covered up—our names—

508   I'm ceded—I've stopped being Theirs—
The name They dropped upon my face
With water, in the country church
Is finished using, now,
And They can put it with my Dolls,
My childhood, and the string of spools,
I've finished threading—too—

Baptized, before, without the choice,
But this time, consciously, of Grace—
Unto supremest name—
Called to my Full—The Crescent dropped—
Existence's whole Arc, filled up,
With one small Diadem.

My second Rank—too small the first—
Crowned—Crowing—on my Father's breast—
A half unconscious Queen—
But this time—Adequate—Erect,
With Will to choose, or to reject,
And I choose, just a Crown—

520   I started Early—Took my Dog—
And visited the Sea—
The Mermaids in the Basement
Came out to look at me—

And Frigates—in the Upper Floor
Extended Hempen Hands—
Presuming Me to be a Mouse—
Aground—upon the Sands—

But no Man moved Me—till the Tide
Went past my simple Shoe—
And past my Apron—and my Belt
And past my Bodice—too—

And made as He would eat me up—
As wholly as a Dew
Upon a Dandelion's Sleeve—
And then—I started—too—

And He—He followed—close behind—
I felt His Silver Heel
Upon my Ankle—Then my Shoes
Would overflow with Pearl—

Until We met the Solid Town—
No One He seemed to know—
And bowing—with a Mighty look—
At me—the Sea withdrew—

536   The Heart asks Pleasure—first—
And then—Excuse from Pain—
And then—those little Anodynes
That deaden suffering—

And then—to go to sleep—
And then—if it should be
The will of its Inquisitor
The privilege to die—

538   'Tis true—They shut me in the Cold—
But then—Themselves were warm
And could not know the feeling 'twas—
Forget it—Lord—of Them—

Let not my Witness hinder Them
In Heavenly esteem—
No Paradise could be—Conferred
Through Their beloved Blame—

The Harm They did—was short—And since
Myself—who bore it—do—
Forgive Them—Even as Myself—
Or else—forgive not me—

579   I had been hungry, all the Years—
My Noon had Come—to dine—
I trembling drew the Table near—
And touched the Curious Wine—

'Twas this on Tables I had seen—
When turning, hungry, Home
I looked in Windows, for the Wealth
I could not hope—for Mine—

I did not know the ample Bread—
'Twas so unlike the Crumb
The Birds and I, had often shared
In Nature's—Dining Room—

153

The Plenty hurt me—'twas so new—
Myself felt ill—and odd—
As Berry—of a Mountain Bush—
Transplanted—to the Road—

Nor was I hungry—so I found
That Hunger—was a way
Of Persons outside Windows—
The Entering—takes away—

612   It would have starved a Gnat—
To live so small as I—
And yet I was a living Child—
With Food's necessity

Upon me—like a Claw—
I could no more remove
Than I could coax a Leech away—
Or make a Dragon—move—

Nor like the Gnat—had I—
The privilege to fly
And seek a Dinner for myself
How mightier He—than I—

Nor like Himself—the Art
Upon the Window Pane
To gad my little Being out—
And not begin—again—

613   They shut me up in Prose—
As when a little Girl
They put me in the Closet—
Because they liked me "still"—

Still! Could themself have peeped—
And seen my Brain—go round—
They might as wise have lodged a Bird
For Treason—in the Pound—

Himself has but to will
And easy as a Star
Abolish his Captivity—
And laugh—No more have I—

640   I cannot live with You—
It would be Life—
And Life is over there—
Behind the Shelf

The Sexton keeps the Key to—
Putting up
Our Life—His Porcelain—
Like a Cup—

Discarded of the Housewife—
Quaint—or Broke—
A newer Sevres pleases—
Old Ones crack—

I could not die—with You—
For One must wait
To shut the Other's Gaze down—
You—could not—

And I—Could I stand by
And see You—freeze—
Without my Right of Frost—
Death's privilege?

Nor could I rise—with You—
Because Your Face
Would put out Jesus'—
That New Grace

Glow plain—and foreign
On my homesick Eye—
Except that You than He
Shone closer by—

They'd judge Us—How—
For You—served Heaven—You know,
Or sought to—
I could not—

Because You saturated Sight—
And I had no more Eyes
For sordid excellence
As Paradise

And were You lost, I would be—
Though My Name
Rang loudest
On the heavenly fame—

And were You—saved—
And I—condemned to be
Where You were not—
That self—were Hell to Me—

So We must meet apart—
You there—I—here—
With just the Door ajar
That Oceans are—and Prayer—
And that White Sustenance—
Despair—

642   Me from Myself—to banish—
Had I Art—
Impregnable my Fortress
Unto All Heart—

But since Myself—assault Me—
How have I peace
Except by subjugating
Consciousness?

And since We're mutual Monarch
How this be
Except by Abdication—
Me—of Me?

650   Pain—has an Element of Blank—
It cannot recollect
When it begun—or if there were
A time when it was not—

It has no future—but itself—
Its Infinite contain
Its Past—enlightened to perceive
New Periods—of Pain.

675   Essential Oils—are wrung—
The Attar from the Rose
Be not expressed by Suns—alone—
It is the gift of Screws—

The General Rose—decay—
But this—in Lady's Drawer
Make Summer—When the Lady lie
In Ceaseless Rosemary—

712   Because I could not stop for Death—
He kindly stopped for me—
The Carriage held but just Ourselves—
And Immortality.

We slowly drove—He knew no haste
And I had put away
My labor and my leisure too,
For His Civility—

We passed the School, where Children strove
At Recess—in the Ring—
We passed the Fields of Gazing Grain—
We passed the Setting Sun—

Or rather—He passed Us—
The Dews drew quivering and chill—
For only Gossamer, my Gown—
My Tippet—only Tulle—

We paused before a House that seemed
A Swelling of the Ground—
The Roof was scarcely visible—
The Cornice—in the Ground—

Since then—'tis Centuries—and yet
Feels shorter than the Day
I first surmised the Horses' Heads
Were toward Eternity—

754   My Life had stood—a Loaded Gun—
In Corners—till a Day
The Owner passed—identified—
And carried Me away—

And now We roam in Sovereign Woods—
And now We hunt the Doe—
And every time I speak for Him—
The Mountains straight reply—

And do I smile, such cordial light
Upon the Valley glow—
It is as a Vesuvian face
Had let its pleasure through—

And when at Night—Our good Day done—
I guard My Master's Head—
'Tis better than the Eider-Duck's
Deep Pillow—to have shared—

To foe of His—I'm deadly foe—
None stir the second time—
On whom I lay a Yellow Eye—
Or an emphatic Thumb—

Though I than He—may longer live
He longer must—than I—
For I have but the power to kill,
Without—the power to die—

1732   My life closed twice before its close—
It yet remains to see
If Immortality unveil
A third event to me

So huge, so hopeless to conceive
As these that twice befell.
Parting is all we know of heaven,
And all we need of hell.

Mathilde Blind (1841-1896)

ATHILDE BLIND'S childhood and youth present a striking contrast to the conventional girlhoods of her English and American contemporaries. Neither the Brontes nor Mathilde's beloved George Eliot could have invented a more romantic beginning, or a more appropriate genesis for the literary heights to which she aspired. Mathilde Blind was born Mathilde Cohen in Mannheim, Germany, the elder of two children of a well-to-do elderly banker and his young vivacious wife. Cohen died in Mathilde's infancy and her mother made a very different second marriage to Karl Blind, a young political writer who became a leader of the Baden insurrections in the '48 revolutions. Blind was jailed for a time. When released he was sent as the people's representative to Paris. As reaction swung him out of favor, he was forced into exile first in Belgium, then in London. The family settled in St. John's Wood when Mathilde was eight.

Throughout the next thirty years the Blind house was a way station for radical exiles and transients. Mathilde's formal education was haphazard, but she was privy to all sorts of momentous meetings. She remembered listening to Garibaldi and Ledru-Rollin reviewing the failure of '48 in France. Louis Blanc commended one of her first serious poetic efforts— a verse tragedy about Robespierre. And Mazzini, whom she preferred to all the others, talked to her seriously about her life, chiding her for "being an aristocrat because I had more feeling for the sufferings of celebrated people than for

those unknown persons." He advised the earnest young woman to make herself "clear about life and the world."

Mathilde needed the discipline of such advice. Left in early adolescence to educate herself, she had steeped herself in literature, principally the Romantic poets. From this "Earthly Paradise which the poets have planted with immortelles" she emerged at about fifteen or sixteen, but noted in retrospect that "art, with the exception of the noble Greek drama, is not a good preparation for life." Her first confrontation with the world occurred in a genteel school for girls run by a faded minister's widow. Mathilde retained a gentle memory of the place:

Whenever I think of that house I am again conscious of the atmosphere that pervaded it. A scent of sandal-wood and lavender is faintly perceptible. The partially drawn blinds diffuse a mellow half light. The air stealing through an open window puffs out the white muslin curtains; lilac bushes and clematis cling to the wall outside. A girl sits at the piano with smooth, light-brown hair slightly fluffed on either side of her face like a dove's wing. She is playing Mendelssohn's "Song without Words." The whole place breathes purity and peace. Girls in fresh spotless gowns move about in the rooms.

She had her first crush on a schoolmate, and with another friend she went through a brief spell of religiosity. This quickly turned into an inquiry about the "truths" of the bible. Mathilde compared Genesis with geology: "I went to work with a headlong eagerness which kept me up night after night for many months till the small hours, reading, comparing, annotating . . . ." Eventually she settled on heresy, was discovered, would not back off and was expelled from the school.

The experience left its mark, for the core of Mathilde Blind's feminism was her belief in female education. She realized that she alone of her circle of acquaintances was adequately educated, and that had been achieved through individual perseverance. Her favorite poem was Mrs. Browning's *Aurora Leigh*, which caught the essence of the "soulless, unspiritual education, where everything is nipped in the bud and crushed to nothingness" that was offered to Victorian girls. Significantly, she felt that *Aurora Leigh* was "the first revelation of the world through poetry" and "a whole, springing from the depths of thought." It is possible that she saw Aurora as a model; the poem was published when Mathilde was fifteen.

In 1859 Mathilde visited Zurich, where she stayed with her mother's brother and took a solitary walking tour through Switzerland. In the Alps, "those Mothers of Europe," she "felt truly free. My body, pliant to my soul, moved rhythmically to the sound of the stream." In Switzerland she met a "group of brilliant revolutionists," and studied Latin, Old and Middle German and philology. Her twenties she spent at home, with frequent trips to the continent and to friends in England. She continued her program of self-education, and worked her way through Kant, the Bible, Shakespeare and Goethe. Her feminism began to assume a political shape—she wrote and spoke in favor of the vote, entry to all professions except military, and education. Her trinity of heroines—George Sand, George Eliot, Elizabeth Barrett Browning—were all women who defied Victorian conventions. Mathilde even tried the lecture platform, but her striking presence and wit, so vivid in the drawing room, did not carry to larger audiences. What was conveyed

was her moral earnestness, and a certain lack of humor that sometimes went with it. Mathilde's political and artistic aspirations became more and more directed towards poetry and prose essays. The effect of an atmosphere of frustrated revolutionary ardor worked very differently on her younger brother Ferdinand. In 1866, Ferdinand attempted to assassinate Bismark and, failing, committed suicide. The year after, when Mathilde's first mature book of poems was published, she was in deep mourning.

By the time she was thirty she had moved out of the family house and set up on her own—another step towards independence. By now she had her own circle of associates, who tended to be English and literary, rather than continental and political. Moncure Conway, the Quaker democrat and biographer, was a close friend, sympathetic to her feminism. She knew the William Rossettis well, and became intimate with Ford Madox Brown and his wife. A beautiful and charismatic woman—if a bit imperious and humorless—she made friends easily and kept their loyalty. Although there was no estrangement from her parents' household it appears that she relied on a core of close friends over the years to keep her going through frequent depressions and periods of ill health. She needed friends psychologically as well as socially, for her way of life gave her no secure place in society. It was not usual for well-brought-up, unmarried Victorian women who were not particularly well-off to live as she did. There was nothing scandalous in it; it was merely not done. Aurora Leigh might live in an attic but most Victorian women of letters were suitably surrounded and protected by family—especially while still young—and, presumably, sexually vulnerable.

The 'seventies and 'eighties were productive years. Mathilde translated Strauss's *The Old Faith and the New* (1873), wrote two long poems, "Prophecy of St. Oran" and "The Heather on Fire" and a prose romance, *Tarantella*. Her most important prose works were two biographies—of George Eliot and Mme. Roland—for the Eminent Women series edited by her friend J. H. Ingram. Mathilde realized the crucial role of propaganda—it was important to publicize the lives of women who had rejected the passive model of wife and mother. Her own chosen way of life was an effort to prove that there were fruitful alternatives. Although she had transformed herself into an Englishwoman, she kept her connection with the continent by frequent trips, particularly in her last years, when the fortune she inherited allowed her to travel in style.

Her last ambitious poem was *The Ascent of Man* (1888), a "celebration" of the theory of evolution. None of the long poems stand up terribly well as sustained poetic efforts. She did not have the verbal dexterity or the wit to carry the reader through a long piece. Yet shorter poems like "The Sower," "Reapers" and "Lassitude" are lovely. Description of a single event, abstraction or feeling was within her reach as a poet, and in these poems she avoids the "grand" style that mars the epic attempts. Into the shorter lyrics as well, is channeled the despair and frustration, the sense of failure that is a common theme with most women poets in the nineteenth century. Their aspirations were given so little support by society that a disproportionate amount of emotional energy went into staying confident and productive. Spells of acute depression and self-doubt were normal results of this strain, and the inevitable expression of these feelings in their poems was a sobering corrective to Victorian optimism. Mathilde wrote: "At Life's crude hands/We ask no gift she understands." Mathilde grew up in an atmosphere of political and literary romanticism with its two conflicting ideals, individual heroism and collective democracy. She saw that most women were barred from both, and tried to live the first while arguing for the second. Some of the poems suggest that the effort was exhausting. An acquaintance remembers Mathilde in her late teens as a "dazzling and vivid beauty" who "simply danced for the enjoyment of dancing." When asked what men would do when women took over the professions and put them out of work, she replied "Emigrate."

An older and more embittered Mathilde would write:

Go, happy Soul! run fluid in the wave,
Vibrate in light, escape thy natal curse;
Go forth no longer as my body-slave
But as the heir of all the universe.

There is no doubt that the "natal curse" was the curse of her sex. And Mathilde, who had turned away, after Ferdinand's death, from revolutionary solutions, thought it could be remedied, at least for middle-class women, by education. She looked for a suitable institution to which she might leave Max Cohen's fortune and, after making a tour of women's schools, settled finally on Newnham College, Cambridge.

The Sower

The winds had hushed at last as by command;
 The quiet sky above,
With its grey clouds spread o'er the fallow land,
 Sat brooding like a dove.

There was no motion in the air, no sound
 Within the tree-tops stirred,
Save when some last leaf, fluttering to the ground,
 Dropped like a wounded bird:

Or when the swart rooks in a gathering crowd
 With clamorous noises wheeled,
Hovering awhile, then swooped with wrangling loud
 Down on the stubbly field.

For now the big-thewed horses, toiling slow
 In straining couples yoked,
Patiently dragged the ploughshare to and fro
 Till their wet haunches smoked.

Till the stiff acre, broken into clods,
 Bruised by the harrow's tooth,
Lay lightly shaken, with its humid sods
 Ranged into furrows smooth.

There looming lone, from rise to set of sun,
 Without or pause or speed,
Solemnly striding by the furrows dun,
 The sower sows the seed.

The sower sows the seed, which mouldering,
 Deep coffined in the earth,
Is buried now, but with the future spring
 Will quicken into birth.

Oh, poles of birth and death! Controlling Powers
 Of human toil and need!
On this fair earth all men are surely sowers,
 Surely all life is seed!

All life is seed, dropped in Time's yawning furrow,
 Which with slow sprout and shoot,
In the revolving world's unfathomed morrow,
 Will blossom and bear fruit.

Reapers

Sun-tanned men and women, toiling there together;
  Seven I count in all, in yon field of wheat,
Where the rich ripe ears in the harvest weather
  Glow an orange gold through the sweltering heat.

Busy life is still, sunk in brooding leisure:
  Birds have hushed their singing in the hushed tree-tops;
Not a single cloud mars the flawless azure;
  Not a shadow moves o'er the moveless crops;

In the grassy shallows, that no breath is creasing,
Chestnut-coloured cows in the rushes dank
Stand like cows of bronze, save when they flick the teasing
  Flies with switch of tail from each quivering flank.

Nature takes a rest—even her bees are sleeping,
  And the silent wood seems a church that's shut;
But these human creatures cease not from their reaping
  While the corn stands high, waiting to be cut.

Soul-Drift

I let my soul drift with the thistledown
  Afloat upon the honeymooning breeze;
My thoughts about the swelling buds are blown,
  Blown with the golden dust of flowering trees.

On fleeting gusts of desultory song,
  I let my soul drift out into the Spring;
The Psyche flies and palpitates among
  The palpitating creatures on the wing.

Go, happy Soul! run fluid in the wave,
  Vibrate in light, escape thy natal curse;
Go forth no longer as my body-slave,
  But as the heir of all the Universe.

Lassitude

I laid me down beside the sea,
Endless in blue monotony;
The clouds were anchored in the sky,
Sometimes a sail went idling by.

Upon the shingles on the beach
Gray linen was spread out to bleach,
And gently with a gentle swell
The languid ripples rose and fell.

A fisher-boy, in level line,
Cast stone by stone into the brine:
Methought I too might do as he,
And cast my sorrows on the sea.

The old, old sorrows in a heap
Dropped heavily into the deep;
But with its sorrow on that day
My heart itself was cast away.

Rest

We are so tired; my heart and I.
Of all things here beneath the sky
Only one thing would please us best—
Endless, unfathomable rest.

We are so tired; we ask no more
Than just to slip out by Life's door;
And leave behind the noisy rout
And everlasting turn about.

Once it seemed well to run on too
With her importunate, fevered crew,
And snatch amid the frantic strife
Some morsel from the board of life.

But we are tired. At Life's crude hands
We ask no gift she understands;
But kneel to him she hates to crave
The absolution of the grave.

Manchester By Night

O'er this huge town, rife with intestine wars,
Whence as from monstrous sacrificial shrines
Pillars of smoke climb heavenward, Night inclines
Black brows majestical with glimmering stars.
Her dewy silence soothes life's angry jars:
And like a mother's wan white face, who pines
Above her children's turbulent ways, so shines
The moon athwart the narrow cloudy bars.

Now toiling multitudes that hustling crush
Each other in the fateful strife for breath,
And, hounded on by divers hungers, rush
Across the prostrate ones that groan beneath,
Are swathed within the universal hush,
As life exchanges semblances with death.

The Dead

The dead abide with us! Though stark and cold
Earth seems to grip them, they are with us still:
They have forged our chains of being for good or ill
And their invisible hands these hands yet hold.
Our perishable bodies are the mould
In which their strong imperishable will—
Mortality's deep yearning to fulfil—
Hath grown incorporate through dim time untold.
Vibrations infinite of life in death,
As a star's travelling light survives its star!
So may we hold our lives, that when we are
The fate of those who then will draw this breath,
They shall not drag us to their judgment bar,
And curse the heritage which we bequeath.

Mourning Women

All veiled in black, with faces hid from sight,
  Crouching together in the jolting cart,
  What forms are these that pass alone, apart,
In abject apathy to life's delight?
The motley crowd, fantastically bright,
  Shifts gorgeous through each dazzling street and mart
  Only these sisters of the suffering heart
Strike discords in this symphony of light.

Most wretched woman! whom your prophet dooms
  To take love's penalties without its prize!
Yes; you shall bear the unborn in your wombs,
  And water dusty death with streaming eyes,
And, wailing, beat your breasts among the tombs;
  But souls ye have none fit for Paradise.

The Sâkiyeh

"How long shall Man be Nature's fool?" Man cries;
  "Be like those great, gaunt oxen, drilled and bound,
  Inexorably driven round and round
To turn the water-wheel with bandaged eyes?
And as they trudge beneath Egyptian skies,
  Watering the wrinkled desert's beggared ground,
  The hoarse Sâkiyeh's lamentable sound
Fills all the land as with a people's sighs?"

Poor Brutes! who in unconsciousness sublime,
  Replenishing the ever-empty jars,
    Endow the waste with palms and harvest gold:
  And men, who move in rhythm with moving stars,
    Should shrink to give the borrowed lives they hold:
Bound blindfold to the groaning wheel of Time.

Emma Lazarus (1849-1887)

MOST AMERICAN school children have read or heard, possibly in the well-known musical setting, the famous final lines of Emma Lazarus' sonnet . . .

"Give me your tired, your poor,
Your huddled masses yearning to breathe
free,
The wretched refuse of your teeming shore.
Send these, the homeless, tempest-tost to me,
I lift my lamp beside the golden door!"

The maternal, aristocratic, slightly patronizing speaker is the Statue of Liberty, "Mother of Exiles." Written in 1883, when America's white middle classes were beginning to feel queasy about receiving the "wretched refuse" with open arms, the poem testifies eloquently to the liberal sympathies of its author. The opening lines are less well-known; they are both more democratic and more subversive of male dominance than the sonnet's closing would suggest:

Not like the brazen giant of Greek fame,
With conquering limbs astride from land to
land;
Here at our sea-washed, sunset gates shall
stand
A mighty woman with a torch, whose flame
Is the imprisoned lightning, and her name
"Mother of Exiles."

No poem of the period better indicates the advance in consciousness which women writers had made by the late nineteenth century. The Statue of Liberty is not simply a classical welcoming mother but stands in direct opposition to that other aggressive, imperialist symbol of nationalism. The energy of the poem rises without hesitation to the phrase "mighty woman." Yet the imaging of the immigrants as homeless children, "wretched refuse," betrays the aristocratic condescension and benevolent bias of the poet. Matriarchy can oppose patriarchy, but the paternalistic bourgeois emphasis is not disturbed.

Given Emma Lazarus' life and background it is remarkable that she came to write such a positive, female-oriented poem at all. The frail daughter of a rich New York industrialist, Emma was educated by private tutors who soon discovered her precociousness. Moses and Hettie Lazarus were of old Jewish-American stock. They had wealth, education, and social position. Emma was a middle child among seven children, and the favorite of six girls. Moses was the central and dominating figure of the household, and at least one biographer sees Emma's lifelong attachment to her father, who was also critic, admirer and friend, as the single most important influence in her life.

Emma started writing poetry and translating from German and French when she was still in her teens. Her translations of Hugo, Schiller and Heine were better than her own juvenilia. They first appeared in 1867 in a privately-printed book called *Poems and Translations*. Searching for some expert opinion outside her family she sent her book, with some misgivings, to Ralph Waldo Emerson, whom she had met the year before. A long correspondence and friendship was begun between the old transcendentalist and the young late romantic. In 1875, however, the friendship reached a crisis: Emerson produced a huge anthology of English and American poetry which excluded Emma while including many less talented poets. Her ego was as frail as her health and she broke down briefly over Emerson's neglect. This breach was eventually repaired and in 1887 she even visited her old friend in Concord. She was then twenty-seven and gaining a literary reputation, but she was a girl still, with very little experience of life outside her family.

Judaism as a religion had not affected her life much. Like many liberal Jews, she had espoused a vague ethical humanism which was close in feeling to Emerson's nonsectarian transcendentalism. However, the pogroms following the assassination of Czar Alexander II suddenly provided an issue with which she could identify ethnically, politically and emotionally. She had been too young to feel much about the Civil War; "politics" had always meant the sordid corruptions of America's Gilded Age. The pogroms set her Jewishness in a new light. They gave Emma an international liberal and romantic cause which she eventually integrated with an unexamined patriotism to her own country. She began to write essays for popular magazines as well as for *The American Hebrew*. A laudatory piece on Disraeli as a representative Jew indicates her basically elitist and naive view of politics, but her eloquent defenses of the victims of the pogroms are much more ably argued. She was an excellent linguist, and she now applied herself to Hebrew so that she could translate from Jewish literature. George Eliot's *Daniel Deronda*, with its Jewish hero and pro-Jewish bias, made the novelist a heroine for Emma Lazarus. Eliot's portrait stood for many years a fixture on Emma's desk.

In 1883 Emma, accompanied by her younger sister Annie, made her first trip abroad. She now had a large circle of literary acquaintances and was provided with introductions. In England she made friends with Browning and developed an even warmer relationship with William Morris. She enjoyed the continent, which she had previously known only through books, but it somehow frightened her. She felt more at home in England.

In 1885 she returned home, where her father was dying. On his deathbed she quoted Poe's lines:

> Ah, broken is the golden bowl! the spirit
> flows forever!
> Let the bell toll!—a saintly soul floats on
> the Stygian River.

Grieving and empty she fled back to Europe. During this last period of her life she continued to write poems about the Jews and it was chiefly the *Songs of a Semite* for which she was known in her own day. She became ill with what must have been cancer during her second European trip and died in 1887 at the home of one of her sisters. A whole issue of *The American Hebrew* was given over to her memory. Her admirers included many of the leading writers of the day, yet her reputation as a poet for any verse other than "The New Colossus" did not last.

Emma Lazarus is certainly one of the most talented and interesting American poets of a generation which produced very few poets of any merit. Perhaps she would have been more at home with the great Victorians—Emily Dickinson, Whitman, Emerson, Thoreau, the Brownings. Emma may have died too young to see beyond the confines of the upper-class late romantic sensibility which dominated her work and the age. Her crusade for the Jews took place in the last flare of liberal romanticism, with its passionate concern for abstract liberty, its love of individual heroes and heroines, and its vague distaste for the unknown masses in whose behalf "liberty" was to be won.

Emma Lazarus' brief life falls into two parts. The first was her "transcendental" romantic phase, in which her poetry gave full vent to ambivalence about herself as a woman and poet. The second begins in the early 1880's, when she submerges her own sense of psychological exile to fight for Jewish exiles. Too "veiled and screened by womanhood" or, more precisely, by the cultural notion of it as embodied in the genteel tradition, her considerable talents both for poetry and polemic were never fully developed. Her father's death, and her last lonely trip to England (which she saw as beginning a new independent life for herself) came too late. Emma Lazarus' poetry is always interesting, often powerful, fresh in language and feeling, if a little tired in form. (She experimented with some blank verse in the manner of Whitman but did not use it enough to make it work for her.) Her life was too full to be judged unfinished, but that, somehow, is the sense that one is left with.

Epochs

"The epochs of our life are not in the visible facts, but in the silent thought by the wayside as we walk."—EMERSON

I. YOUTH.

Sweet empty sky of June without a stain,
　Faint, gray-blue dewy mists on far-off hills,
Warm, yellow sunlight flooding mead and plain,
　That each dark copse and hollow overfills;
　The rippling laugh of unseen, rain-fed rills,
Weeds delicate-flowered, white and pink and gold,
A murmur and a singing manifold.

The gray, austere old earth renews her youth
　With dew-lines, sunshine, gossamer, and haze.
How still she lies and dreams, and veils the truth,
　While all is fresh as in the early days!
　What simple things be these the soul to raise
To bounding joy, and make young pulses beat,
With nameless pleasure finding life so sweet.

On such a golden morning forth there floats,
　Between the soft earth and the softer sky,
In the warm air adust with glistening motes,
　The mystic winged and flickering butterfly,
　A human soul, that hovers giddily
Among the gardens of earth's paradise,
Nor dreams of fairer fields or loftier skies.

II. REGRET.

Thin summer rain on grass and bush and hedge,
　Reddening the road and deepening the green
On wide, blurred lawn, and in close-tangled sedge;
　Veiling in gray the landscape stretched between
　These low broad meadows and the pale hills seen
But dimly on the far horizon's edge.

In these transparent-clouded, gentle skies,
　Where through the moist beams of the soft June sun
Might any moment break, no sorrow lies,
　No note of grief in swollen brooks that run,
　No hint of woe in this subdued, calm tone
Of all the prospect unto dreamy eyes.

Only a tender, unnamed half-regret
　For the lost beauty of the gracious morn;
A yearning aspiration, fainter yet,
　For brighter suns in joyous days unborn,
　Now while brief showers ruffle grass and corn,
And all the earth lies shadowed, grave, and wet;

Space for the happy soul to pause again
　From pure content of all unbroken bliss,
To dream the future void of grief and pain,
　And muse upon the past, in reveries
　More sweet for knowledge that the present is
Not all complete, with mist and clouds and rain.

III. LONGING.

Look westward o'er the steaming rain-washed slopes,
  Now satisfied with sunshine, and behold
Those lustrous clouds, as glorious as our hopes,
  Softened with feathery fleece of downy gold,
  In all fantastic, huddled shapes uprolled,
Floating like dreams, and melting silently,
In the blue upper regions of pure sky.

The eye is filled with beauty, and the heart
  Rejoiced with sense of life and peace renewed;
And yet at such an hour as this, upstart
  Vague myriad longings, restless, unsubdued,
  And causeless tears from melancholy mood,
Strange discontent with earth's and nature's best,
Desires and yearnings that may find no rest.

IV. STORM.

Serene was morning with clear, winnowed air,
  But threatening soon the low, blue mass of cloud
Rose in the west, with mutterings faint and rare
  At first, but waxing frequent and more loud.
  Thick sultry mists the distant hill-tops shroud;
The sunshine dies; athwart black skies of lead
Flash noiselessly thin threads of lightning red.

Breathless the earth seems waiting some wild blow,
  Dreaded, but far too close to ward or shun.
Scared birds aloft fly aimless, and below
  Naught stirs in fields whence light and life are gone,
  Save floating leaves, with wisps of straw and down,
Upon the heavy air; 'neath blue-black skies,
Livid and yellow the green landscape lies.

And all the while the dreadful thunder breaks,
  Within the hollow circle of the hills,
With gathering might, that angry echoes wakes,
  And earth and heaven with unused clamor fills.
  O'erhead still flame those strange electric thrills.
A moment more,—behold! yon bolt struck home,
And over ruined fields the storm hath come!

V. SURPRISE.

When the stunned soul can first lift tired eyes
  On her changed world of ruin, waste, and wrack,
Ah, what a pang of aching sharp surprise
  Brings all sweet memories of the lost past back,
With wild self-pitying grief of one betrayed,
Duped in a land of dreams where Truth is dead!

Are these the heavens that she deemed were kind?
  Is this the world that yesterday was fair?
What painted images of folk half-blind
  Be these who pass her by, as vague as air?
What go they seeking? there is naught to find.
  Let them come nigh and hearken her despair.

A mocking lie is all she once believed,
   And where her heart throbbed, is a cold dead stone.
This is a doom she never preconceived,
   Yet now she cannot fancy it undone.
Part of herself, part of the whole hard scheme,
All else is but the shadow of a dream.

VI. GRIEF.

There is a hungry longing in the soul,
   A craving sense of emptiness and pain,
She may not satisfy nor yet control,
   For all the teeming world looks void and vain.
No compensation in eternal spheres,
She knows the loneliness of all her years.

There is no comfort looking forth nor back,
   The present gives the lie to all her past.
Will cruel time restore what she doth lack?
   Why was no shadow of this doom forecast?
Ah! she hath played with many a keen-edged thing;
Naught is too small and soft to turn and sting.

In the unnatural glory of the hour,
   Exalted over time, and death, and fate,
No earthly task appears beyond her power,
   No possible endurance seemeth great.
She knows her misery and her majesty,
And recks not if she be to live or die.

VII. ACCEPTANCE.

Yea, she hath looked Truth grimly face to face,
   And drained unto the lees the proffered cup.
This silence is not patience, nor the grace
   Of resignation, meekly offered up,
But mere acceptance fraught with keenest pain,
Seeing that all her struggles must be vain.

Her future clear and terrible outlies,—
   This burden to be borne through all her days,
This crown of thorns pressed down above her eyes,
   This weight of trouble she may never raise.
No reconcilement doth she ask nor wait;
Knowing such things are, she endures her fate.

No brave endeavor of the broken will
   To cling to such poor strays as will abide
(Although the waves be wild and angry still)
   After the lapsing of the swollen tide.
No fear of further loss, no hope of gain,
Naught but the apathy of weary pain.

VIII. LONELINESS.

All stupor of surprise hath passed away;
   She sees, with clearer vision than before,
A world far off of light and laughter gay,
   Herself alone and lonely evermore.
Folk come and go, and reach her in no wise,
Mere flitting phantoms to her heavy eyes.

All outward things, that once seemed part of her,
    Fall from her, like the leaves in autumn shed.
She feels as one embalmed in spice and myrrh,
    With the heart eaten out, a long time dead;
Unchanged without, the features and the form;
Within, devoured by the thin red worm.

By her own prowess she must stand or fall,
    This grief is to be conquered day by day.
Who could befriend her? who could make this small,
    Or her strength great? she meets it as she may.
A weary struggle and a constant pain,
She dreams not they may ever cease nor wane.

IX. SYMPATHY.
It comes not in such wise as she had deemed,
    Else might she still have clung to her despair.
More tender, grateful than she could have dreamed,
    Fond hands passed pitying over brows and hair,
    And gentle words borne softly through the air,
Calming her weary sense and wildered mind,
By welcome, dear communion with her kind.

Ah! she forswore all words as empty lies;
    What speech could help, encourage, or repair?
Yet when she meets these grave, indulgent eyes,
    Fulfilled with pity, simplest words are fair,
    Caressing, meaningless, that do not dare
To compensate or mend, but merely soothe
With hopeful visions after bitter Truth.

One who through conquered trouble had grown wise,
    To read the grief unspoken, unexpressed,
The misery of the blank and heavy eyes,—
    Or through youth's infinite compassion guessed
    The heavy burden,—such a one brought rest,
And bade her lay aside her doubts and fears,
While the hard pain dissolved in blessed tears.

X. PATIENCE.
The passion of despair is quelled at last;
    The cruel sense of undeservéd wrong,
The wild self-pity, these are also past;
    She knows not what may come, but she is strong;
She feels she hath not aught to lose nor gain,
Her patience is the essence of all pain.

As one who sits beside a lapsing stream,
    She sees the flow of changeless day by day,
Too sick and tired to think, too sad to dream,
    Nor cares how soon the waters slip away,
Nor where they lead; at the wise God's decree,
She will depart or bide indifferently.

173

There is a deeper pathos in the mild
    And settled sorrow of the quiet eyes,
Than in the tumults of the anguish wild,
    That made her curse all things beneath the skies;
No question, no reproaches, no complaint,
Hers is the holy calm of some meek saint.

XI. HOPE.

Her languid pulses thrill with sudden hope,
    That will not be forgot nor cast aside,
And life in statelier vistas seems to ope,
    Illimitably lofty, long, and wide.
What doth she know? She is subdued and mild,
Quiet and docile "as a weanéd child."

If grief came in such unimagined wise,
    How may joy dawn? In what undreamed-of hour,
May the light break with splendor of surprise,
    Disclosing all the mercy and the power?
A baseless hope, yet vivid, keen, and bright,
As the wild lightning in the starless night.

She knows not whence it came, nor where it passed,
    But it revealed, in one brief flash of flame,
A heaven so high, a world so rich and vast,
    That, full of meek contrition and mute shame,
In patient silence hopefully withdrawn,
She bows her head, and bides the certain dawn.

XII. COMPENSATION.

'Tis not alone that black and yawning void
    That makes her heart ache with this hungry pain,
But the glad sense of life hath been destroyed,
    The lost delight may never come again.
Yet myriad serious blessings with grave grace
Arise on every side to fill their place.

For much abides in her so lonely life,—
    The dear companionship of her own kind,
Love where least looked for, quiet after strife,
    Whispers of promise upon every wind,
And quickened insight, in awakened eyes,
For the new meaning of the earth and skies.

The nameless charm about all things hath died,
    Subtle as aureole round a shadow's head,
Cast on the dewy grass at morning-tide;
    Yet though the glory and the joy be fled,
'T is much her own endurance to have weighed,
And wrestled with God's angels, unafraid.

XIII. FAITH.

She feels outwearied, as though o'er her head
    A storm of mighty billows broke and passed.
Whose hand upheld her? Who her footsteps led
    To this green haven of sweet rest at last?

What strength was hers, unreckoned and unknown?
What love sustained when she was most alone?

Unutterably pathetic her desire,
   To reach, with groping arms outstretched in prayer,
Something to cling to, to uplift her higher
   From this low world of coward fear and care,
Above disaster, that her will may be
At one with God's, accepting his decree.

Though by no reasons she be justified,
   Yet strangely brave in Evil's very face,
She deems this want must needs be satisfied,
   Though here all slips from out her weak embrace.
And in blind ecstasy of perfect faith,
With her own dream her prayer she answereth.

XIV. WORK

Yet life is not a vision nor a prayer,
   But stubborn work; she may not shun her task.
After the first compassion, none will spare
   Her portion and her work achieved, to ask.
She pleads for respite,—she will come ere long
When, resting by the roadside, she is strong.

Nay, for the hurrying throng of passers-by
   Will crush her with their onward-rolling stream.
Much must be done before the brief light die;
   She may not loiter, rapt in this vain dream.
With unused trembling hands, and faltering feet,
She staggers forth, her lot assigned to meet.

But when she fills her days with duties done,
   Strange vigor comes, she is restored to health.
New aims, new interests rise with each new sun,
   And life still holds for her unbounded wealth.
All that seemed hard and toilsome now proves small,
And naught may daunt her,—she hath strength for all.

XV. VICTORY.

How strange, in some brief interval of rest,
   Backward to look on her far-stretching past.
To see how much is conquered and repressed,
   How much is gained in victory at last!
The shadow is not lifted,—but her faith,
Strong from life's miracles, now turns toward death.

Though much be dark where once rare splendor shone,
   Yet the new light has touched high peaks unguessed
In her gold, mist-bathed dawn, and one by one
   New outlooks loom from many a mountain crest.
She breathes a loftier, purer atmosphere,
And life's entangled paths grow straight and clear.

Nor will Death prove an all-unwelcome guest;
  The struggle has been toilsome to this end,
Sleep will be sweet, and after labor rest,
  And all will be atoned with him to friend.
Much must be reconciled, much justified,
And yet she feels she will be satisfied.

XVI. PEACE.
The calm outgoing of a long, rich day,
  Checkered with storm and sunshine, gloom and light,
Now passing in pure, cloudless skies away,
  Withdrawing into silence of blank night.
  Thick shadows settle on the landscape bright,
Like the weird cloud of death that falls apace
On the still features of the passive face.

Soothing and gentle as a mother's kiss,
  The touch that stopped the beating of the heart.
A look so blissfully serene as this,
  Not all the joy of living could impart.
  Patient to bide, yet willing to depart,
With dauntless faith and courage therewithal,
The Master found her ready at his call.

On such a golden evening forth there floats,
  Between the grave earth and the glowing sky
In the clear air, unvexed with hazy motes,
  The mystic-winged and flickering butterfly,
  A human soul, that drifts at liberty,
Ah! who can tell to what strange paradise,
To what undreamed-of fields and lofty skies!

Magnetism   By the impulse of my will,
  By the red flame in my blood,
By my nerves' electric thrill,
  By the passion of my mood,
My concentrated desire,
  My undying, desperate love,
I ignore Fate, I defy her,
  Iron-hearted Death I move.
When the town lies numb with sleep,
  Here, round-eyed I sit; my breath
Quickly stirred, my flesh a-creep,
  And I force the gates of death.
I nor move nor speak—you'd deem
  From my quiet face and hands,
I were tranced—but in her dream,
  She responds, she understands.
I have power on what is not,
  Or on what has ceased to be,
From that deep, earth-hollowed spot,
  I can lift her up to me.

And, or ere I am aware
    Though the closed and curtained door,
Comes my lady white and fair,
    And embraces me once more.
Though the clay clings to her gown,
    Yet all heaven is in her eyes;
Cool, kind fingers press mine eyes,
    To my soul her soul replies.
But when breaks the common dawn,
    And the city wakes—behold!
My shy phantom is withdrawn,
    And I shiver lone and cold.
And I know when she has left,
    She is stronger far than I,
And more subtly spun her weft,
    Than my human wizardry.
Though I force her to my will,
    By the red flame in my blood,
By my nerves' electric thrill,
    By the passion of my mood,
Yet all day a ghost am I.
    Nerves unstrung, spent will, dull brain.
I achieve, attain, but die,
    And she claims me hers again.

From: In Memoriam Rev. J. J. Lyons

Hark! through the quiet evening air, their song
    Floats forth with wild sweet rhythm and glad refrain.
They sing the conquest of the spirit strong,
    The soul that wrests the victory from pain;
The noble joys of manhood that belong
    To comrades and to brothers.   In their strain
Rustle of palms and Eastern streams one hears,
And the broad prairie melts in mist of tears.

Echoes

Late-born and woman-souled I dare not hope,
The freshness of the elder lays, the might
Of manly, modern passion shall alight
Upon my Muse's lips, nor may I cope
(Who veiled and screened by womanhood must grope)
With the world's strong-armed warriors and recite
The dangers, wounds, and triumphs of the fight;
Twanging the full-stringed lyre through all its scope.
But if thou ever in some lake-floored cave
O'erbrowed by rocks, a wild voice wooed and heard,
Answering at once from heaven and earth and wave,
Lending elf-music to thy harshest word,
Misprize thou not these echoes that belong
To one in love with solitude and song.

Success

Oft have I brooded on defeat and pain,
The pathos of the stupid, stumbling throng.
These I ignore to-day and only long
To pour my soul forth in one trumpet strain,
One clear, grief-shattering, triumphant song,
For all the victories of man's high endeavor,
Palm-bearing, laureled deeds that live forever,
The splendor clothing him whose will is strong.
Hast thou beheld the deep, glad eyes of one
Who has persisted and achieved?   Rejoice!
On naught diviner shines the all-seeing sun.
Salute him with free heart and choral voice,
'Midst flippant, feeble crowds of spectres wan,
The bold, significant, successful man.

The New Colossus

Not like the brazen giant of Greek fame,
With conquering limbs astride from land to land;
Here at our sea-washed, sunset gates shall stand
A mighty woman with a torch, whose flame
Is the imprisoned lightning, and her name
Mother of Exiles.   From her beacon-hand
Glows world-wide welcome; her mild eyes command
The air-bridged harbor that twin cities frame.
"Keep, ancient lands, your storied pomp!" cries she
With silent lips.   "Give me your tired, your poor,
Your huddled masses yearning to breathe free,
The wretched refuse of your teeming shore.
Send these, the homeless, tempest-tost to me,
I lift my lamp beside the golden door!"

Venus of the Louvre

Down the long hall she glistens like a star,
The foam-born mother of Love, transfixed to stone,
Yet none the less immortal, breathing on.
Time's brutal hand hath maimed but could not mar.
When first the enthralled enchantress from afar
Dazzled mine eyes, I saw not her alone,
Serenely poised on her world-worshipped throne,
As when she guided once her dove-drawn car,—
But at her feet a pale, death-stricken Jew,
Her life adorer, sobbed farewell to love.
Here *Heine* wept!   Here still he weeps anew,
Nor ever shall his shadow lift or move,
While mourns one ardent heart, one poet-brain,
For vanished Hellas and Hebraic pain.

In Exile

*Since that day till now our life is one unbroken paradise. We live a true brotherly life. Every evening after supper we take a seat under the mighty oak and sing our songs.—
Extract from a letter of a Russian refugee in Texas.*

Twilight is here, soft breezes bow the grass,
  Day's sounds of various toil break slowly off,
The yoke-freed oxen low, the patient ass
  Dips his dry nostril in the cool, deep trough.
Up from the prairie the tanned herdsmen pass
  With frothy pails, guiding with voices rough
Their udder-lightened kine.   Fresh smells of earth,
The rich, black furrows of the glebe send forth.

After the Southern day of heavy toil,
  How good to lie, with limbs relaxed, brows bare
To evening's fan, and watch the smoke-wreaths coil
  Up from one's pipe-stem through the rayless air.
So deem these unused tillers of the soil,
  Who stretched beneath the shadowing oak-tree, stare
Peacefully on the star-unfolding skies,
And name their life unbroken paradise.

The hounded stag that has escaped the pack,
  And pants at ease within a thick-leaved dell:
The unimprisoned bird that finds the track
  Through sun-bathed space, to where his fellows dwell;
The martyr, granted respite from the rack,
  The death-doomed victim pardoned from his cell,—
Such only know the joy these exiles gain,—
Life's sharpest rapture is surcease of pain.

Strange faces theirs, wherethrough the Orient sun
  Gleams from the eyes and glows athwart the skin.
Grave lines of studious thought and purpose run
  From curl-crowned forehead to dark-bearded chin.
And over all the seal is stamped thereon
  Of anguish branded by a world of sin,
If fire and blood through ages on their name,
Their seal of glory and the Gentiles' shame.

Freedom to love the law that Moses brought,
  To sing the songs of David, and to think
The thoughts Gabirol to Spinoza taught,
  Freedom to dig the common earth, to drink
The universal air—for this they sought
  Refuge o'er wave and continent, to link
Egypt with Texas in their mystic chain,
And truth's perpetual lamp forbid to wane.

Alice Meynell (1847-1922)

ALICE MEYNELL'S mother Christiana was a talented pianist and artist for whom Charles Dickens had a long-standing and, perhaps, romantic admiration. Her parents intended Christiana for the concert stage, but at twenty she married a friend of Dickens', Thomas James Thompson, a widower with an independent income. The Thompsons had two daughters in rapid succession: Elizabeth, born in 1846, and Alice in 1847. Much of Alice's childhood was spent in Italy, where the family lived in a relaxed bohemian style which astonished and amused visitors. Thomas educated the children and the fey Christiana played and painted. Unconventional, democratic and stimulating, this happy childhood and youth was nomadic but full of affectionate relationships. Alice described her father in a delicate Jamesian portrait—

> Loving literature, he never lifted a pen except to write a letter. He was not inarticulate, he was only silent. He had an exquisite style from which to refrain. . . . It was by holding session among so many implicit safeguards that he taught, rather than by precepts. . . . It was a subtle education, for it persuaded insensibly to a conception of my own.

Alice inherited her mother's beauty and father's reserve and "quick" nerves. She was writing poetry in her teens and experiencing, during a dull stay at Henley when she was eighteen, adolescent depression. Her analysis of her mood is mature, detached and political.

> How unhealthy it is to depend as I do so much on my own thoughts and moods and feelings for employment, for excitement. A young man, occupied with study or business or laborious pleasures has no time to watch and ponder on every half-shade of thought and feeling that flits over his heart, and if the subtle perceptions of his soul are kept in abeyance, the more material mind, as it were, grows strong, grand and healthy.
> A girl, on the other hand, thrills through every nerve and fibre of her self-consciousness at the touch of the slightest joy or pain. If these nerves are tolerably in tune with one another she becomes a great woman—a writer, say, famous for laying bare the melancholy secrets of the female heart to the curious gaze of man; if the chords jar, she dwindles into a miserably self-conscious melancholy which feeds upon itself. Of all the crying evils in the depraved earth, aye of all the sins of which the cry must surely come to Heaven, the greatest, judged by all the laws of God and humanity, is the miserable selfishness of men that keeps women from work—work, the salvation of the world, the winner of the dreamless sleep, and the dreamless thought too, the strengthener of mind and body. . . . O my dream, my dream! When will you be realized to gladden my soul, to redeem my trampled and polluted sex? O my sisters, are you content to make bricks so long, sitting by your fleshpots?

This early feminism is romantic, unconsciously elitist, heavily influenced by Elizabeth Barrett Browning and Christina Rossetti. Yet Alice Thompson was mature enough to turn with disgust and contempt from the frayed nervous sensibility of a Victorian lady with nothing to do. She began to write seriously, although she said of her "rhyming faculty" that "whatever I write will be melancholy and self-conscious, as are all women's poems."

Christiana had become a Catholic when the girls were young; the two daughters, first Alice and then Elizabeth, a talented artist, followed her. The conversion gave a moral order to their lives and served to keep melancholy at bay.

Alice's first book, *Preludes*, was published when she was twenty-eight. Ruskin, one of her earliest critics and a family friend, admired it. In 1876 she met and married a young Catholic journalist, Wilfred Meynell. They discussed setting up a magazine together, and in 1880 they actually did so. *The Pen* was a short-lived venture, but soon after Wilfred began an eighteen-year stint as editor of *The Weekly Register*, a Catholic periodical. Alice helped, but wrote her own critical articles for *Spectator* and *Saturday Review*. The Meynells founded a new, nonsectarian periodical called *Merry England* to which the poets Coventry Patmore and Hilaire Belloc contributed. Patmore's admiring friendship with Alice eventually became so cloying that the reserved Alice began to avoid him. Through the medium of *Merry England* the Meynells also discovered and befriended the eccentric poet, Francis Thompson.

Alice had prayed for work, and work she had. A busy, crowded life of writing, editing and child-rearing followed her marriage. She had eight children, seven of whom survived. She was an excellent critic who led rather than followed fashion. Her judgments were aggressively stated: "The eighteenth century, admired for its measure, moderation and good sense, should be considered rather an age of extravagance, because, in it, imagination, which needs no exaggeration, failed." Instead of the Augustan writers she offered her public the rediscovered lyrics of the sixteenth and seventeeth centuries. Meynell's essays are still an immense pleasure to read. *Woman and Books* includes a masterly defense, against the condemnation of Macaulay and others, of Dr. Johnson's wife—"The meanest man is generally allowed his own counsel as to his own wife; one of the greatest men has been denied it." The prejudice, she thought, was deeply sexist —the woman was older than Johnson and not educated. Johnson "chose, for love, a woman who had the wit to admire him at first meeting, and in spite of first sight. . . . let us remember what was the aspect of Johnson's form and face, even in his twenties, and how little he could have touched the senses of a widow fond of externals."

Mrs. Meynell's feminism was as penetrating as her literary insights. She moved right to the core of her argument.

See the curious history of the political rights of women under the Revolution. On the scaffold she enjoyed an ungrudged share in the fortunes of party. Political life might be denied her, but that seems a trifle when you consider how generously she was permitted political death. She was to spin and cook for her citizen in the obscurity of her living hours; but to the hour of her death was granted a part in the largest interests, social, national, international. The blood wherewith she should, according to Robespierre, have blushed to be seen or heard in the tribune, was exposed in the public sight unsheltered by her veins. . . . Women might be, and were, duly silenced when, by the mouth of Olympe de Gouges, they claimed a 'right to concur in the choice of representatives for the formation of the laws'. . . . Olympe de Gouges was guillotined. Robespierre thus made her public and complete amends.

Alice Meynell was, of course, a suffragette. Although she never joined the window-smashing militants of the S.P.U.C., her son Everard supported the extreme radical group. However, family and friends, all for the vote, were equally divided about violent tactics.

Vita Sackville-West, in an excellent biographical essay on Alice Meynell, regards her with something like awe: the devoted Victorian wife and mother, the perfect lady, the poet with the precision of a jeweler, who wrote "with an etching pen." But Sackville-West is also sensitive to certain problems in Meynell's writing. She notes the recurrence in Meynell's poetry of "the idea of 'wildness' and the corrective symbol of the shepherd or shepherdess," and the conflict, central in women's poetry since Charlotte Smith, between wild and tame nature. Sackville-West also quotes the revealing passage from Meynell's essay "The Colour of Life"—"... the true colour of life is not red: Red is the colour of violence, or of life broken open." She interprets this passage as a sign that the poet had an aversion to passions of all sorts, but in fact Alice Meynell met the violence of the World War with outraged horror, and her "England, 1914" is one of the best poems about the war.

Always keen to expose male literary prejudice, Meynell picked up Dryden's praise of Anne Killegrew, "Her father was transfused into her blood," and turned this unconscious sexism into a weapon against father-caused wars. It is not true, as she once wrote of herself, that she was "a poet of one mood." She grew as a poet and her most powerful poems—whether religious, political or purely descriptive—are her last ones, written in the war decade. She was as skilful with a small descriptive poem "A Rainy Summer" as with her more ambitious themes.

The rifled flowers are cold as ocean shells
Bees, humming in the storm, carry their cold
Wild honey to cold cells.

Here she makes a garden physically and emotionally sinister, almost out of nature, by the triple repetition of the word "cold," and the placing of it in conjunction with "wild" and "cells."

Sackville-West calls her poetry "an integral expression of a complete personality—authentic, delicate, and fine." The emphasis here seems wrong. Alice Meynell may have been the perfect lady, content with Victorian standards of dress and behavior, but she was a hard-working professional. She had an egalitarian marriage that seemed to work well, and her children emerged, as far as one can see, emotionally healthy. Her imagination escaped the delicacy and fineness that characterized the Victorian conception of women. More important, Meynell wrote some of the best self-consciously feminist verse after Mrs. Browning.

A good Catholic, Meynell joined the Church and tolerated its dogma in order to have a "guide in morals": she thought that "Christian morality is infinitely the greatest of moralities." She mistrusted Bolshevism because she thought it "heretical in the practice of right and wrong." Yet the framework of her morality included neither false piety nor prudery, and her feminism is not without its social and political analysis. To a bigoted doctor who objected to women physicians she wrote, "The different modesty assigned to the woman doctor who is to be condemned and to the nurse who is to be used, must be explained by a difference of social caste. Fastidiousness as to the modesty of a lady is not respect for purity, but respect for caste."

Alice Meynell died on November 27, 1922. She hated death-beds and the morbid Victorian pleasure taken in them, hated her children to see her ill. But she was able to say, when she knew death was certain, "This is not tragic. I am happy."

A Letter from a Girl to Her Own Old Age

Listen, and when thy hand this paper presses,
O time-worn woman, think of her who blesses
What thy thin fingers touch, with her caresses.

O mother, for the weight of years that break thee!
O daughter, for slow time must yet awake thee,
And from the changes of my heart must make thee!

O fainting traveller, morn is grey in heaven.
Dost thou remember how the clouds were driven?
And are they calm about the fall of even?

Pause near the ending of thy long migration,
For this one sudden hour of desolation
Appeals to one hour of thy meditation.

Suffer, O silent one, that I remind thee
Of the great hills that stormed the sky behind thee,
Of the wild winds of power that have resigned thee.

Know that the mournful plain where thou must wander
Is but a grey and silent world, but ponder
The misty mountains of the morning yonder.

Listen:—the mountain winds with rain were fretting,
And sudden gleams the mountain-tops besetting.
I cannot let thee fade to death, forgetting.

What part of this wild heart of mine I know not
Will follow with thee where the great winds blow not,
And where the young flowers of the mountain grow not.

Yet let my letter with my lost thoughts in it
Tell what the way was when thou didst begin it,
And win with thee the goal when thou shalt win it.

Oh, in some hour of thine my thoughts shall guide thee.
Suddenly, though time, darkness, silence, hide thee,
This wind from thy lost country flits beside thee,—

Telling thee: all thy memories moved the maiden,
With thy regrets was morning over-shaden,
With sorrow, thou hast left, her life was laden.

But whither shall my thoughts turn to pursue thee?
Life changes, and the years and days renew thee.
Oh, Nature brings my straying heart unto thee.

Her winds will join us, with their constant kisses
Upon the evening as the morning tresses,
Her summers breathe the same unchanging blisses.

185

And we, so altered in our shifting phases,
Track one another 'mid the many mazes
By the eternal child-breath of the daisies.

I have not writ this letter of divining
To make a glory of thy silent pining,
A triumph of thy mute and strange declining.

Only one youth, and the bright life was shrouded.
Only one morning, and the day was clouded.
And one old age with all regrets is crowded.

O hush, O hush! Thy tears my words are steeping.
Oh hush, hush, hush! So full, the fount of weeping?
Poor eyes, so quickly moved, so near to sleeping?

Pardon the girl; such strange desires beset her.
Poor woman, lay aside the mournful letter
That breaks thy heart; the one who wrote, forget her:

The one who now thy faded features guesses,
With filial fingers thy grey hair caresses,
With morning tears thy mournful twilight blesses.

A Poet of One Mood

A poet of one mood in all my lays,
  Ranging all life to sing one only love,
  Like a west wind across the world I move,
Sweeping my harp of floods mine own wild ways.
The countries change, but not the west-wind days
  Which are my songs. My soft skies shine above,
  And on all seas the colours of a dove,
And on all fields a flash of silver greys.

I make the whole world answer to my art
  And sweet monotonous meanings. In your ears
I change not ever, bearing, for my part,
  One thought that is the treasure of my years—
A small cloud full of rain upon my heart
  And in mine arms, clasped, like a child in tears.

The Shepherdess

She walks—the lady of my delight—
  A shepherdess of sheep.
Her flocks are thoughts. She keeps them white;
  She guards them from the steep;
She feeds them on the fragrant height,
  And folds them in for sleep.

She roams maternal hills and bright,
  Dark valleys safe and deep.
Into that tender breast at night
  The chastest stars may peep.
She walks—the lady of my delight—
  A shepherdess of sheep.

She holds her little thoughts in sight,
   Though gay they run and leap.
She is so circumspect and right;
   She has her soul to keep.
She walks—the lady of my delight—
   A shepherdess of sheep.

Parentage

"When Augustus Cæsar legislated against the unmarried citizens of Rome, he declared them to be, in some sort, slayers of the people."

   Ah! no, not these!
These, who were childless, are not they who gave
So many dead unto the journeying wave,
The helpless nurslings of the cradling seas;
Not they who doomed by infallible decrees
Unnumbered man to the innumerable grave.

   But those who slay
Are fathers. Theirs are armies. Death is theirs—
The death of innocences and despairs;
The dying of the golden and the grey.
The sentence, when these speak it, has no Nay.
And she who slays is she who bears, who bears.

Chimes

Brief, on a flying night,
   From the shaken tower
A flock of bells take flight,
   And go with the hour.

Like birds from the cote to the gales,
   Abrupt—O hark!
A fleet of bells set sails,
   And go to the dark.

Sudden the cold airs swing.
   Alone, aloud,
A verse of bells takes wing
   And flies with the cloud.

In Manchester Square

In Memoriam T. H.

The paralytic man has dropped in death
   The crossing-sweeper's brush to which he clung,
One-handed, twisted, dwarfed, scanted of breath,
   Although his hair was young.

I saw this year the winter vines of France,
   Dwarfed, twisted goblins in the frosty drouth—
Gnarled, crippled, blackened little stems askance
   On long hills to the South.

Great green and golden hands of leaves ere long
   Shall proffer clusters in that vineyard wide.
And O his might, his sweet, his wine, his song,
   His stature, since he died!

Summer in England, 1914

On London fell a clearer light;
  Caressing pencils of the sun
Defined the distances, the white
  Houses transfigured one by one,
The 'long, unlovely street' impearled.
O what a sky has walked the world!

Most happy year! And out of town
  The hay was prosperous, and the wheat;
The silken harvest climbed the down:
  Moon after moon was heavenly-sweet,
Stroking the bread within the sheaves,
Looking 'twixt apples and their leaves.

And while this rose made round her cup,
  The armies died convulsed. And when
This chaste young silver sun went up
  Softly, a thousand shattered men,
One wet corruption, heaped the plain,
After a league-long throb of pain.

Flower following tender flower; and birds,
  And berries; and benignant skies
Made thrive the serried flocks and herds—
  Yonder are men shot through the eyes.
       Love, hide thy face
From man's unpardonable race.

Who said "No man hath greater love than this,
  To die to serve his friend"?
So these have loved us all unto the end.
  Chide thou no more, O thou unsacrificed!
The soldier dying dies upon a kiss,
  The very kiss of Christ.

A Father of Women

Ad sororem E. B.

"Thy father was transfused into thy blood."
DRYDEN: *Ode to Mrs. Anne Killigrew.*

    Our father works in us,
The daughters of his manhood. Not undone
Is he, not wasted, though transmuted thus,
    And though he left no son.

    Therefore on him I cry
To arm me: "For my delicate mind a casque,
A breastplate for my heart, courage to die,
    Of thee, captain, I ask.

    "Nor strengthen only; press
A finger on this violent blood and pale,
Over this rash will let thy tenderness
    A while pause, and prevail.

    "And shepherd-father, thou
Whose staff folded my thoughts before my birth,
Control them now I am of earth, and now
    Thou art no more of earth.

"O liberal, constant, dear,
Crush in my nature the ungenerous art
Of the inferior; set me high, and here,
    Here garner up thy heart!"

Like to him now are they,
The million living fathers of the War—
Mourning the crippled world, the bitter day—
    Whose striplings are no more.

The crippled world! Come then,
Fathers of women with your honour in trust,
Approve, accept, know them daughters of men,
    Now that your sons are dust.

The Watershed

Lines written between Munich and Verona

Black mountains pricked with pointed pine
    A melancholy sky.
Out-distanced was the German vine,
    The sterile fields lay high.
From swarthy Alps I travelled forth
Aloft; it was the north, the north;
    Bound for the Noon was I.

I seemed to breast the streams that day;
    I met, opposed, withstood
The northward rivers on their way,
    My heart against the flood—
My heart that pressed to rise and reach,
And felt the love of altering speech,
    Of frontiers, in its blood.

But O the unfolding South! the burst
    Of summer! O to see
Of all the southward brooks the first!
    The travelling heart went free
With endless streams; that strife was stopped;
And down a thousand vales I dropped,
    I flowed to Italy.

The Rainy Summer

There's much afoot in heaven and earth this year;
    The winds hunt up the sun, hunt up the moon,
Trouble the dubious dawn, hasten the drear
    Height of a threatening noon.

No breath of boughs, no breath of leaves, of fronds,
    May linger or grow warm; the trees are loud;
The forest, rooted, tosses in her bonds,
    And strains against the cloud.

No scents may pause within the garden-fold;
    The rifled flowers are cold as ocean-shells;
Bees, humming in the storm, carry their cold
    Wild honey to cold cells.

189

Charlotte Mew (1870-1928)

ONE POEM of Charlotte Mew's small treasury of exquisite verse survives in the standard anthologies. "The Farmer's Bride" is the tragedy of a middle-aged farmer whose teenaged wife, hastily woo'd and wed, has "turned afraid" of love "and all things human." It is significant that this poem, which is told by the frustrated husband, should be Mew's standard anthology piece. Many of Charlotte Mew's poems are dramatic and narrative but most are spoken by women. In "Madeleine in Church," "The Quiet House," and "Monsieur Qui Passe," the women reach for God and grace but remain earthbound, held by fathers, lovers, husbands and the passions they engender. The language of the poems is sensuous, even violent— "A purple blot against the dead white door"—and female sensuality is a common theme. Seen against Charlotte Mew's spotless and secluded life, these preoccupations, so fully rendered and emotionally accurate, seem a little strange.

She was born on November 15, 1869 in London, and she lived in that city all her life. Her architect father gave his four children a comfortable gay childhood but died, "having spent all his available capital on living," when Charlotte was in her late twenties. Some joy had gone out of the house before then: the two youngest children went mad and ended their lives in asylums. As a result Charlotte and her sister Anne determined never to marry, lest they pass the weakness on. After Fred Mew's death Charlotte, Anne and their mother—all slight and in frail health—continued to live in the Gordon Square house where the girls had grown up, but now in straitened circumstances. Charlotte, who had been respectably educated at Lucy Harrison's School for Girls, wrote stories and poems for the English magazines *Temple Bar*, *The Egoist*, *The English Woman*, *Yellow Book*, and sometimes *The Nation*. Anne, who was a talented artist, redecorated antique furniture for "a sweated wage." The upper part of the house was let out, and the women barely managed to get along. Both Anne and Charlotte were committed to keeping up a certain standard lest their mother feel humiliated by the loss of social and economic status. In spite of this genteel poverty Charlotte, who had spent time in France when a girl and occasionally returned there, was no recluse. After her "discovery" by Harold and Alida Monroe of the Poetry Bookshop and the publication of *The Farmer's Bride* (1916), she became known to the literati, and developed warm friendships with other writers. Absolutely circumspect in her own life, she was equally rigorous about the sexual morality of her friends and would drop anyone whom scandal had touched.

Both sisters were lively, entertaining women; Charlotte was a great story-teller, and a dramatic figure altogether. Alida Monroe describes her in her forties and fifties: dressed in her long tweed topcoat with a velvet collar, a pork pie hat set straight on her fine white hair, a rolled umbrella under one arm and her tiny feet (she was under five feet in height and very finely made) in size-two custom-made boots.

In 1923, on the recommendation of John Masefield, Walter de la Mare and Thomas

Hardy, she was given a Civil List pension of seventy-five pounds a year. Hardy in particular thought Charlotte a fine poet; after his death a copy of her "Fin de Fête," written out in his own hand on the back of a British Museum reading room slip, was found among his possessions and given to Charlotte.

After 1916 Charlotte wrote no more prose and little new verse. In the twenties life began to fall apart. The lease on the Gordon Square house ran out, and the three women moved to Delancey Street near Regent's Park. Old Mrs. Mew died the year after the move and Charlotte tried, for the sake of economy, to live with Anne at her studio. Anne too died shortly after, and the loss of her family broke Charlotte mentally and physically. She took poison and died in a nursing home in 1928. So little known to the general public was this retiring Edwardian lady that the local press, reporting her death, described her as "Charlotte New [sic], said to be a writer."

In 1953 the Monroes brought out a complete edition of her poems, including a memoir from which is drawn the biographical data. Her prose has never been collected. It is not condescending to say that Charlotte Mew's life was a period piece which her verse wholly transcends and explains but for which no belated recognition can make amends.

In spite of the religious-moral axis of her verse, Charlotte Mew never sought the consolation of any organized religion. The Christ so often called upon in her poems is an enigmatic deity, from whom her fallen women beg in vain for explanation and expiation.

There are two kinds of tragic women in her poems: those who have bartered their souls for the comforts of sexual love and those who have not, whom experience has passed by. We see the first sort in "Madeleine," where this familiar nineteenth-century theme is treated with unusual frankness. In "Fame" the speaker sees her lost dreams as "A frail dead, new born lamb, ghostly and pitiful and white,/A blot upon the night,/The moon's dropped child!" The history of this characteristically female image (Christina Rossetti among others uses lambs and sheep in a similar way) reaches back to Charlotte Smith and her ambivalent use of nature. White in Charlotte Mew's verse is chastity and death; red, crimson and scarlet suggest sexuality and sin, but also life. Linked with the rose—the flower which for both sexes symbolizes female sensuality, life and fecundity—redness produces in "The Quiet House" one of the most painful and powerful passages in any poem by a woman. "The Quiet House" is semi-autobiographical. The remaining daughter of a blasted family lives locked in with her silent father. She muses that:

> Red is the strangest pain to bear;
> In Spring the leaves on the budding trees;
> In Summer the roses are worse than these,
>   More terrible than they are sweet:
> A rose can stab you across the street
> Deeper than any knife:
> And the crimson haunts you everywhere—
> Thin shafts of sunlight, like the ghosts of
>   reddened swords have struck our stair
> As if, coming down, you had spilt your life.

The Narrow Door

The narrow door, the narrow door
  On the three steps of which the café children play
Mostly at shop with pebbles from the shore,
It is always shut this narrow door
But open for a little while to-day.

And round it, each with pebbles in his hand,
A silenced crowd the café children stand
To see the long box jerking down the bend
Of twisted stair; then set on end,
Quite filling up the narrow door
Till it comes out and does not go in any more.

    Along the quay you see it wind,
The slow black line. Someone pulls up the blind
Of the small window just above the narrow door—
    "Tiens! que veux-tu acheter?" Renée cries,
    "Mais, pour quat'sous, des oignons," Jean replies,
And one pays down with pebbles from the shore.

Madeleine in Church

Here, in the darkness, where this plaster saint
  Stands nearer than God stands to our distress,
And one small candle shines, but not so faint
  As the far lights of everlastingness,
I'd rather kneel than over there, in open day
  Where Christ is hanging, rather pray
    To something more like my own clay,
      Not too divine;
    For, once, perhaps my little saint
    Before he got his niche and crown,
Had one short stroll about the town;
It brings him closer, just that taint—
    And any one can wash the paint
Off our poor faces, his and mine!

Is that why I see Monty now? equal to any saint, poor boy, as good as gold,
But still, with just the proper trace
Of earthliness on his shining wedding face;
And then gone suddenly blank and old
The hateful day of the divorce:
Stuart got his, hands down, of course
Crowing like twenty cocks and grinning like a horse:
But Monty took it hard. All said and done I liked him best,—
He was the first, he stands out clearer than the rest.
        It seems too funny all we other rips
    Should have immortal souls; Monty and Redge quite damnably
    Keep theirs afloat while we go down like scuttled ships.—

It's funny too, how easily we sink,
One might put up a monument, I think
To half the world and cut across it "Lost at Sea!"
I should drown Jim, poor little sparrow, if I netted him to-night—
No, it's no use this penny light—
Or my poor saint with his tin-pot crown—
The trees of Calvary are where they were,
When we are sure that we can spare
The tallest, let us go and strike it down
And leave the other two still standing there.
I, too, would ask Him to remember me
If there were any Paradise beyond this earth that I could see.
Oh! quiet Christ who never knew
The poisonous fangs that bite us through
And make us do the things we do,
See how we suffer and fight and die,
How helpless and how low we lie,
God holds You, and You hang so high,
Though no one looking long at You,
Can think You do not suffer too,
But, up there, from your still, star-lighted tree
What can You know, what can You really see
Of this dark ditch, the soul of me!

We are what we are: when I was half a child I could not sit
Watching black shadows on green lawns and red carnations burning
    in the sun,
Without paying so heavily for it
That joy and pain, like any mother and her unborn child were
    almost one.
I could hardly bear
The dreams upon the eyes of white geraniums in the dusk,
The thick, close voice of musk,
The jessamine music on the thin night air,
Or, sometimes, my own hands about me anywhere—
The sight of my own face (for it was lovely then) even the scent of my
    own hair,
Oh! there was nothing, nothing that did not sweep to the high seat
Of laughing gods, and then blow down and beat
My soul into the highway dust, as hoofs do the dropped roses of the
    street.
I think my body was my soul,
And when we are made thus
Who shall control
Our hands, our eyes, the wandering passion of our feet,
Who shall teach us
To thrust the world out of our heart: to say, till perhaps in death,
When the race is run,
And it is forced from us with our last breath
"Thy will be done"?
If it is Your will that we should be content with the tame, bloodless things.
As pale as angels smirking by, with folded wings—
Oh! I know Virtue, and the peace it brings!
The temperate, well-worn smile
The one man gives you, when you are evermore his own:

And afterwards the child's, for a little while,
                   With its unknowing and all-seeing eyes
      So soon to change, and make you feel how quick
    The clock goes round. If one had learned the trick—
                 (How does one though?)quite early on,
      Of long green pastures under placid skies,
      One might be walking now with patient truth.
What did we ever care for it, who have asked for youth,
      When, oh! my God! This is going or has gone?

      There is a portrait of my mother, at nineteen,
      With the black spaniel, standing by the garden seat,
      The dainty head held high against the painted green
And throwing out the youngest smile, shy, but half haughty and half sweet.
      Her picture then: but simply Youth, or simply Spring
         To me to-day: a radiance on the wall,
         So exquisite, so heart-breaking a thing
      Beside the mask that I remember, shrunk and small,
         Sapless and lined like a dead leaf,
All that was left of oh! the loveliest face, by time and grief!

      And in the glass, last night, I saw a ghost behind my chair—
      Yet why remember it, when one can still go moderately gay—?
         Or could—with any one of the old crew,
           But oh! these boys! the solemn way
         They take you and the things they say—
         This "I have only as long as you"
      When you remind them you are not precisely twenty-two—
      Although at heart perhaps—God! if it were
           Only the face, only the hair!
         If Jim had written to me as he did to-day
         A year ago — and now it leaves me cold—
           I know what this means, old, old, *old:*
           Et avec ça—mais on a vécu, tout se paie.

That is not always true: there was my Mother (well at least the dead are
        free!)
      Yoked to the man that Father was; yoked to the woman I am, Monty
        too;
      The little portress at the Convent School, stewing in hell so patiently;
The poor, fair boy who shot himself at Aix. And what of me — and
        what of me?
      But I, I paid for what I had, and they for nothing. No, one cannot see
        How it shall be made up to them in some serene eternity.
If there were fifty heavens God could not give us back the child who
        went or never came;
      Here, on our little patch of this great earth, the sun of any darkened
        day,
Not one of all the starry buds hung on the hawthorn trees of last year's
        May,
         No shadow from the sloping fields of yesterday;
      For every hour they slant across the hedge a different way,
         The shadows are never the same.

      "Find rest in Him!" One knows the parsons' tags—
      Back to the fold, across the evening fields, like any flock of baa-ing
        sheep:

195

Yes, it may be, when He has shorn, led us to slaughter, torn the
bleating soul in us to rags,
For so He giveth His belovèd sleep.
Oh! He will take us stripped and done,
Driven into His heart. So we are won:
Then safe, safe are we? in the shelter of His everlasting wings—
I do not envy Him his victories, His arms are full of broken things.

But I shall not be in them. Let Him take
The finer ones, the easier to break.
And they are not gone, yet, for me, the lights, the colours, the perfumes,
Though now they speak rather in sumptuous rooms,
In silks and in gem-like wines;
Here, even, in this corner where my little candle shines
And overhead the lancet-window glows
With golds and crimsons you could almost drink
To know how jewels taste, just as I used to think
There was the scent in every red and yellow rose
Of all the sunsets. But this place is grey,
And much too quiet. No one here,
Why, this is awful, this is fear!
Nothing to see, no face,
Nothing to hear except your heart beating in space
As if the world was ended. Dead at last!
Dead soul, dead body, tied together fast.
These to go on with and alone, to the slow end:
No one to sit with, really, or to speak to, friend to friend:
Out of the long procession, black or white or red
Not one left now to say "Still I am here, then see you, dear, lay here
your head".
Only the doll's house looking on the Park
To-night, all nights, I know, when the man puts the lights out,
very dark.
With, upstairs, in the blue and gold box of a room, just the maids'
footsteps overhead,
Then utter silence and the empty world—the room—the bed—
The corpse! No, not quite dead, while this cries out in me,
But nearly: very soon to be
A handful of forgotten dust—
There must be someone. Christ! there must,
Tell me there *will* be someone. Who?
If there were no one else, could it be You?

How old was Mary out of whom you cast
So many devils? Was she young or perhaps for years
She had sat staring, with dry eyes, at this and that man going past
Till suddenly she saw You on the steps of Simeon's house
And stood and looked at You through tears.
I think she must have known by those
The thing, for what it was that had come to her
For some of us there is a passion, I suppose,
So far from earthly cares and earthly fears
That in its stillness you can hardly stir
Or in its nearness, lift your hand,
So great that you have simply got to stand
Looking at it through tears, through tears.

Then straight from these there broke the kiss,
I think You must have known by this
The thing, for what it was, that had come to You:
She did not love You like the rest,
It was in her own way, but at the worst, the best,
She gave You something altogether new.
And through it all, from her, no word,
She scarcely saw You, scarcely heard:
Surely You knew when she so touched You with her hair,
Or by the wet cheek lying there,
And while her perfume clung to You from head to feet all through the day
That You can change the things for which we care,
But even You, unless You kill us, not the way.

This, then was peace for her, but passion too.
I wonder was it like a kiss that once I knew,
The only one that I would care to take
Into the grave with me, to which, if there were afterwards, to wake.
Almost as happy as the carven dead
In some dim chancel lying head by head
We slept with it, but face to face, the whole night through—
One breath, one throbbing quietness, as if the thing behind our lips was
endless life,
Lost, as I woke, to hear in the strange earthly dawn, his "Are you there?"
And lie still, listening to the wind outside, among the firs.

So Mary chose the dream of Him for what was left to her of night and day,
It is the only truth: it is the dream in us that neither life nor death nor any
other thing can take away:
But if she had not touched Him in the doorway of the dream could she
have cared so much?
She was a sinner, we are what we are: the spirit afterwards, but first the
touch.

And He has never shared with me my haunted house beneath the trees
Of Eden and Calvary, with its ghosts that have not any eyes for tears,
And the happier guests who would not see, or if they did, remember these,
Though they lived there a thousand years.
Outside, too gravely looking at me, He seems to stand,
And looking at Him, if my forgotten spirit came
Unwillingly back, what could it claim
Of those calm eyes, that quiet speech,
Breaking like a slow tide upon the beach,
The scarred, not quite human hand?—
Unwillingly back to the burden of old imaginings
When it has learned so long not to think, not to be,
Again, again it would speak as it has spoken to me of things
That I shall not see!

I cannot bear to look at this divinely bent and gracious head:
When I was small I never quite believed that He was dead:
And at the Convent school I used to lie awake in bed
Thinking about His hands. It did not matter what they said,

He was alive to me, so hurt, so hurt! And most of all in Holy Week
When there was no one else to see
I used to think it would not hurt me too, so terribly,
If He had ever seemed to notice me
Or if, for once, He would only speak.

Monsieur qui Passe

Quai Voltaire

A purple blot against the dead white door
In my friend's rooms, bathed in their vile pink light,
I had not noticed her before
She snatched my eyes and threw them back at me:
She did not speak till we came out into the night,
Paused at this bench beside the kiosk on the quay.

God knows precisely what she said—
I left to her the twisted skein,
Though here and there I caught a thread,—
Something, at first, about "the lamps along the Seine,
And Paris, with that witching card of Spring
Kept up her sleeve,—why you could see
The trick done on these freezing winter nights!
While half the kisses of the Quay—
Youth, hope,—the whole enchanted string
Of dreams hung on the Seine's long line of lights".

Then suddenly she stripped, the very skin
Came off her soul,—a mere girl clings
Longer to some last rag, however thin,
When she has shown you—well—all sorts of things:
"If it were daylight—oh! one keeps one's head—
But fourteen years!—No one has ever guessed—
The whole thing starts when one gets to bed—
Death?—If the dead would tell us they had rest!
But your eyes held it as I stood there by the door—
One speaks to Christ—one tries to catch His garment's hem—
One hardly says as much to Him—no more:
It was not you, it was your eyes—I spoke to them".

She stopped like a shot bird that flutters still,
And drops, and tries to run again, and swerves.
The tale should end in some walled house upon a hill.
My eyes, at least, won't play such havoc there,—
Or hers——But she had hair!—blood dipped in gold;
And here she left me throwing back the first odd stare.
Some sort of beauty once, but turning yellow, getting old.
Pouah! These women and their nerves!
God! but the night *is* cold!

Fame

Sometimes in the over-heated house, but not for long,
Smirking and speaking rather loud,
I see myself among the crowd,
Where no one fits the singer to his song,

Or sifts the unpainted from the painted faces
Of the people who are always on my stair;
They were not with me when I walked in heavenly places;
            But could I spare
In the blind Earth's great silences and spaces,
        The din, the scuffle, the long stare
            If I went back and it was not there?
Back to the old known things that are the new,
The folded glory of the gorse, the sweet-briar air,
To the larks that cannot praise us, knowing nothing of what we do,
        And the divine, wise trees that do not care.
Yet, to leave Fame, still with such eyes and that bright hair!
God! If I might! And before I go hence
            Take in her stead
            To our tossed bed
One little dream, no matter how small, how wild.
Just now, I think I found it in a field, under a fence—
A frail, dead, new-born lamb, ghostly and pitiful and white,
            A blot upon the night,
The moon's dropped child!

The Quiet House

When we were children old Nurse used to say,
The house was like an auction or a fair
Until the lot of us were safe in bed.
    It has been quiet as the country-side
    Since Ted and Janey and then Mother died
And Tom crossed Father and was sent away.
After the lawsuit he could not hold up his head,
    Poor Father, and he does not care
    For people here, or to go anywhere.

To get away to Aunt's for that week-end
    Was hard enough; (since then, a year ago,
    He scarcely lets me slip out of his sight—)
At first I did not like my cousin's friend,
    I did not think I should remember him:
    His voice has gone, his face is growing dim
And if I like him now I do not know.
    He frightened me before he smiled—
    He did not ask me if he might—
    He said that he would come one Sunday night,
    He spoke to me as if I were a child.

No year has been like this that has just gone by;
    It may be that what Father says is true,
If things are so it does not matter why:
    But everything has burned, and not quite through.
    The colours of the world have turned
    To flame, the blue, the gold has burned
In what used to be such a leaden sky.
When you are burned quite through you die.

Red is the strangest pain to bear;
In Spring the leaves on the budding trees;
In Summer the roses are worse than these,
   More terrible than they are sweet:
   A rose can stab you across the street
      Deeper than any knife:
   And the crimson haunts you everywhere—
Thin shafts of sunlight, like the ghosts of reddened swords have struck
      our stair
As if, coming down, you had spilt your life.

      I think that my soul is red
Like the soul of a sword or a scarlet flower:
      But when these are dead
      They have had their hour.

   I shall have had mine, too,
      For from head to feet
   I am burned and stabbed half through,
      And the pain is deadly sweet.

   The things that kill us seem
      Blind to the death they give:
   It is only in our dream
      The things that kill us live.

The room is shut where Mother died,
   The other rooms are as they were,
The world goes on the same outside,
   The sparrows fly across the Square,
   The children play as we four did there,
   The trees grow green and brown and bare,
The sun shines on the dead Church spire,
   And nothing lives here but the fire.
While Father watches from his chair
            Day follows day
The same, or now and then a different grey,
            Till, like his hair,
Which Mother said was wavy once and bright,
            They will all turn white.

   To-night I heard a bell again—
Outside it was the same mist of fine rain,
The lamps just lighted down the long, dim street,
            No one for me—
   I think it is myself I go to meet:
I do not care; some day I *shall* not think; I shall not *be*

The Farmer's Bride   Three Summers since I chose a maid,
Too young maybe—but more's to do
At harvest-time than bide and woo.
      When us was wed she turned afraid

Of love and me and all things human;
Like the shut of a winter's day
Her smile went out, and 'twadn't a woman—
    More like a little frightened fay.
        One night, in the Fall, she runned away.

"Out 'mong the sheep, her be," they said,
'Should properly have been abed;
But sure enough she wadn't there
Lying awake with her wide brown stare.
So over seven-acre field and up-along across the down
We chased her, flying like a hare
Before our lanterns. To Church-Town
    All in a shiver and a scare
We caught her, fetched her home at last
    And turned the key upon her, fast.

She does the work about the house
As well as most, but like a mouse:
    Happy enough to chat and play
    With birds and rabbits and such as they,
    So long as men-folk keep away.

"Not near, not near!" her eyes beseech
When one of us comes within reach.
    The women say that beasts in stall
    Look round like children at her call.
    I've hardly heard her speak at all.

Shy as a leveret, swift as he,
Straight and slight as a young larch tree,
Sweet as the first wild violets, she,
To her wild self. But what to me?

The short days shorten and the oaks are brown,
    The blue smoke rises to the low grey sky,
One leaf in the still air falls slowly down,
    A magpie's spotted feathers lie
On the black earth spread white with rime,
The berries redden up to Christmas-time.
    What's Christmas-time without there be
    Some other in the house than we!

She sleeps up in the attic there
    Alone, poor maid. 'Tis but a stair
Betwixt us. Oh! my God! the down,
The soft young down of her, the brown,
The brown of her—her eyes, her hair, her hair!

Amy Lowell (1874-1925)

AMY LOWELL, one of the founders of the Imagist movement and a promoter of the "new" twentieth-century poetry, came to her profession relatively late in life; her first book of poems was not published until 1912, when she was 38. Her need to acquire a profession was determined more by family tradition than by economic need. The Lowells, one of the first families in New England, had produced intellectuals of all sorts. Her grandfather was the poet James Russell Lowell; one of her brothers, Abbott Lawrence, was a political scientist and president of Harvard from 1909 to 1933.

In adolescence Amy began to put on weight, a result of a glandular condition which both shortened her life and put an end, by her mid-twenties, to any hopes of matrimony and "normal" family life. She wrote a long poem in blank verse inspired by the actress Eleanora Duse and, so she reports, discovered her true vocation. The Lowell standards were high; Amy spent the next ten years or so learning her craft. Her models were the Romantic poets and their interpreters; Keats in particular caught her imagination. She saw her place in modern poetry when she read a poem by H.D. signed "H. D. Imagiste." Imagism was the product of a group of Anglo-American poets, led by Ezra Pound, who were trying to break free from Victorian critical standards in verse. They espoused free verse, new rhythms, common speech, exact words and compression as the essence of poetry. They rejected "cosmic" poets and, by implication, cosmic themes.

Imagism as a movement was short-lived; its precepts were at once too general and too confining for the smallish group of poets who adhered to them. Amy Lowell and Pound soon quarreled over the meaning of the term. It succeeded, however, in encouraging young poets to drop Browning and Tennyson as arbiters of poetic taste. If Imagism was, as so many of its critics suggest, self-conscious and anemic in its choice of subjects, it did better in its attempt to reform the language of verse, to achieve poetry that was "hard and clear."

Miss Lowell published eight books of poems between 1912 and 1922, and three more individual collections came out after her death in 1925. It was a prodigious output, considering that she was in ill health much of the time and was simultaneously writing critical prose and a mammoth biography of Keats. The poetry includes a wide variety of experiments, few entirely original except perhaps for her attempts at polyphonic prose. There are successful imitations of Oriental poetry, first-person narratives in American rural working-class dialect, sonnets, and A Critical Fable affectionately mocking her poet contemporaries in the manner of James Russell Lowell's A Fable for Critics. Not all the poetry is good. There is too much of it, and one often has an uncomfortable sensation that considerable technical skill has gone into the treatment of subjects about which the poet lacked both first-hand knowledge and imaginative feeling.

Amy Lowell was eccentric with the eccentricity permitted privilege. When she came into her inheritance her home in Sevenels ran to the hours she dictated; she smoked (in private) small cigars. In other respects she was a good conservative New Englander. God may have been dead, but the social and moral conventions lived on. She disapproved intensely of the political feminism of her time, but the poems which deal specifically with the condition of women as poets, wives or historical figures are, as a group, more closely observed and felt than those dealing with other subjects. As a critic of other poets she was witty and sharp. *A critical Fable* (1922) remains rewarding and funny.

Lowell used her wealth and influence to promote the careers of other young poets, notably D. H. Lawrence. *What O'Clock* won the Pulitzer Prize in 1926. Her aggressive self-confidence, a product of the particular class and family from which she came, made her for a time a leader of aesthetic fashions. Competitive and ambitious, she was one of the first women poets to catch and ride the new tide in literary modes.

Meeting-House Hill

I must be mad, or very tired,
When the curve of a blue bay beyond a railroad track
Is shrill and sweet to me like the sudden springing of a tune,
And the sight of a white church above thin trees in a city square
Amazes my eyes as though it were the Parthenon.
Clear, reticent, superbly final,
With the pillars of its portico refined to a cautious elegance,
It dominates the weak trees,
And the shot of its spire
Is cool, and candid,
Rising into an unresisting sky.
Strange meeting-house
Pausing a moment upon a squalid hilltop.
I watch the spire sweeping the sky,
I am dizzy with the movement of the sky,
I might be watching a mast
With its royals set full
Straining before a two-reef breeze.
I might be sighting a tea-clipper,
Tacking into the blue bay,
Just back from Canton
With her hold full of green and blue porcelain,
And a Chinese coolie leaning over the rail
Gazing at the white spire
With dull, sea-spent eyes.

On Looking at a Copy of Alice Meynell's Poems, Given Me, Years Ago, by a Friend

Upon this greying page you wrote
A whispered greeting, long ago.
Faint pencil-marks run to and fro
Scoring the lines I loved to quote.

A sea-shore of white, shoaling sand,
Blue creeks zigzagging through marsh-grasses,
Sand pipers, and a wind which passes
Cloudily silent up the land.

Upon the high edge of the sea
A great four-master sleeps; three hours
Her bowsprit has not cleared those flowers.
I read and look alternately.

It all comes back again, but dim
As pictures on a winking wall
Hidden save when the dark clouds fall
Or crack to show the moon's bright rim.

I well remember what I was,
And what I wanted. You, unwise
With sore unwisdom, had no eyes
For what was patently the cause.

So are we sport of others' blindness,
We who could see right well alone.
What were you made of—wood or stone?
Yet I remember you with kindness.

You gave this book to me to ease
The smart in me you could not heal.
Your gift a mirror—woe or weal.
We sat beneath the apple-trees.

And I remember how they rang,
These words, like bronze cathedral bells
Down ancient lawns, or citadels
Thundering with gongs where choirs sang.

Silent the sea, the earth, the sky,
And in my heart a silent weeping.
Who has not sown can know no reaping!
Bitter conclusion and no lie.

O heart that sorrows, heart that bleeds,
Heart that was never mine, your words
Were like the pecking Autumn birds
Stealing away my garnered seeds.

No future where there is no past!
O cherishing grief which laid me bare,
I wrapped you like a wintry air
About me. Poor enthusiast!

How strange that tumult, looking back.
The ink is pale, the letters fade.
The verses seem to be well made,
But I have lived the almanac.

And you are dead these drifted years,
How many I forget. And she
Who wrote the book, her tragedy
Long since dried up its scalding tears.

I read of her death yesterday,
Frail lady whom I never knew
And knew so well. Would I could strew
Her grave with pansies, blue and grey.

Would I could stand a little space
Under a blowing, brightening sky,
And watch the sad leaves fall and lie
Gently upon that lonely place.

So cried her heart, a feverish thing.
But clay is still, and clay is cold,
And I was young, and I am old,
And in December what birds sing!

Go, wistful book, go back again
Upon your shelf and gather dust.
I've seen the glitter through the rust
Of old, long years, I've known the pain.

I've recollected both of you,
But I shall recollect no more.
Between us I must shut the door.
The living have so much to do.

Streets

*(Adapted from the poet
Yakura Sanjin, 1769)*

As I wandered through the eight hundred and eight streets of the city,
I saw nothing so beautiful
As the Women of the Green Houses,
With their girdles of spun gold,
And their long-sleeved dresses,
Coloured like the graining of wood.
As they walk,
The hems of their outer garments flutter open,
And the blood-red linings glow like sharp-toothed maple leaves
In Autumn.

Reaping

You want to know what's the matter with me, do yer?
My! Ain't men blinder'n moles?
It ain't nothin' new, be sure o' that.
Why, ef you'd had eyes you'd ha' seed
Me changin' under your very nose,
Each day a little diff'rent.
But you never see nothin', you don't.
Don't touch me, Jake,
Don't you dars't to touch me,
I ain't in no humour.
That's what's come over me;
Jest a change clear through.
You lay still, an' I'll tell yer,
I've had it on my mind to tell yer
Fer some time.
It's a strain livin' a lie from mornin' till night,
An' I'm goin' to put an end to it right now.

207

An' don't make any mistake about one thing,
When I married yer I loved yer.
Why, your voice 'ud make
Me go hot and cold all over,
An' your kisses most stopped my heart from beatin'.
Lord! I was a silly fool.
But that's the way 'twas.
Well, I married yer
An' thought Heav'n was comin'
To set on the door-step.
Heav'n didn't do no settin',
Though the first year warn't so bad.
The baby's fever threw you off some, I guess,
An' then I took her death real hard,
An' a mopey wife kind o' disgusts a man.
I ain't blamin' yer exactly.
But that's how 'twas.
Do lay quiet,
I know I'm slow, but it's harder to say'n I thought.
There come a time when I got to be
More wife agin than mother.
The mother part was sort of a waste
When we didn't have no other child.
But you'd got used ter lots o' things,
An' you was all took up with the farm.
Many's the time I've laid awake
Watchin' the moon go clear through the elm-tree,
Out o' sight.
I'd foller yer around like a dog,
An' set in the chair you'd be'n settin' in,
Jest to feel its arms around me,
So long's I didn't have yours.
It preyed on me, I guess,
Longin' and longin'
While you was busy all day, and snorin' all night.
Yes, I know you're wide awake now,
But now ain't then,
An' I guess you'll think diff'rent
When I'm done.
Do you mind the day you went to Hadrock?
I didn't want to stay home for reasons,
But you said someone'd have to be here
'Cause Elmer was comin' to see t' th' telephone.
An' you never see why I was so set on goin' with yer,
Our married life hadn't be'n any great shakes,
Still marriage is marriage, an' I was raised God-fearin'.
But, Lord, you didn't notice nothin',
An' Elmer hangin' around all Winter!
'Twas a lovely mornin'.
The apple-trees was just elegant

With their blossoms all flared out,
An' there warn't a cloud in the sky.
You went, you wouldn't pay no 'tention to what I said,
An' I heard the Ford chuggin' for most a mile,
The air was so still.
Then Elmer come.
It's no use your frettin', Jake,
I'll tell you all about it.
I know what I'm doin',
An' what's worse, I know what I done.
Elmer fixed th' telephone in about two minits,
An' he didn't seem in no hurry to go,
An' I don't know as I wanted him to go either,
I was awful mad at your not takin' me with yer,
An' I was tired o' wishin' and wishin'
An' gittin' no comfort.
I guess it ain't necessary to tell yer all the things.
He stayed to dinner,
An' he helped me do the dishes,
An' he said a home was a fine thing,
An' I said dishes warn't a home
Nor yet the room they're in.
He said a lot o' things,
An' I fended him off at first,
But he got talkin' all around me,
Clost up to the things I'd be'n thinkin',
What's the use o' me goin' on, Jake,
You know.
He got all he wanted,
An' I give it to him,
An' what's more, I'm glad!
I ain't dead, anyway,
An' somebody thinks I'm somethin'.
Keep away, Jake,
You can kill me to-morrer if you want to,
But I'm goin' to have my say.
Funny thing! Guess I ain't made to hold a man.
Elmer ain't be'n here for more'n two months.
I don't want to pretend nothin',
Mebbe if he'd be'n lately
I shouldn't have told yer.
I'll go away in the mornin', o' course.
What you want the light fer?
I don't look no diff'rent.
Ain't the moon bright enough
To look at a woman that's deceived yer by?
Don't Jake, don't, you can't love me now!
It ain't a question of forgiveness.

Why! I'd be thinkin' o' Elmer ev'ry minute;
It ain't decent.
Oh, my God! It ain't decent any more either way!

The Sisters Taking us by and large, we're a queer lot
We women who write poetry. And when you think
How few of us there've been, it's queerer still.
I wonder what it is that makes us do it,
Singles us out to scribble down, man-wise,
The fragments of ourselves. Why are we
Already mother-creatures, double-bearing,
With matrices in body and in brain?
I rather think that there is just the reason
We are so sparse a kind of human being;
The strength of forty thousand Atlases
Is needed for our every-day concerns.
There's Sapho, now I wonder what was Sapho.
I know a single slender thing about her:
That, loving, she was like a burning birch-tree
All tall and glittering fire, and that she wrote
Like the same fire caught up to Heaven and held there,
A frozen blaze before it broke and fell.
Ah, me! I wish I could have talked to Sapho,
Surprised her reticences by flinging mine
Into the wind. This tossing off of garments
Which cloud the soul is none too easy doing
With us to-day. But still I think with Sapho
One might accomplish it, were she in the mood
To bare her loveliness of words and tell
The reasons, as she possibly conceived them,
Of why they are so lovely. Just to know
How she came at them, just to watch
The crisp sea sunshine playing on her hair,
And listen, thinking all the while 'twas she
Who spoke and that we two were sisters
Of a strange, isolated little family.
And she is Sapho—Sapho—not Miss or Mrs.,
A leaping fire we call so for convenience;
But Mrs Browning—who would ever think
Of such presumption as to call her "Ba."
Which draws the perfect line between sea-cliffs
And a close-shuttered room in Wimpole Street.
Sapho could fly her impulses like bright
Balloons tip-tilting to a morning air
And write about it. Mrs. Browning's heart
Was squeezed in stiff conventions. So she lay
Stretched out upon a sofa, reading Greek

And speculating, as I must suppose,
In just this way on Sapho; all the need,
The huge, imperious need of loving, crushed
Within the body she believed so sick.
And it was sick, poor lady, because words
Are merely simulacra after deeds
Have wrought a pattern; when they take the place
Of actions they breed a poisonous miasma
Which, though it leave the brain, eats up the body.
So Mrs. Browning, aloof and delicate,
Lay still upon her sofa, all her strength
Going to uphold her over-topping brain.
It seems miraculous, but she escaped
To freedom and another motherhood
Than that of poems. She was a very woman
And needed both.
                    If I had gone to call,
Would Wimpole Street have been the kindlier place,
Or Casa Guidi, in which to have met her?
I am a little doubtful of that meeting,
For Queen Victoria was very young and strong
And all-pervading in her apogee
At just that time. If we had stuck to poetry,
Sternly refusing to be drawn off by mesmerism
Or Roman revolutions, it might have done.
For, after all, she is another sister,
But always, I rather think, an older sister
And not herself so curious a technician
As to admit newfangled modes of writing—
"Except, of course, in Robert, and that is neither
Here nor there for Robert is a genius."
I do not like the turn this dream is taking,
Since I am very fond of Mrs. Browning
And very much indeed should like to hear her
Graciously asking me to call her "Ba."
But then the Devil of Verisimilitude
Creeps in and forces me to know she wouldn't.
Convention again, and how it chafes my nerves,
For we are such a little family
Of singing sisters, and as if I didn't know
What those years felt like tied down to the sofa.
Confounded Victoria, and the slimy inhibitions
She loosed on all of us Anglo-Saxon creatures!
Suppose there hadn't been a Robert Browning,
No "Sonnets from the Portuguese" would have been written.
They are the first of all her poems to be,
One might say, fertilized. For, after all,
A poet is flesh and blood as well as brain

And Mrs. Browning, as I said before,
Was very, very woman. Well, there are two
Of us, and vastly unlike that's for certain.
Unlike at least until we tear the veils
Away which commonly gird souls. I scarcely think
Mrs. Browning would have approved the process
In spite of what had surely been relief;
For speaking souls must always want to speak
Even when bat-eyed, narrow-minded Queens
Set prudishness to keep the keys of impulse.
Then do the frowning Gods invent new banes
And make the need of sofas. But Sapho was dead
And I, and others, not yet peeped above
The edge of possibility. So that's an end
to speculating over tea-time talks
Beyond the movement of pentameters
With Mrs. Browning.
                                    But I go dreaming on,
In love with these my spiritual relations.
I rather think I see myself walk up
A flight of wooden steps and ring a bell
And send a card in to Miss Dickinson.
Yet that's a very silly way to do.
I should have taken the dream twist-ends about
And climbed over the fence and found her deep
Engrossed in the doing of a hummingbird
Among nasturtiums. Not having expected strangers,
She might forget to think me one, and holding up
A finger say quite casually: "Take care.
Don't frighten him, he's only just begun."
"Now this," I well believe I should have thought,
"Is even better than Sapho. With Emily
You're really here, or never anywhere at all
In range of mind." Wherefore, having begun
In the strict centre, we could slowly progress
To various circumferences, as we pleased.
We could, but should we? That would quite depend
On Emily. I think she'd be exacting,
Without intention possibly, and ask
A thousand tight-rope tricks of understanding.
But, bless you, I would somersault all day
If by so doing I might stay with her.
I hardly think that we should mention souls
Although they might just round the corner from us
In some half-quizzical, half-wistful metaphor.
I'm very sure that I should never seek
To turn her parables to stated fact.
Sapho would speak, I think, quite openly,
And Mrs. Browning guard a careful silence,

But Emily would set doors ajar and slam them
And love you for your speed of observation.

Strange trio of my sisters, most diverse,
And how extraordinarily unlike
Each is to me, and which way shall I go?
Sapho spent and gained; and Mrs. Browning,
After a miser girlhood, cut the strings
Which tied her money-bags and let them run;
But Emily hoarded—hoarded—only giving
Herself to cold, white paper. Starved and tortured,
She cheated her despair with games of patience
And fooled herself by winning. Frail little elf,
The lonely brain-child of a gaunt maturity,
She hung her womanhood upon a bough
And played ball with the stars—too long—too long—
The garment of herself hung on a tree
Until at last she lost even the desire
To take it down. Whose fault? Why let us say,
To be consistent, Queen Victoria's.
But really, not to over-rate the queen,
I feel obliged to mention Martin Luther,
And behind him the long line of Church Fathers
Who draped their prurience like a dirty cloth
About the naked majesty of God.
Good-bye, my sisters, all of you are great,
And all of you are marvellously strange,
And none of you has any word for me.
I cannot write like you, I cannot think
In terms of Pagan or of Christian now.
I only hope that possibly some day
Some other woman with an itch for writing
May turn to me as I have turned to you
And chat with me a brief few minutes. How
We lie, we poets! It is three good hours
I have been dreaming. Has it seemed so long
To you? And yet I thank you for the time
Although you leave me sad and self-distrustful,
For older sisters are very sobering things.
Put on your cloaks, my dears, the motor's waiting.
No, you have not seemed strange to me, but near,
Frightfully near, and rather terrifying.
I understand you all, for in myself—
Is that presumption? Yet indeed it's true—
We are one family. And still my answer
Will not be any one of yours, I see.
Well, never mind that now. Good night! Good night!

Elinor Wylie (1885-1928)

ELINOR WYLIE was born Elinor Morton Hoyt in Somerville, New Jersey, the eldest of the five children of Henry Morton and Anne Hoyt. Elinor's father was Assistant Attorney General in McKinley's cabinet. She grew up in Philadelphia and, until 1910, lived life as the bright, beautiful, genteel daughter of a socially prominent minor political figure. She went to finishing school, traveled to Europe and in 1905 was married (within her own social milieu) to Philip Hichborn, the son of an admiral. They had a son. In 1910 she broke the conventional pattern of her life and ran off with Horace Wylie, thus scandalizing polite society. They lived under an assumed name in England for two years. It was here that Elinor's first poems, *Incidental Numbers*, were privately printed. In 1915 the couple returned to Boston, and the next year they were married. By the end of the war they had settled in Washington and Elinor had begun to make literary friendships. In 1921 her first proper book, *Nets to Catch the Wind*, was published. It was a success and Elinor, now in New York, served for a while as poetry editor of *Vanity Fair*. In 1923 she was divorced from Wylie and married poet-critic William Rose Benet. Her last years were particularly productive. By her death at the age of forty-four she had brought out four novels and three more volumes of verse.

Wylie's brief but bright career was shadowed by a personal history that would today seem unremarkable, even commonplace. It is hard to grasp the provincialism of America in these years.

When the League of American Penwomen read Miss Wylie out of their lists, her friend Edna Millay rallied to her cause with splendid scorn: "Strike me too from your lists, and permit me, I beg you, to share with Elinor Wylie a brilliant exile from your fusty province." Less easy to understand or excuse is Amy Lowell, who, while congratulating Miss Wylie on her third marriage, warned that if she were to marry again, society would never forgive her. To understand her poetry it must be read against this background of sexual prejudice, possibly envy, which sadly came as much from other women as from men. Acquaintances found her beautiful, witty and vain. Yet her poems are an extended and ruthless self-portrait in which she criticizes and interprets her egoism. In her finest poems, "Wild Peaches" for example, she picks up on Imagist techniques by evoking tactile and visual sensations, but the poems always associate the images with personal meaning. She describes herself as drawn to a "lotus-eating" sensuous existence; she imagines herself in an Edenic world with her lover, swimming "in milk and honey till we drown." Once she has evoked it, however, the speaker draws back from this sensuous, highly colored paradise. In "the Puritan marrow" of her bones she wants the "austere, immaculate." In another poem she sees herself sentenced by her early conditioning in love, to a mistrustful isolation. She erects defenses "Against love's violence" even while lying next to her lover.

Though the poet-speaker is condemned to a kind of loneliness she is not without power. In "Atavism" and "Wild Peaches" part of the pleasure of the poem is the imaginative control which the speaker seems to have over the landscapes she invents or describes. Yet we are reminded that there are limitations imposed by nature and sex. "I was, being human, born alone/I am, being woman, hard beset." Wylie's poetic voice is always female, ironic and defiant but never defeated:

In masks outrageous and austere
The years go by in single file
But none has merited my fear,
And none has quite escaped my smile.

Shortly after Wylie's death Edna St. Vincent Millay wrote a tender letter to William Rose Benet which confirms Wylie's self-assessment: "how delightful she was and how funny, so gay and splendid about tragic things, so comically serious about silly ones. Oh, she was lovely! There was nobody like her at all. I am grateful for all she gave me."

Atavism

I always was afraid of Somes's Pond:
Not the little pond, by which the willow stands,
Where laughing boys catch alewives in their hands
In brown, bright shallows; but the one beyond.
There, when the frost makes all the birches burn
Yellow as cow-lilies, and the pale sky shines
Like a polished shell between black spruce and pines,
Some strange thing tracks us, turning where we turn.

You'll say I dream it, being the true daughter
Of those who in old times endured this dread.
Look! Where the lily-stems are showing red
A silent paddle moves below the water,
A sliding shape has stirred them like a breath;
Tall plumes surmount a painted mask of death.

Wild Peaches

1
When the world turns completely upside down
You say we'll emigrate to the Eastern Shore
Aboard a river-boat from Baltimore;
We'll live among wild peach trees, miles from town,
You'll wear a coonskin cap, and I a gown
Homespun, dyed butternut's dark gold colour.
Lost, like your lotus-eating ancestor,
We'll swim in milk and honey till we drown.

The winter will be short, the summer long,
The autumn amber-hued, sunny and hot,
Tasting of cider and of scuppernong;
All seasons sweet, but autumn best of all.
The squirrels in their silver fur will fall
Like falling leaves, like fruit, before your shot.

2
The autumn frosts will lie upon the grass
Like bloom on grapes of purple-brown and gold.
The misted early mornings will be cold;
The little puddles will be roofed with glass.
The sun, which burns from copper into brass,
Melts these at noon, and makes the boys unfold
Their knitted mufflers; full as they can hold,
Fat pockets dribble chestnuts as they pass.

Peaches grow wild, and pigs can live in clover;
A barrel of salted herrings lasts a year;
The spring begins before the winter's over.
By February you may find the skins
Of garter snakes and water moccasins
Dwindled and harsh, dead-white and cloudy-clear.

3

When April pours the colours of a shell
Upon the hills, when every little creek
Is shot with silver from the Chesapeake
In shoals new-minted by the ocean swell,
When strawberries go begging, and the sleek
Blue plums lie open to the blackbird's beak,
We shall live well—we shall live very well.

The months between the cherries and the peaches
Are brimming cornucopias which spill
Fruits red and purple, sombre-bloomed and black;
Then, down rich fields and frosty river beaches
We'll trample bright persimmons, while you kill
Bronze partridge, speckled quail, and canvasback.

4

Down to the Puritan marrow of my bones
There's something in this richness that I hate.
I love the look, austere, immaculate,
Of landscapes drawn in pearly monotones.
There's something in my very blood that owns
Bare hills, cold silver on a sky of slate,
A thread of water, churned to milky spate
Streaming through slanted pastures fenced with stones.

I love those skies, thin blue or snowy gray,
Those fields sparse-planted, rendering meagre sheaves;
That spring, briefer than apple-blossom's breath,
Summer, so much too beautiful to stay,
Swift autumn, like a bonfire of leaves,
And sleepy winter, like the sleep of death.

Confession of Faith

I lack the braver mind
That dares to find
The lover friend, and kind.

I fear him to the bone;
I lie alone
By the beloved one,

And, breathless for suspense,
Erect defense
Against love's violence

Whose silences portend
A bloody end
For lover never friend.

But, in default of faith,
In futile breath,
I dream no ill of Death.

Let No Charitable Hope

Now let no charitable hope
Confuse my mind with images
Of eagle and of antelope:
I am in nature none of these.

I was, being human, born alone;
I am, being woman, hard beset;
I live by squeezing from a stone
The little nourishment I get.

In masks outrageous and austere
The years go by in single file;
But none has merited my fear,
And none has quite escaped my smile.

Cold-blooded Creatures

Man, the egregious egoist
(In mystery the twig is bent),
Imagines, by some mental twist,
That he alone is sentient

Of the intolerable load
Which on all living creatures lies,
Nor stoops to pity in the toad
The speechless sorrow of its eyes.

He asks no questions of the snake,
Nor plumbs the phosphorescent gloom
Where lidless fishes, broad awake,
Swim staring at a night-mare doom.

Epitaph

For this she starred her eyes with salt
And scooped her temples thin,
Until her face shone pure of fault
From the forehead to the chin.

In coldest crucibles of pain
Her shrinking flesh was fired
And smoothed into a finer grain
To make it more desired.

Pain left her lips more clear than glass;
It coloured and cooled her hand.
She lay a field of scented grass
Yielded as pasture land.

For this her loveliness was curved
And carved as silver is:
For this she was brave: but she deserved
A better grave than this.

Nebuchadnezzar

My body is weary to death of my mischievous brain;
I am weary forever and ever of being brave;
Therefore I crouch on my knees while the cool white rain
Curves the clover over my head like a wave.

The stem and the frosty seed of the grass are ripe;
I have devoured their strength; I have drunk them deep;
And the dandelion is gall in a thin green pipe,
But the clover is honey and sun and the smell of sleep.

Full Moon

My bands of silk and miniver
Momently grew heavier;
The black gauze was beggarly thin;
The ermine muffled mouth and chin;
I could not suck the moonlight in.

Harlequin in lozenges
Of love and hate, I walked in these
Striped and ragged rigmaroles;
Along the pavement my footsoles
Trod warily on living coals.

Shouldering the thoughts I loathed,
In their corrupt disguises clothed,
Mortality I could not tear
From my ribs, to leave them bare
Ivory in silver air.

There I walked, and there I raged;
The spiritual savage caged
Within my skeleton, raged afresh
To feel, behind a carnal mesh,
The clean bones crying in the flesh.

A Proud Lady

Hate in the world's hand
Can carve and set its seal
Like the strong blast of sand
Which cuts into steel.

I have seen how the finger of hate
Can mar and mould
Faces burned passionate
And frozen cold.

Sorrowful faces worn
As stone with rain,
Faces writhing with scorn
And sullen with pain.

But you have a proud face
Which the world cannot harm,
You have turned the pain to a grace
And the scorn to a charm.

You have taken the arrows and slings
Which prick and bruise
And fashioned them into wings
For the heels of your shoes.

From the world's hand which tries
To tear you apart
You have stolen the falcon's eyes
And the lion's heart.

What has it done, this world,
With hard finger-tips,
But sweetly chiselled and curled
Your inscrutable lips?

HD (Hilda Doolittle) (1886-1961)

THE PROTAGONISTS of Hilda Doolittle's poems are often female figures out of Greek myth whom she represents in conflict with the first of Western patriarchies. This conflict takes place on an heroic scale. Its significance for Hilda, however, may arise from the domestic pattern of oppression which she found in her own childhood. In *Tribute to Freud*, the breathy, semi-autobiographical study she wrote of her psychoanalysis, Hilda recalls the atmosphere of her astronomer father's household in Philadelphia.

> *My father's study was lined with books. . . . There was one picture, a photograph of Rembrandt's Dissection, and a skull on the top of my father's highest set of shelves. There was a white owl under a bell-jar. I could sit on the floor with a doll or a folder of paper dolls, but I must not speak to him when he was writing at his table. . . . I must not speak to my father when he lay stretched out on the couch, because he worked at night and so must not be disturbed when he lay down on the couch and closed his eyes by day.*

Childhood was a series of don'ts. Hilda's mother was equally inaccessible, busy with friends, preferring the brother to the sister, and only really devoting time and attention to Hilda if she was ill. She saw herself as

> *. . . a girl between two boys; but, ironically, it was wispey and mousey, while the boys were glowing and gold. It was not pretty, they said. Then they said it was—pretty— but suddenly, it shot up like a weed. They said, surprised, "She is really very pretty, but isn't it a pity she's so tall?"*

Something of the alienating power of this experience can be sensed in the fact that Hilda relates it in the third person neuter. From this alienation she was, presumably, emancipated by Freud, whom she called the "blameless physician." Between the floor of Charles Leander Doolittle's study and the Vienna couch of Sigmund Freud there was a long passage of years in which moments of despair were balanced, even outweighed, by periods of happiness and success.

If family life was formal and cold, at least Hilda's parents did not discourage female intellect. She read voraciously, gobbling up Hawthorne's *Tanglewood Tales* and "all fairy tales." School taught her the Romantic and Victorian writers, but her preference for classical and neo-classical literature established itself when she was very young. At fifteen she met Ezra Pound, who lived nearby. Pound, who was a year older than Hilda, fell in love with her and, more important, supervised her reading. He brought her, she remembered, "(literally) armfuls of books to read. Among others, there were some rather old de luxe volumes of Renaissance Latin poets." From these poets she found her way back to the classics. Between 1906 and 1908 Hilda attended Bryn Mawr; ill health forced her to leave after her second year. She spent five years following her withdrawal from college at home, learning to write. William Carlos Williams, who met her through Pound in 1905, described her as "tall, blond and with a long jaw but gay blue eyes. . . . She dressed indifferently, almost sloppily and looked to a young man, not inviting—she had nothing of that—but irritating, with a smile." Williams also gives us the family at dinner: the silent, gaunt scientist who "never focused upon anything nearer, literally, than the moon" and the deferential mother who "would silence everyone with a look when she found her husband prepared to talk." It must have been a strain. Leander had focused on Pound long enough to declare him "nothing but a nomad" and emphatically not a match for his daughter. That, plus his expatriation to England in 1908, caused a three-year hiatus in Pound's friendship with Hilda. In 1911 she saw her own means of escape. She and some friends went on holiday to the continent. Hilda remet Pound in his new milieu, and at the end of the summer wrote to her father that she wished to live abroad. She was in her mid-twenties and Professor Doolittle was not Edward Moulton Barrett. He agreed to send her a small allowance. She never lived in America again.

Settled in England, Hilda was introduced by Pound to the poet Richard Aldington, who shared her interest in Greek poetry. They were married in 1913. Meanwhile, Pound had just been appointed the European agent for Harriet Monroe's newly-founded magazine, *Poetry*. His friend T. E. Hulme had recently come back from Bologna full of Bergson's theory of the Image, and Pound, looking for a package to sell a group of related but finally very disparate talents to Monroe, hit on the term "Imagiste." He persuaded Hilda to sign her first published poems, "H.D., Imagiste," and the movement (as well as Hilda's career) was born. Seven of H.D.'s poems and ten of Aldington's went into their first anthology *Des Imagistes*, published in 1914. The movement soon dropped the pretentious final "e" after hoots of laughter from the critics. H.D. survived all the splits in the loosely-connected group of poets; her poems appeared in all three of Amy Lowell's annual collections *Some Imagist Poets* (1915, 1916, 1917). In 1916 her first book of poetry *Sea Garden* was published. In that same year Aldington was drafted, and she replaced him as editor of *The Egoist*, a journal taken over from the feminist movement by the new poets.

Then in rhythm with the mounting chaos of the war, H.D.'s new life began to disintegrate. Her brother, of whom she was very fond, was killed in action in France in 1918, and her father died a year later. Both deaths affected her profoundly. She had had one miscarriage. Now, with the marriage going badly— Aldington had started an affair with the girl in the downstairs flat—she was pregnant again, living on her own, and ill. From this situation she was fortuitously rescued by a new friend, Winifred Ellerman, the rebellious daughter of a rich English businessman. Winifred had already assumed the pen name Bryher, under which she would become a successful historical novelist. She promised H.D. that she would look after both her and the baby. After Perdita's birth the trio traveled in Greece, America and Egypt, settling after a few years in Switzerland. H.D. and Bryher lived in nearby houses. Under this arrangement both women established stable and productive lives. Trips to England and Paris broke up the occasional monotony of life in Switzerland. Hilda's analysis with Freud in the early thirties was, of course, a central event, and she spent the war years in England. *Collected Poems of H.D.* appeared in 1925 and represented all her early Imagist work. Three novels, several books of poems, a children's story called *The Hedghog*, a translation of Euripides' *Ion* and *Tribute to Freud* were written in later

years. She received the Helen Haire
Levinson Prize for poetry offered by
Poetry Magazine in 1938, the Brandeis
University Creative Arts Award for
Poetry in 1959 and was the first woman
to receive the Award of Merit Medal for
Poetry of the American Academy of Arts
and Letters in 1960.

The poetry presents problems that are
best approached from the vantage point
of *Tribute to Freud*. H.D.'s interpretation
of her analysis was a long time in
preparation, and her quarrels with Freud
are consistent with the philosophical views
expressed in her verse. Freud and H.D.
tangled when it came to placing the
meaning of the unconscious in a total
world view. H.D. was eager to fit it into a
mystical, religious schema of her own.
She was interested in the eternal,
archetypal models suggested by psycho-
analytic theory, convinced that Freud
had proved that "all nations and races
met in the universal world of the
dream. . . ."

It is not at all clear that that was what
Freud did mean, but H.D.'s reading of
him provides a clue to her hellenism,
which is often criticized for having very
little to do with Greece. For her, Greece
was the source of western culture; there
were set the psycho-social patterns which
would be realized again and again in
subsequent eras. The Greeks lived through
these models of experience in a pure
form (without ornament, like classical
Greek poetry and art) and therefore we
can see the conflicts acted out in the
original in Greek drama and myth. In her
reworking of the myth of Phaedra, for
example, H.D. emphasizes the Cretan
princess' materialist perspective on the
Greek world.

> *O how I hate*
> *this world, this west, this power*

> *that strives to reach*
> *through river, town or flower,*
> *the god or spirit that inhabit it;*
> *O, is it not enough to greet*
> *the red-rose*
> *for the red, red, sweet of it?*
> *must we encounter*
> *with each separate flower,*
> *some god, some goddess?*

Phaedra represents one side of the divided
female self, which is a central theme in
H.D.'s work. The other side, the cold
intellectual ego, is often associated with
freedom and represented by a goddess
such as Artemis.

In her hellenic poems H.D. has found a
concretely conceived counterpart for the
body/soul, man/woman conflict that
interested her. These poems fulfil the
Imagist criteria better than purely descriptive verses like "Oread" which are
beautifully designed Christmas ornaments
without a tree—evoking, finally, neither
pines nor oceans. The hellenic poems are
"straight talk" as Pound suggested; the
diction is simple, uses everyday speech,
heightened slightly by repetition, rhythm
and the occasional rhyme; there is no
useless ornament. They reject the Imagist
criteria by their concern with the didactic,
with the "message" always presented as a
statement attached to a specific object—
—Helen's face, the rose, Callypso's gift.
Each poem suggests, too, the shifting
meaning of objects. The rose is one thing
to Phaedra, another to Hippolytus;
Callypso's gifts have an ominously
different significance to her and to
Odysseus. The reader must choose between Callypso's excessive anger and
Odysseus' obtuse satisfaction, between
Phaedra and Artemis, between Helen's
genuinely frightening beauty and the
Greek's vicious fear of it. She suggests
how heavily sexual role is involved with

these opposed views. The choice is not obvious, nor does H.D. mean it to be. These early poems have a strong feminist thrust which is quite different from the Victorian use of classical themes. Here the sexual conflicts are totally exposed, not masked as in the nineteenth century, by the metaphor of history.

William Carlos Williams commented that Hilda was "much like her father, though I never saw her pay him any particular attention." In her own philosophy H.D. sought, through Freudian theory, to give eternal human truths a scientific base. Her transcendentalism is a bit naive if seen simply as a piece of eclectic theology. If seen, however, as the raw beginnings of a theory about women's relation to art and to symbols in a patriarchal society where men control the symbol-making, it is considerably more impressive. She never sat passive under her analysis but argued continuously with Freud. He was seventy-seven, she forty-seven, when they met. Just before his death he wrote her a moving letter. "What you gave me was not praise, was affection and I need not be ashamed of my satisfaction." Her own best work has precision, hard edges, and analytic distance as well as the element missing from her childhood—the passion of felt experience.

Oread

Whirl up, sea—
whirl your pointed pines,
splash your great pines
on our rocks,
hurl your green over us,
cover us with your pools of fir.

Helen

All Greece hates
the still eyes in the white face,
the lustre as of olives
where she stands,
and the white hands.

All Greece reviles
the wan face when she smiles,
hating it deeper still
when it grows wan and white,
remembering past enchantments
and past ills.

Greece sees, unmoved,
God's daughter, born of love,
the beauty of cool feet
and slenderest knees,
could love indeed the maid,
only if she were laid,
white ash amid funereal cypresses.

Callypso Speaks *Callypso.*

O you clouds,
here is my song;
man is clumsy and evil
a devil

O you sand,
this is my command,
drown all men in slow breathless suffocation—
then they may understand.

O you winds,
beat his sails flat,
shift a wave sideways
that he suffocate,

O you waves
run counter to his oars,
waft him to blistering shores,
where he may die of thirst

O you skies
send rain
to wash salt from my eyes,

and witness, all earth and heaven,
it was of my heart-blood
his sails were woven;

Odysseus (on the sea)   witness, river and sea and land;

you, you must hear me—
man is a devil,
man will not understand.

She gave me fresh water in an earth-jar,
strange fruits
to quench thirst,
a golden zither
to work magic on the water;

she gave me wine in a cup
and white wine in a crystal shell;
she gave me water and salt,
wrapped in a palm-leaf,
and palm dates:

she gave me wool and a pelt of fur,
she gave me a pelt of a silver-fox,
and a brown soft skin of a bear,

she gave me an ivory comb for my hair,
she washed brine and mud from my body,
and cool hands
held balm
for a rust-wound;

she gave me water
and fruit in a basket,
and shallow
baskets of pulse and grain, and a ball
of hemp
for mending the sail;

she gave me a willow-basket
for letting into the shallows
for eels,

she gave me peace in her cave.

Callypso (from land)	He has gone, he has forgotten; he took my lute and my shell of crystal— he never looked back—
Odysseus (on the sea)	She gave me a wooden flute and a mantle, she wove this wool—
Callypso (from land)	For man is a brute and a fool.

Hippolytus Temporizes

I worship the greatest first—
(it were sweet, the couch,
the brighter ripple of cloth
over the dipped fleece;
the thought: her bones
under the flesh are white
as sand which along a beach
covers but keeps the print
of the crescent shapes beneath:
I thought:
between cloth and fleece,
so her body lies.)

I worship first, the great—
(ah, sweet, your eyes—
what God, invoked in Crete,
gave them the gift to part
as the Sidonian myrtle-flower
suddenly, wide and swart,
then swiftly,
the eye-lids having provoked our hearts—
as suddenly beat and close.)

I worship the feet, flawless,
that haunt the hills—
(ah, sweet, dare I think,
beneath fetter of golden clasp,
of the rhythm, the fall and rise
of yours, carven, slight
beneath straps of gold that keep
their slender beauty caught,
like wings and bodies
of trapped birds.)

I worship the greatest first—
(suddenly into my brain—
the flash of sun on the snow,
the fringe of light and the drift,
the crest and the hill-shadow—

ah, surely now I forget,
ah splendour, my goddess turns:
or was it the sudden heat,
beneath quivering of molten flesh,
of veins, purple as violets?)

Phaedra   Think, O my soul,
of the red sand of Crete;
think of the earth; the heat
burnt fissures like the great
backs of the temple serpents;
think of the world you knew;
as the tide crept, the land
burned with a lizard-blue
where the dark sea met the sand.

Think, O my soul—
what power has struck you blind—
is there no desert-root, no forest-berry
pine-pitch or knot of fir
known that can help the soul
caught in a force, a power,
passionless, not its own?

So I scatter, so implore
Gods of Crete, summoned before
with slighter craft;
ah, hear my prayer:

Grant to my soul
the body that it wore,
trained to your thought,
that kept and held your power,
as the petal of black poppy,
the opiate of the flower.

For art undreamt in Crete,
strange art and dire,
in counter-charm prevents my charm
limits my power:
pine-cone I heap,
grant answer to my prayer.

No more, my soul—
as the black cup, sullen and dark with fire,
burns till beside it, noon's bright heat
is withered, filled with dust—
and into that noon-heat
grown drab and stale,

suddenly wind and thunder and swift rain,
till the scarlet flower is wrecked
in the slash of the white hail.

The poppy that my heart was,
formed to bind all mortals,
made to strike and gather hearts
like flame upon an altar,
fades and shrinks, a red leaf
drenched and torn in the cold rain.

She Contrasts With Herself Hippolyta

Can flame beget white steel—
ah no, it could not take
within my reins its shelter;
steel must seek steel,
or hate make out of joy
a whet-stone for a sword;
sword against flint,
Theseus sought Hippolyta;
she yielded not nor broke,
sword upon stone,
from the clash leapt a spark,
Hippolytus, born of hate.

What did she think
when all her strength
was twisted for his bearing;
did it break,
even within her sheltered heart, a song,
some whispered note,
distant and faint as this:

Love that I bear
within my breast
how is my armour melted
how my heart:
as an oak-tree
that keeps beneath the snow,
the young bark fresh
till the spring cast
from off its shoulders
the white snow
so does my armour melt.

Love that I bear
within my heart, O speak;
tell how beneath the serpent-spotted shell,
the cygnets wait,
how the soft owl
opens and flicks with pride,
eye-lids of great bird-eyes,
when underneath its breast
the owlets shrink and turn.

You have the power,
(then did she say) Artemis,
benignity to grant
forgiveness that I gave
no quarter to an enemy who cast
his armour on the forest-moss,
and took, unmatched in an uneven contest,
Hippolyta who relented not,
returned and sought no kiss.

Then did she pray: Artemis,
grant that no flower
be grafted alien on a broken stalk,
no dark flame-laurel on the stricken crest
of a wild mountain-poplar;
grant in my thought,
I never yield but wait,
entreating cold white river,
She Rebukes Hippolyta   mountain-pool and salt:
let all my veins be ice,
until they break
(strength of white beach,
rock of mountain land,
forever to you, Artemis, dedicate)
from out my reins,
those small, cold hands.

Was she so chaste?

Swift and a broken rock
clatters across the steep shelf
of the mountain slope,
sudden and swift
and breaks as it clatters down
into the hollow breach
of the dried water-course:
far and away
(though fire I see it,
and smoke of the dead, withered stalks
of the wild cistus-brush)
Hippolyta, frail and wild,

galloping up the slope
between great boulder and rock
and group and cluster of rock.

Was she so chaste,
(I see it, sharp, this vision,
and each fleck on the horse's flanks
of foam, and bridle and bit,
silver, and the straps,
wrought with their perfect art,
and the sun,
striking athwart the silver-work,
and the neck, strained forward, ears alert,
and the head of a girl
flung back and her throat.)

Was she so chaste—
(Ah, burn my fire, I ask
out of the smoke-ringed darkness
enclosing the flaming disk
of my vision)
I ask for a voice to answer:
was she chaste?

Who can say—
the broken ridge of the hills
was the line of a lover's shoulder,
his arm-turn, the path to the hills,
the sudden leap and swift thunder
of mountain boulders, his laugh.

She was mad—
as no priest, no lover's cult
could grant madness;
the wine that entered her throat
with the touch of the mountain rocks
was white, intoxicant:
she, the chaste,
was betrayed by the glint
of light on the hills,
the granite splinter of rocks,
the touch of the stone
where heat melts
toward the shadow-side of the rocks.

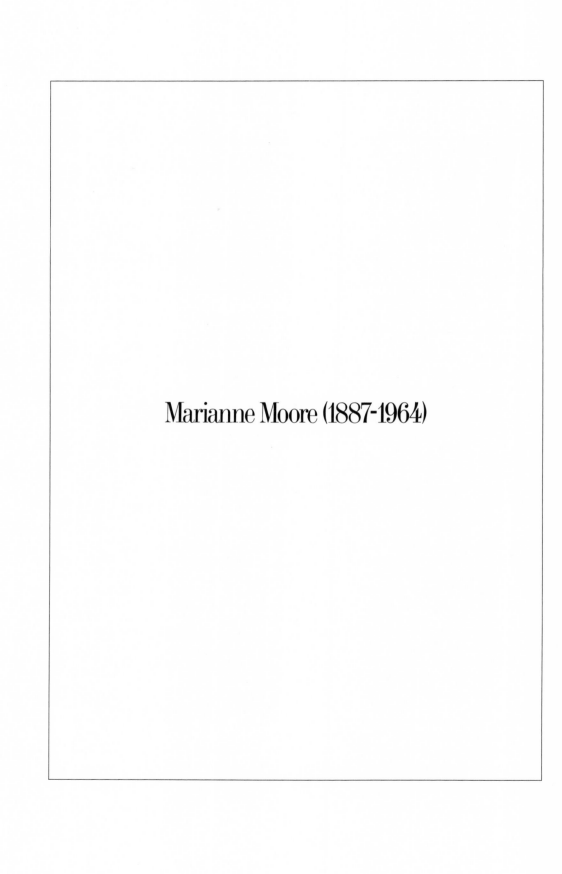

Marianne Moore (1887-1964)

W HAT I WRITE," said Marianne Moore, "could only be called poetry because there is no other category in which to put it." For many years she "disliked the term poetry" for any "but Chaucer's or Shakespeare's or Dante's." While her contemporaries among the "new" poets were hammering out the rules of the Modernist movement, the eccentric Miss Moore was beginning her own experiments with "syllabic" verse. She followed her own notions of form and developed a technique that gradually became as much a part of Modernism as the innovations of Pound and Eliot. Other women writers— Emma Lazarus, Amy Lowell, and Gertrude Stein, among them—had been drawn to the idea of a poetic form that was something between prose and verse. Emma Lazarus and Amy Lowell treated this form in a rather conventional way: they wanted the paragraph, like the stanza, to work as a unit of feeling as well as meaning.

Marianne Moore was always more concerned with the phrase and the sentence. "I am governed by the pull of the sentence as the pull of the fabric is governed by gravity." Her models were the great prose writers: Sir Thomas Browne, Francis Bacon, Dr. Johnson, Edmund Burke, Henry James. Instead of enriching her own poetic language by borrowing from other poets, she would build a poem around a prose quotation. Quotations—from her father, a taxidriver, a statesman, a journalist—these as well as literature could supply a text for comment and expansion. The often-anthologized "Blessed is the Man" is a pastiche of quotations from several sources; yet the structure and central idea of the poem, rather than leaning on the borrowed text, has a new sound and meaning of its own. Miss Moore was the granddaughter of a Presbyterian minister, and the sermon form, delivered over long childhood Sundays, may have had an impact on her.

All of Miss Moore's poetry is public and moral with an emphasis on liberty and individualism. While she blesses "the unaccomodating man" there is no single sentiment in her poetry that deviates from the comfortable center of American liberal wisdom. The poems warn us against war, materialism, the destruction of buildings, egocentricity, the rape of nature. It is all plain fare, embellished with words rather than thought. Yet without being either snobbish or introverted it is very self-consciously "class" poetry—meant for "literary" audiences as fascinated with words in themselves as Miss Moore was.

Marianne Moore had a passion for baseball, which she compared to writing. The worst thing that can be said of her poetry is that it is most often a sort of game, in which words and cultural attitudes are placed on a diamond and made to run rings around each other. Louise Bogan finds her later poetry "warmer and more direct." This judgment seems hard to sustain. There are warm and direct poems scattered through her *oeuvre*: "The Steeple Jack" and "In Distrust of Merits" are two. But on the whole the very precision of the words, the merry attention she calls to language, to arrangement, to half-rhymes, leads us toward some abstraction called literature and away from life.

Or, perhaps, this preoccupation with language was the real focus of Marianne Moore's life. "I think books are chiefly responsible for my doggedly self-determined efforts to write; books and verisimilitude."

Marianne Moore was born in Kirkwood, Missouri near St. Louis on November 15, 1887. She was the second child of Mary and John Milton Moore. Her engineer father, having suffered a nervous breakdown after the failure of business plans, retreated to his own family. Mrs. Moore did the same. When her father died in 1894 Mrs. Moore took her children to Carlisle, Pennsylvania where she stretched a small inheritance by teaching English at Carlisle's Metzger Institute. Miss Moore attended Metzger and entered Bryn Mawr in 1905. H.D. was her classmate there. Although she wrote poetry in college, Miss Moore said that on graduation she had not decided on a career, and had even thought of painting. From 1911 until 1915 she taught at Carlisle Indian School in Carlisle, Pennsylvania. But the rich cultural life of New York City drew her. A visit in 1916 confirmed a determination to live there. She set up house in Greenwich Village with her mother, and in 1929 they moved to Brooklyn.

Moore got a job as a librarian at the New York Public Library. She became more and more involved with the world of poetry and the poets who lived in and around Greenwich Village. By 1915 Harriet Monroe and the Aldingtons were soliciting her verse for *Poetry* and the *Egoist*; she contributed as well to *Others*, Seymour Kreymbourg's annual. Success came early but did not much change the pattern of her life. She wrote poetry and served as critic and acting editor of *The*

Dial from 1925 to 1929. She knew almost everyone, and the calm of her private life in the chaotic literary culture of the 'twenties and 'thirties made her a point of reference and stability in the circles in which she moved.

Critics have connected Miss Moore's poetry with William Carlos Williams, Wallace Stevens and the Objectivist focus on "the thing itself." Poems describe objects and objects indicate their own meaning. This was, of course, part of Imagist theory too, but neither the Imagists nor Williams, Stevens and Moore follow it very strictly. In Moore's case, technical skill often gilds a mundane idea. Her skill is highly developed, almost overdeveloped. The super-literary quality of the poems, a kind of facile cleverness, betrays a certain intellectual insecurity. Her observations of personal relationships are formal, even superficial.

In one of her translated fables of La Fontaine, Miss Moore says that

Love is a curious mastery,
In name alone a felicity.
Better know of than know the thing.
If too personal and thus trespassing.

Of all the women poets born in the 'eighties and 'nineties Miss Moore seems the only one who is truly emancipated from "trespassing" love and, in a way, from all strong emotion. It is good to see a female poet living an idiosyncratic life who has escaped the emotional coercions of her culture. Marianne Moore's considerable place in modern poetry makes her an heir to the atmosphere of liberation which swept America in the 'teens and 'twenties, and allowed women not only an entrée to literature but considerable influence over its critical reception. Her *Collected Poems* (1952) received the

National Book Award, the Pulitzer Prize and the Bollingen Award. No higher recognition from the literary establishment could have been possible. It is tempting—though decidedly unkind—to suggest that Miss Moore's popularity in critical circles was due in part to her avoidance of "female" themes. One of her most successful poetic ventures was her translation of *The Fables of La Fontaine*. Her two books of criticism, *Predilections* and *Idiosyncrasy and Technique*, are absorbing reading.

Miss Moore came out of Henry James's world—just the sort of eccentric, naive American woman he would have liked to draw. Her own admiration for Burke, Johnson and James was probably more than just a delight in their prose styles. She was attracted, too, to their essential social conservatism. Yet even James, that aesthetic spinster, invested his writing with something more succulent than we find in Miss Moore. Still, the poetry she wrote gives so many incidental pleasures, is so witty, so linguistically surprising, that it is almost churlish to complain that its scent is dry—the zest of the lemon without the juice.

The Steeple-Jack

(Revised, 1961)

Dürer would have seen a reason for living
     in a town like this, with eight stranded whales
to look at; with the sweet air coming into your house
on a fine day, from water etched
     with waves as formal as the scales
on a fish.

One by one in two's and three's, the seagulls keep
     flying back and forth over the town clock,
or sailing around the lighthouse without moving their wings—
rising steadily with a slight
     quiver of the body—or flock
mewing where

a sea the purple of the peacock's neck is
     paled to greenish azure as Dürer changed
the pine green of the Tyrol to peacock blue and guinea
gray. You can see a twenty-five-
     pound lobster; and fishnets arranged
to dry. The

whirlwind fife-and-drum of the storm bends the salt
     marsh grass, disturbs stars in the sky and the
star on the steeple; it is a privilege to see so
much confusion. Disguised by what
     might seem the opposite, the sea-
side flowers and

trees are favored by the fog so that you have
     the tropics at first hand: the trumpet-vine,
fox-glove, giant snap-dragon, a salpiglossis that has
spots and stripes; morning-glories, gourds,
     or moon-vines trained on fishing-twine
at the back

door; cat-tails, flags, blueberries and spiderwort,
     stripped grass, lichens, sunflowers, asters, daisies—
yellow and crab-claw ragged sailors with green bracts—toad-plant,
petunias, ferns; pink lilies, blue
     ones, tigers; poppies; black sweet-peas.
The climate

is not right for the banyan, frangipani, or
     jack-fruit trees; or an exotic serpent
life. Ring lizard and snake-skin for the foot, if you see fit;
but here they've cats, not cobras, to
     keep down the rats. The diffident
little newt

with white pin-dots on black horizontal spaced
        out bands lives here; yet there is nothing that
ambition can buy or take away. The college student
named Ambrose sits on the hillside
        with his not-native books and hat
and sees boats

at sea progress white and rigid as if in
        a groove. Liking an elegance of which
the source is not bravado, he knows by heart the antique
sugar-bowl shaped summer-house of
        interlacing slats, and the pitch
of the church

spire, not true, from which a man in scarlet lets
        down a rope as a spider spins a thread;
he might be part of a novel, but on the sidewalk a
sign says C. J. Poole, Steeple Jack,
        in black and white; and one in red
and white says

Danger. The church portico has four fluted
        columns, each a single piece of stone, made
modester by white-wash. This would be a fit haven for
waifs, children, animals, prisoners,
        and presidents who have repaid
sin-driven

senators by not thinking about them. The
        place has a school-house, a post-office in a
store, fish-houses, hen-houses, a three-masted
        schooner on
the stocks. The hero, the student,
        the steeple-jack, each in his way,
is at home.

It could not be dangerous to be living
        in a town like this, of simple people,
who have a steeple-jack placing danger-signs by the church
while he is gilding the solid-
        pointed star, which on a steeple
stands for hope.

Rigorists

"We saw reindeer
browsing," a friend who'd been in Lapland, said:
"finding their own food; they are adapted

to scant *reino*
or pasture, yet they can run eleven
miles in fifty minutes; the feet spread when

the snow is soft,
and act as snow-shoes. They are rigorists,
however handsomely cutwork artists

of Lapland and
Siberia elaborate the trace
or saddle-girth with saw-tooth leather lace.

One looked at us
with its firm face part brown, part white,—a queen
of alpine flowers. Santa Claus' reindeer, seen

at last, had gray-
brown fur, with a neck like edelweiss or
lion's foot,—*leontopodium* more

exactly." And
this candelabrum-headed ornament
for a place where ornaments are scarce, sent

to Alaska,
was a gift preventing the extinction
of the Eskimo. The battle was won

by a quiet man,
Sheldon Jackson, evangel to that race
whose reprieve he read in the reindeer's face.

Sojourn in the Whale

Trying to open locked doors with a sword, threading
    the points of needles, planting shade trees
        upside down; swallowed by the opaqueness of one whom
            the seas
love better than they love you, Ireland—

you have lived and lived on every kind of shortage.
    You have been compelled by hags to spin
        gold thread from straw and have heard men say: "There
            is a feminine
temperament in direct contrast to

240

ours which makes her do these things. Circumscribed by a
    heritage of blindness and native
      incompetence, she will become wise and will be forced
        to give
in. Compelled by experience, she

will turn back; water seeks its own level'': and you
    have smiled. ''Water in motion is far
      from level.'' You have seen it, when obstacles happened
        to bar
the path, rise automatically.

Silence My father used to say,
"Superior people never make long visits,"
have to be shown Longfellow's grave
or the glass flowers at Harvard.
Self-reliant like the cat—
that takes its prey to privacy,
the mouse's limp tail hanging like a shoelace from its mouth—
they sometimes enjoy solitude,
and can be robbed of speech
by speech which has delighted them.
The deepest feeling always shows itself in silence;
not in silence, but restraint.
Nor was he insincere in saying, "Make my house your inn."
Inns are not residences.

Edna St. Vincent Millay (1892-1950)

No OTHER American writing poetry in the first half of the twentieth century had as much impact on the general reading public and on other poets as Edna St. Vincent Millay. She "made poetry seem so easy that we could all do it," Dorothy Parker said, adding, "but of course we couldn't." The fluent lyrics that she wrote in her youth did sound deceptively easy; here, as in the verse drama she also wrote, she managed a language which was elegant yet colloquial. Like Elizabeth Barrett Browning, Millay was primarily a poet of ideas. Much of her verse explored and anatomized feelings that were political as well as personal. Her language at its best is so well trained to serve the idea as to be almost invisible. In her love poetry, especially, it is the whole argument, rather than a particular phrase, that remains as the after-image when you lift your eyes from the page. She achieved this effect through a lifelong apprenticeship to her craft and an ear not only for poetry in English but for Latin, French, Spanish and Russian verse as well.

Edna St. Vincent Millay was born the eldest of three daughters in Rockland, Maine in 1892. Her mother, Cora Millay, was a remarkable woman: trained as a singer and divorced from her feckless husband when Edna was eight, she supported her family by nursing. Cora recognized and encouraged her eldest daughter's talent. When she was twenty, Millay submitted a long poem, "Renascence," to a poetry contest. Though she came in only fourth, she attracted the attention of one of the judges and several of the contributors to *The Lyric Year*, a poetry annual. Caroline Dow of the YWCA saw that she got to college—Barnard for a year of solid reading and Vassar afterwards. She graduated in 1917 at the age of 25. The next year her first book of poems was published. Millay lived in Greenwich Village, wrote and acted for the Provincetown Players, had several love affairs, and traveled in Europe. In 1923 she returned home, ill. In that same year she won the Pulitzer Prize for poetry and married Eugen Jan Boissevain. Two years later the couple bought a farm near Austerlitz in upstate New York, where they lived most of the rest of their lives.

Reading through her collected poems is an odd experience. With the combined arrogance and insecurity of the educated New Englander, she assumes that all of the language from the Elizabethans onwards belongs to her. She uses archaisms in order to include in the sensibility of the speaker—and, by implication, the listener—that history of thought and feeling which should be accessible to any literate person. It is a hard trick to pull off without sounding both derivative and pretentious. The wonder is that her mature style not only survives the attempt, but—like all fine poetry—is as individual as a fingerprint and as accessible as an outstretched hand.

Together with other women poets of her generation Millay made a determined frontal assault on the genteel image of the woman poet. She wrote not only about love but about lust, about woman's right to stalk and choose as well as adore and suffer. These poems are witty and apt, but they come across as a little too rhetorical: the need to project the particular didactic message is more apparent than the need to write a good poem about it. Poems like "My candle burns at both ends . . ." are deliberate shockers; verse posters for the sexual revolution. In contrast, later work (notably from *Huntsman, What Quarry*) is the product of intense and varied emotional experience. These later poems assume the freedom that the young Millay demanded for her sisters, but they concentrate on the constraints and consequences involved in the exercise of such freedom. The sonnet sequence "Fatal Interview" and the less ambitious but perhaps more consistently successful "Theme and Variations" detail the course of a love affair. No other modern poet has come so near to such a sustained lyrical presentation of the shifting moods and perspectives of that common experience.

In early Millay emotions are romantic and generalized. "Renascence," written when Millay was nineteen, describes a spiritual crisis, death and rebirth. The poet is hemmed in by the landscape: "three long mountains and a wood" and "three islands in a bay." She lies back and touches the sky, comes in contact with Infinity, and, feeling the suffering of the universe, craves death. She is pushed symbolically underground and, in this demi-death, realizes that she can cope with the "multi-colored multi-form" world. The rain washes away her grave. Reborn, she discovers that

The heart can push the sea and land
Farther away on either hand;
The soul can split the sky in two,
And let the face of God shine through.

If we compare this arrogant Romantic testament to the power of the female spirit with the frustration expressed by nineteenth-century women poets from Charlotte Smith onwards, we can see that Millay has made a psychological and imaginative breakthrough. The poems of her late teens and twenties, even when they record broken love affairs, retain this exuberant sense of power over self and nature—"Oh World, I cannot hold thee close enough!"

In her early poems Millay had not yet found her best style, and seemed for a while stuck with a popular but trivial one which uses flowery, self-indulgent and abstract language, easy meters and jingly rhymes. Modernity seemed sometimes apparent only in the sentiments, and even they were too often shallow or cynical. But after 1925 her poetry begins to change. Millay does not abandon the high style, but the grand gestures become genuinely heroic and there is an increasing use of homely detail to counterbalance the "poetic" blasts. She writes more political poetry. Her attitudes toward both nature and love are slowly revised. Gardens, seasons and flowers figure throughout her verse as major symbols, but in her early poetry the relationship between symbol and self seems forced and mechanical. The rose that "budded, bloomed and shattered" or "bastard Daisies" are clumsy counters for lost love or sexual irregularity. Just as her view of passion becomes more complex and shadowed in the later verse, so her use of nature as an analogue for the human condition become infinitely more flexible and interesting, as well as more cautious and even bitter. Of a bird (herself) she writes,

Though Time refeather the wing,
Ankle slip the ring,
The once-confined thing
Is never again free.

Seasons are not used simply to evoke

mood or contrast the condition of the speaker with the weather. In the last poem of "Theme and Variations" Millay begins,

The time of year ennobles you.
The death of autumn draws you in.

The death of those delights I drew
From such a cramped and troubled source
Ennobles all, including you,
Involves you as a matter of course.

Winter is not mentioned. "The death of autumn," itself a dying season, is ironically linked to the end of the "cramped and troubled" love affair. The whole effort of "Theme and Variations" is to turn formless anguish into formal distanced images, to use will against regressive feelings, against the helpless attachment to the "unworthy" lover. At best, the fight is a draw; but the effort is ennobling and hopeful.

The young Millay was a Romantic revolutionary; the old Millay was a seasoned campaigner and a different sort of radical. "Logic alone, all love laid by,/ Must calm this crazed and plunging star." Her ideas about love and politics begin with the assertion of a crude Romantic optimism more appropriate to the early nineteenth than the early twentieth century. This is not simply attributable to youth, naivete or provincialism. It took a whole century for women to assert their own right to transform and control the world. The brashness of early Millay reflects the confident mood that followed suffragist triumphs. Later poems, sadder and mellower, suggest that control and transcendence over nature has been recognized as a dubious goal. Love is not the key to power. Power is not the object of struggle. Sexual independence is not all it is cracked up to be, yet love is still a final, profound value. Millay's rhetoric acquires historic resonances. In "Modern Declaration" the speaker declares her love incorruptible, announcing

That I shall love you always.
No matter what party is in power;
No matter what temporarily expedient
combination of allied interests win the war;
Shall love you always.

In spite of continued bouts of bad health in her thirties and forties—a nervous breakdown in 1944 brought on by war work—Millay remained a public person throughout her life. She read her poetry around the country and on the radio. She picketed for Sacco and Vanzetti and wrote propaganda during the war. Her feminism is strongly expressed in her poetry, and, like all her convictions, acted out in life. When New York University awarded her an honorary degree in 1937, she discovered too late to back out that she was to be excluded from the all-male dinner preceding the ceremony. Her letter of protest concludes with the eloquent hope that she "may be the last woman so honored to be required to swallow from the very cup of the honor the gall of the humiliation."

To her friends she offered deep personal loyalty and acute criticism of their work. With younger writers she was helpful and generous. In 1950, a year after her husband's death from cancer, she was found dead at Steepletop, book in hand.

Never May the Fruit Be Plucked

Never, never may the fruit be plucked from the bough
And gathered into barrels.
He that would eat of love must eat it where it hangs.
Though the branches bend like reeds,
Though the ripe fruit splash in the grass or wrinkle on the tree,
He that would eat of love may bear away with him
Only what his belly can hold,
Nothing in the apron,
Nothing in the pockets.
Never, never may the fruit be gathered from the bough
And harvested in barrels.
The winter of love is a cellar of empty bins,
In an orchard soft with rot.

To the Wife of a Sick Friend

Shelter this candle from the wind.
Hold it steady. In its light
The cave wherein we wander lost
Glitters with frosty stalactite,
Blossoms with mineral rose and lotus,
Sparkles with crystal moon and star,
Till a man would rather be lost than found:
We have forgotten where we are.

Shelter this candle. Shrewdly blowing
Down the cave from a secret door
Enters our only foe, the wind.
Hold it steady. Lest we stand,
Each in a sudden, separate dark,
The hot wax spattered upon your hand,
The smoking wick in my nostrils strong,
The inner eyelid red and green
For a moment yet with moons and roses,—
Then the unmitigated dark.

Alone, alone, in a terrible place,
In utter dark without a face,
With only the dripping of the water on the stone,
And the sound of your tears, and the taste of my own.

Justice Denied in Massachusetts

Let us abandon then our gardens and go home
And sit in the sitting-room.
Shall the larkspur blossom or the corn grow under this cloud?
Sour to the fruitful seed
Is the cold earth under this cloud,
Fostering quack and weed, we have marched upon but cannot conquer;
We have bent the blades of our hoes against the stalks of them.

Let us go home, and sit in the sitting-room.
Not in our day
Shall the cloud go over and the sun rise as before,
Beneficent upon us
Out of the glittering bay,
And the warm winds be blown inward from the sea
Moving the blades of corn
With a peaceful sound.
Forlorn, forlorn,
Stands the blue hay-rack by the empty mow.
And the petals drop to the ground,
Leaving the tree unfruited.
The sun that warmed our stooping backs and withered the weed uprooted—
We shall not feel it again.
We shall die in darkness, and be buried in the rain.

What from the splendid dead
We have inherited—
Furrows sweet to the grain, and the weed subdued—
See now the slug and the mildew plunder.
Evil does overwhelm
The larkspur and the corn;
We have seen them go under.

Let us sit here, sit still,
Here in the sitting-room until we die;
At the step of Death on the walk, rise and go;
Leaving to our children's children this beautiful doorway,
And this elm,
And a blighted earth to till
With a broken hoe.

Dirge Without Music

I am not resigned to the shutting away of loving hearts in the hard
    ground.
So it is, and so it will be, for so it has been, time out of mind:
Into the darkness they go, the wise and the lovely. Crowned
With lilies and with laurel they go; but I am not resigned.

Lovers and thinkers, into the earth with you.
Be one with the dull, the indiscriminate dust.
A fragment of what you felt, of what you knew,
A formula, a phrase remains,—but the best is lost.

The answers quick and keen, the honest look, the laughter, the love,—
They are gone. They are gone to feed the roses. Elegant and curled
Is the blossom. Fragrant is the blossom. I know. But I do not approve.
More precious was the light in your eyes than all the roses in the world.

Down, down, down into the darkness of the grave
Gently they go, the beautiful, the tender, the kind;
Quietly they go, the intelligent, the witty, the brave.
I know. But I do not approve. And I am not resigned.

Apostrophe to Man

*(on reflecting that the world is
ready to go to war again)*

Detestable race, continue to expunge yourself, die out.
Breed faster, crowd, encroach, sing hymns, build bombing airplanes;
Make speeches, unveil statues, issue bonds, parade;
Convert again into explosives the bewildered ammonia and the
    distracted cellulose;
Convert again into putrescent matter drawing flies
The hopeful bodies of the young; exhort,
Pray, pull long faces, be earnest, be all but overcome, be photographed;
Confer, perfect your formulae, commercialize
Bacteria harmful to human tissue,
Put death on the market;
Breed, crowd, encroach, expand, expunge yourself, die out,
Homo called *sapiens.*

Intention to Escape from Him

I think I will learn some beautiful language, useless for commercial
Purposes, work hard at that.
I think I will learn the Latin name of every songbird, not only in
    America but wherever they sing.
(Shun meditation, though; invite the controversial:
Is the world flat? Do bats eat cats?) By digging hard I might deflect that
    river, my mind, that uncontrollable thing.
Turgid and yellow, strong to overflow its banks in spring, carrying
    away bridges;
A bed of pebbles now, through which there trickles one clear narrow
    stream, following a course henceforth nefast—

Dig, dig; and if I come to ledges, blast.

Theme and Variations

I
Not even my pride will suffer much;
Not even my pride at all, maybe,
If this ill-timed, intemperate clutch
Be loosed by you and not by me,
Will suffer; I have been so true
A vestal to that only pride
Wet wood cannot extinguish, nor
Sand, nor its embers scattered, for,
See all these years, it has not died.

And if indeed, as I dare think,
You cannot push this patient flame,
By any breath your lungs could store,
Even for a moment to the floor
To crawl there, even for a moment crawl,
What can you mix for me to drink
That shall deflect me? What you do
Is either malice, crude defense
Of ego, or indifference:
I know these things as well as you;
You do not dazzle me at all.

Some love, and some simplicity,
Might well have been the death of me.

II
Heart, do not bruise the breast
That sheltered you so long;
Beat quietly, strange guest.

Or have I done you wrong
To feed you life so fast?
Why, no; digest this food
And thrive. You could outlast
Discomfort if you would.

You do not know for whom
These tears drip through my hands.
You thus in the bright room
Darkly. This pain demands
No action on your part,
Who never saw that face.

These eyes, that let him in,
(Not you, my guiltless heart)
These eyes, let them erase
His image, blot him out
With weeping, and go blind.

Heart, do not stain my skin
With bruises; go about
Your simple function. Mind,
Sleep now; do not intrude;
And do not spy; be kind.

Sweet blindness, now begin.

III

Rolled in the trough of thick desire,
No oars, and no sea-anchor out
To bring my bow into the pyre
Of sunset, suddenly chilling out
To shadow over sky and sea,
And the boat helpless in the trough;
No oil to pour; no power in me
To breast these waves, to shake them off:

I feel such pity for the poor,
Who take the fracas on the beam—
Being ill-equipped, being insecure—
Daily; and caulk the opening seam
With strips of shirt and scribbled rhyme;
Who bail disaster from the boat
With a pint can; and have no time,
Being so engrossed to keep afloat,
Even for quarrelling (that chagrined
And lavish comfort of the heart),
Who never came into the wind,
Who took life beam-on from the start.

IV

And do you think that love itself,
Living in such an ugly house,
Can prosper long?

        We meet and part;
Our talk is all of heres and nows,
Our conduct likewise; in no act
Is any future, any past;
Under our sly, unspoken pact,
I know with whom I saw you last,
But I say nothing; and you know
At six-fifteen to whom I go.

Can even love be treated so?

I know, but I do not insist,
Having stealth and tact, though not enough,
What hour your eye is on your wrist.
No wild appeal, no mild rebuff
Deflates the hour, leaves the wine flat.

Yet if you drop the picked-up book
To intercept my clockward look—
Tell me, can love go on like that?

Even the bored, insulted heart,
That signed so long and tight a lease,
Can break its contract, slump in peace.

V

I had not thought so tame a thing
Could deal me this bold suffering.

I have loved badly, loved the great
Too soon, withdrawn my words too late;
And eaten in an echoing hall
Alone and from a chipped plate
The words that I withdrew too late.
Yet even so, when I recall
How ardently, ah! and to whom
Such praise was given, I am not sad:
The very rafters of this room
Are honoured by the guests it had.

You only, being unworthy quite
And specious,—never, as I think,
Having noticed how the gentry drink
Their poison, how administer
Silence to those they would inter—
Have brought me to dementia's brink.
Not that this blow be dealt to *me*:
But by thick hands, and clumsily.

VI

Leap now into this quite grave.
How cool it is. Can you endure
Packed men and their hot rivalries—
The plodding rich, the shiftless poor,
The bold inept, the weak secure—
Having smelt this grave, how cool it is?

Why, here's a house, why, here's a bed
For every lust that drops its head
In sleep, for vengeance gone to seed,
For the slashed vein that will not bleed,
The jibe unheard, the whip unfelt,
The mind confused, the smooth pelt
Of the breast, compassionate and brave.
Pour them into this quiet grave.

VII

Now from a stout and more imperious day
Let dead impatience arm me for the act.

We bear too much. Let the proud past gainsay
This tolerance. Now, upon the sleepy pact
That bound us two as lovers, now in the night
And ebb of love, let me with stealth proceed,
Catch the vow nodding, harden, feel no fright,
Bring forth the weapon sleekly, do the deed.

I know—and having seen, shall not deny—
This flag inverted keeps its colour still;
This moon in wane and scooped against the sky
Blazes in stern reproach. Stare back, my Will—
We can out-gaze it; can do better yet:
We can expunge it. I will not watch it set.

VIII
The time of year ennobles you.
The death of autumn draws you in.

The death of those delights I drew
From such a cramped and troubled source
Ennobles all, including you,
Involves you as a matter of course.

You are not, you have never been
(Nor did I ever hold you such),
Between your banks, that all but touch,
Fit subject for heroic song . . .
The busy stream not over-strong,
The flood that any leaf could dam . . .

Yet more than half of all I am
Lies drowned in shallow water here:
And you assume the time of year.

I do not say this love will last:
Yet Time's perverse, eccentric power
Has bound the hound and stag so fast
That strange companions mount the tower
Where Lockhart's fate with Keats' is cast,
And Booth with Lincoln shares the hour.

That which has quelled me, lives with me,
Accomplice in catastrophe.

Say that We Saw Spain Die

Say that we saw Spain die. O splendid bull, how well you fought!
Lost from the first.

       . . . the tossed, the replaced, the
  watchful *torero* with gesture elegant and spry,

Before the dark, the tiring but the unglazed eye deploying the
    bright cape,
Which hid for once not air, but the enemy indeed, the authentic
    shape,
A thousand of him, interminably into the ring released . . .
    the turning beast at length between converging colours
    caught.

Save for the weapons of its skull, a bull
Unarmed, considering, weighing, charging
Almost a world, itself without ally.

Say that we saw the shoulders more than the mind confused, so
    profusely
Bleeding from so many more than the accustomed barbs, the
    game gone vulgar, the rules abused.

Say that we saw Spain die from loss of blood, a rustic reason, in
    a reinforced
And proud punctilious land, no *espada*—
A hundred men unhorsed,
A hundred horses gored, and the afternoon aging, and the crowd
    growing restless (all, all so much later than planned),
And the big head heavy, sliding forward in the sand, and the
    tongue dry with sand,—no *espada*
Toward that hot neck, for the delicate and final thrust, having
    dared trust forth his hand.

Underground System

Set the foot down with distrust upon the crust of the world—it is thin.
Moles are at work beneath us; they have tunnelled the sub-soil
With separate chambers, which at an appointed knock
Could be as one, could intersect and interlock. We walk on the skin
Of life. No toil
Of rake or hoe, no lime, no phosphate, no rotation of crops, no irrigation
    of the land,
Will coax the limp and flattened grain to stand
On that bad day, or feed to strength the nibbled roots of our nation.

Ease has demoralized us, nearly so; we know
Nothing of the rigours of winter: the house has a roof against—
    the car a top against—the snow.
All will be well, we say; it is a habit, like the rising of the sun,
For our country to prosper; who can prevail against us? No one.

The house has a roof; but the boards of its floor are rotting, and hall
    upon hall
The moles have built their palace beneath us: we have not far to fall.

Love is not blind. I see with single eye
Your ugliness and other women's grace.
I know the imperfection of your face,—
The eyes too wide apart, the brow too high
For beauty. Learned from earliest youth am I
In loveliness, and cannot so erase
Its letters from my mind, that I may trace
You faultless, I must love until I die.
More subtle is the sovereignty of love:
So am I caught that when I say, "Not fair,"
'Tis but as if I said, "Not here—not there—
Not risen—not writing letters." Well I know
What is this beauty men are babbling of;
I wonder only why they prize it so.

I, being born a woman and distressed
By all the needs and notions of my kind,
Am urged by your propinquity to find
Your person fair, and feel a certain zest
To bear your body's weight upon my breast:
So subtly is the fume of life designed,
To clarify the pulse and cloud the mind,
And leave me once again undone, possessed.
Think not for this, however, the poor treason
Of my stout blood against my staggering brain,
I shall remember you with love, or season
My scorn with pity,—let me make it plain:
I find this frenzy insufficient reason
For conversation when we meet again.

Alcestis to her husband, just before, with his tearful approbation, she dies in order that he may live.

Admetus, from my marrow's core I do
Despise you: wherefore pity not your wife,
Who, having seen expire her love for you
With heaviest grief, today gives up her life.
You could not with your mind imagine this:
One might surrender, yet continue proud.
Not having loved, you do not know: the kiss
You sadly beg, is impious, not allowed.
Of all I loved,—how many girls and men
Have loved me in return?—speak!—young or old—
Speak!—sleek or famished, can you find me then
One form would flank me, as this night grows cold?
I am at peace, Admetus—go and slake
Your grief with wine. I die for my own sake.

Gazing upon him now, severe and dead,
It seemed a curious thing that she had lain
Beside him many a night in that cold bed,
And that had been which would not be again.
From his desirous body the great heat
Was gone at last, it seemed, and the taut nerves
Loosened forever. Formally the sheet
Set forth for her today those heavy curves
And lengths familiar as the bedroom door.
She was as one who enters, sly, and proud,
To where her husband speaks before a crowd,
And sees a man she never saw before—
The man who eats his victuals at her side,
Small, and absurd, and hers: for once, not hers, unclassified.

Vita Sackville-West (1892-1962)

VITA SACKVILLE-WEST'S novels and poetry are largely unread today. If she is immortalized in fiction it is because her lover and friend Virginia Woolf used her as the model for the hero-heroine of *Orlando*. Her son, Nigel Nicolson, has made her confessional autobiography public property by including it in a book about his famous parents, *Portrait of a Marriage*. Both *Orlando* and *Portrait of a Marriage* emphasize Vita's bold bisexuality, and she is in danger of being transformed historically into an androgynous messenger of sexual liberation and forgotten as a writer. The special nature of her sexual rebellion is obliquely reflected in her prose and poetry. Its full significance, however, emerges only when Vita's life and work are compared with those of other contemporary women writers and set within the context of the upper class society which bred her, and enjoyed, vicariously, her scandalous adventures.

Vita Sackville-West was born and grew up at Knole, near Sevenoaks, Kent. Her lineage was as eccentric as it was aristocratic. Her mother Victoria, a great beauty, was the illegitimate child of Lionel Sackville-West and a half-gypsy dancer. Victoria married her cousin, also Lionel, but her marriage gave neither happiness nor emotional security. Both partners amused themselves elsewhere, and in 1919 Lady Sackville left her husband for good. Vita grew up regarding the domestic situation as normal, though she preferred her father to her highstrung mother. She was athletic and intellectually precocious and started to write poetry and plays in early adolescence.

Harold Nicolson was already a promising young diplomat when she met him in 1910. They were married in 1913 after an extended courtship which was conducted largely by post. The courtship coincided with a lesbian affair, Vita's first, with a pretty, docile friend named Rosamund Grosvenor. The clinging, tearful, Rosamund was no match for Harold, and she eventually became maid of honor at Vita's wedding. For some years Vita and Harold, posted to Constantinople, lived out the roles of a handsome, happily married young couple, though Harold too was bisexual. They had two children, Ben and Nigel. Then in 1918 Vita remet an old school friend, Violet Keppel. It was Violet who seduced Vita but the resulting passion threatened to destroy both women's marriages. The two spent a great deal of time in France; Vita, masquerading as "Julian," left her young boys with her mother. Intimations of the affair hit English shores and started rumors in English society. Eventually the affair burnt itself out and both marriages survived, though not sexually. Vita and Harold continued to have homosexual relationships while remaining closely dependent on each other.

In spite of her adventures and her literary friendships, Vita remained bound up in her own class attitudes. There was nothing political in her rebellion; it was an act which she could not have realized without a broad base of privilege. Vita, on her way to a Paris farewell with Violet, notes that "there was a dreary slut scrubbing the doorstep, for it was very early, and I stepped in over the soapy pail, and saw Violet in the morning-room." Loving women did not extend in any social sense to sympathy for woman.

As a poet Sackville-West is most usefully compared to Elinor Wylie and Edna St. Vincent Millay. Collectively the three women represent an attack on the Victorian ideal of sexual propriety. Their poems project a notion of female autonomy in love. All three share a basically Romantic vision of female individualism, although only in Miss Millay's work is this vision part of a wider liberal humanism. Elinor Wylie and Vita Sackville-West belonged to the aristocracies of their respective countries; next to Vita's Byronic adventuress, Edna Millay seems a hardworking bourgeois Keats. The allusion to the Romantics is not casual either. It took a whole century for women poets to assert the personal freedom that male writers of comparable class had had in Regency England. Wylie, Sackville-West, and Amy Lowell were all busy remaking, with new techniques and twentieth-century sensibilities, a relationship to nature that was begun by Wordsworth, Keats, Shelley and Coleridge. Both in Wylie and in Sackville-West nature is a mirror and a refuge for the female speaker. The seasons and the countryside represent the poet's mood and situation as well as places and times which they seem to possess through appreciation. In "On the Lake" and in "Black Tarn" Sackville-West renders successfully both the psychic and physical experience of being in nature. Sackville-West's poetry also generates a powerful sensual connection between the poet and the natural world. In "The Owl" Vita's own divided consciousness is explained. The speaker seems to be protecting her "loves" and the "timorous small colony" of mice against the predatory bird, but her language betrays her ambivalence. The Owl, female of course, is "Soft and nocturnal, creamy as a moth. . . . Such silent beauty taloned with a knife" is so patently admired that calling her a "dire spirit" a few lines later is a very weak exorcism. Trapped with her loved ones, the poet admires and identifies with the bird, "soundless and swift."

At their best, the poems remind us that the world of the writer is one of special privilege. In a poem demanding sanctuary for everyone the final verse, which Vita could have written from personal experience, shows how few people, male or female, could acquire such a splendid retreat:

Within the acres that I rule,
The little patch of peace I vaunt,
Where ways are safe and shadows cool,
Shall come no scarlet-coated fool
To tease my foxes from their haunt.

The narrow social vision of this poem is typical of Sackville-West. In fact, as she grew older Vita Sackville-West stayed mostly in the countryside, letting her public husband bring the news from town. In her best poems the liberation she achieved is made more available to the common reader and does at least hint at a more profound rejection of male values than is often apparent in her work. Her poetry has the attraction of luxury; it is essentially a poetry of private sensibility and *liaisons dangereuses*. For her "The small immediate candle in the prow,/Burns brighter in the water than any star."

To Any M.F.H.　Sanctuary should exist on earth;
Some private place, where life may be.
Some private place for death and birth,
For boisterous love and puppy mirth
Between the bracken and the tree.

In such a place, a girdled place,
The refuge of the small pursued,
Shall some similitude of grace
Be caught within the fenced embrace
That guards my leafy solitude;

And no white horse or scarlet sleeve
Shall sprinkle down the woodland ride
Where paths between the chestnuts cleave,
And mists the morning stories thieve
From men in different mood astride.

In such a place my foxes should
Live free to mate and breed and kill
Within the ambush of my wood,
Scorning the huntsman's hardihood
Hallooing on the stranger's hill.

Though warring men must stain the west
Doubly with sunset's barbarous dye,
Leaving the plumes of manhood's crest,
A shameful yet a proud bequest,
In trails of blood across the sky,

Within the acres that I rule,
The little patch of peace I vaunt,
Where ways are safe and shadows cool,
Shall come no scarlet-coated fool
To tease my foxes from their haunt.

The Owl　Each dusk I saw, while those I loved the most
Chattered of present or of alien things,
The rhythmic owl returning like a ghost
Across the orchard cruising on wide wings.

She went, she came, she swooped, she sought the height
Where her young brood hid snoring for the mouse;
Tirelessly weaving on her silent flight
Between the laden branches and the house,

Soft and nocturnal, creamy as a moth;
But to the timorous small colony
Crouched in the grass, as fatal as a Goth
Ranging the plains in armèd panoply.

Such beauty and such cruelty were hers,
Such silent beauty, taloned with a knife;
Such innocence and fearfulness were theirs,
The little denizens intent on life,

That, terror swooping on my heart's alarm,
I wondered what dire spirit, hushed, adrift,
Might go abroad to do my loves most harm,
Silent and pouncing, ruinous and swift?

On The Lake

A candle lit in darkness of black waters,
A candle set in the drifting prow of a boat,
And every tree to itself a separate shape,
Now plumy, now an arch; tossed trees
Still and dishevelled; dishevelled with past growth,
Forgotten storms; left tufted, tortured, sky-rent,
Even now in stillness; stillness on the lake,
Black, reflections pooled, black mirror
Pooling a litten candle, taper of fire;
Pooling the sky, double transparency
Of sky in water, double elements,
Lying like lovers, light above, below;
Taking, from one another, light; a gleaming,
A glow reflected, fathoms deep, leagues high,
Two distances meeting at a film of surface
Thin as a membrane, sheet of surface, fine
Smooth steel; two separates, height and depth,
Able to touch, giving to one another
All their profundity, all their accidents,
—Changeable mood of clouds, permanent stars,—
Like thoughts in the mind hanging a long way off,
Revealed between lovers, friends. Peer in the water
Over the boat's edge; seek the sky's night-heart;
Are they near, are they far, those clouds, those stars
Given, reflected, pooled? are they so close
For a hand to clasp, to lift them, feel their shape,
Explore their reality, take a rough possession?

Oh no! too delicate, too shy for handling,
They tilt at a touch, quiver to other shapes,
Dance away, change, are lost, drowned, scared;
Hands break the mirror, speech's crudity
The surmise, the divining;
Such things so deeply held, so lightly held,
Subtile, imponderable, as stars in water
Or thoughts in another's thoughts.
Are they near, are they far, those stars, that knowledge?
Deep? shallow? solid? rare? The boat drifts on,
And the litten candle single in the prow,
The small, immediate candle in the prow,
Burns brighter in the water than any star.

Sometimes When Night . . .

Sometimes when night has thickened on the woods,
And we in the house's square security
Read, speak a little, read again,
Read life at second-hand, speak of small things,
Being content and withdrawn for a little hour
From the dangers and fears that are either wholly absent
Or wholly invading,—sometimes a shot rings out,
Sudden and sharp; complete. It has no sequel,
No sequel for us, only the sudden crack
Breaking a silence followed by a silence,
Too slight a thing for comment; slight, and usual,
A shot in the dark, fired by a hand unseen
At a life unknown; finding, or missing, the mark?
Bringing death? bringing hurt? teaching, perhaps, escape,
Escape from a present threat, a threat recurrent,
Or ending, once and for all? But we read on,
Since the shot was not at our hearts, since the mark was not
Your heart or mine, not this time, my companion.

Black Tarn

For Pat Dansey

The road ends with the hills.
No track continues the fair and easy way
That leads in safety beside the valley lake,
Skirting the lake, the lake of candid waters
Sleek among rising fells. It is a valley
Veined by one road, one smooth and certain road,
Walled on the fell-side, walled against the boulders,
The rough fell-side, where few penurious sheep
Find a scrimp pasture, stray, crop, wander;
A road whence the traveller may scan the valley,
Seeing the lake, the prospect north and south,
The foot of the fells; and, lifting up his eyes,
Their heads, mist-dwelling;

He may explore the ferns, the little lichens,
The tiny life at fell's foot, peaty pools,
Learning their detail, finding out their habit;
This, and the general prospect of the valley,
Lie and proportion of the fells, sky, waters,
All from the road. But the road ends with the hills.

At the valley's head the road ends, making no curve
To return whence it came, but, bluntly barred,
Stops with the slope. The road's crisp gravel
Softens to turf, to swamps of spongy peat,
Boulders flung down in anger, brown streams poured
From inaccessible sources. Dull brute hills
Mount sullen, trackless; who would climb, must climb
Finding a way; steps tentative,
Thoughtful, and irrelated, steps of doubt,
Sometimes of exultation. Now see the lake
With its companion road, safe in the valley,
That bird's-eye, easy conquest. Left below
That known, seen, travelled region. Sagging clouds
Veil the high hills, raze the peaks level,
Wimple in white the hidden tors, the final
Pricking of height towards sky; still through the mist
Each conquered patch spreads visible, unrolls
Its footing of turf or stone.
Faith knows the shrouded peaks, their composition,
Granite and shale, their sundered rock
Like an axe's cleavage, wedge of scars.
Faith knows they wait there, may be scaled.
But few climb higher than these middle reaches,
Difficult, wild enough; slopes to be won
Nor wholly relinquished, even when steps return
To the easy lowland, to the calm lake's shore,
For they abide in the mind, as a value held,
A gain achieved.
                    Most certainly I remember
A lonely tarn in the hills, a pool in a crater,
Lustrous as armour, wet rocks, and still, round pool.
Lustrous, but with a sheen not taken from heaven,
Not with a light as lit the lake below
In the open valley, frank and susceptible,
Receiving and giving back; but inward, sullen,
In the crater's cup, as drawing out
Some dark effulgence from subterranean depths,

Self-won, self-suffered. Stones I threw
Sank, forced the surface to a ripple,
But like a plummet dropped into earth's bowels
Were swallowed, and the satanic darkness closed
As though no wound had been.
                                        I have seen Black Tarn,
Shivered it for an instant, been afraid.
Looked into its waters, seen there my own image
As an upturned mask that floated
Just under the surface, within reach, beyond reach.
There are tarns among hills, for all who climb the hills,
Tarns suddenly stumbled on, sudden points of meaning
Among the rough negative hills, reward
Precious and fearful, leaving a discontent
With the lake in the valley, and the road beside the lake,
And the dwellings of men, the safety, and the ease.

The Aquarium, San Francisco

Many a curious mortal have I seen,
Some bald, some hairy, dwarfish, tall, fat, lean;
And some who sought for gold, and some who sought
At second-hand for other people's thought,
And some who sought for nothing on this earth
But how to pass the time twixt death and birth,
And many with their passions and their pranks,
But none so strange as these who came in tanks
From some Pacific atoll of the main
To swim behind a milky opal pane,
Stared at, but never staring back again.

Lengthen imagination to assent
To these conceits that Nature did invent;
Extravagant and freakish holiday
When on an impulse tropical and gay
(Shaking herself from obligation free,)
Nature upset her paint-box in the sea.
A sudden fling of wit, a giddy quirk,
A respite from the solemn serious work
Of making pink, unornamental men,
Forbears of banker and of citizen.

Within that wet, that other element
Sufficient to itself, as different
From sapient life as dream-deluded sleep,
(Life in a prism, luminously deep,)
Content to Be, without a question why,
With gaping gill and lidless open eye,
With frolic fin by waving streamers draped,
Thin as a coin, fantastically shaped,
Fresh as a toy, and sinuous as an imp,
Tiny and exquisite beyond the scrimp
Imagination of a human poet
Who can't devise a thing unless he know it
Already fixed and ready to his pen,
A docketed and handy specimen,
These fish, I say, though fish sound bloodless, cold,
With unreality all rigmaroled,
Now striped, now stippled, speckled, shot, and starre
Pied, painted, dappled, boneless, brindled, barred,
Slim, thoughtless, free and finite, water-wise,
Single and speechless though in shoals they rise
Within the prisoned freedom of the glass,
Between the coral and the reeds they pass.

And some, less arrowy and less gymnastic,
But in their lethargy no less fantastic,
Stalk-eyed and mailed, malevolently slow
As some antennaed, armèd daimio,
Crawl horny on the floor of silver-sand,
And to defend their corner of that strand
Fight with stiff joints and chelate nipper claws
Against the slow transgressor of their laws.
And some, less sinister and much less big,
—Sea-horses, looped and pensive on a sprig,
Mindful of currents that will never come
Here in their tank to bear them far from home,—
With still philosophy accept their lot,
Submissive victims of a human plot;
A plot to frame them all within a square
Neatly supplied with bubbles of fresh air.

Was it for this that Nature lost her wish
To make a man, and made, instead, a fish?

Sea-Sonnet   We have forgot, who safe in cities dwell,
The waters that a labouring planet bore;
Forgot to trace in their primeval lore
The shapeless epochs fluted to a shell.
Their old chaotic voices chronicle
The first confusion, and the dark, before
The first adventurer with spear and oar
Towards the unknown pushed out his coracle.

Yet, to the requiem of a dying earth,
When man has passed, his fever and his pride,
Still shall the constellations find a grave
In that Pacific whence the moon had birth,
And that same moon shall heap the desolate tide
Beneath the night's unchanging architrave.

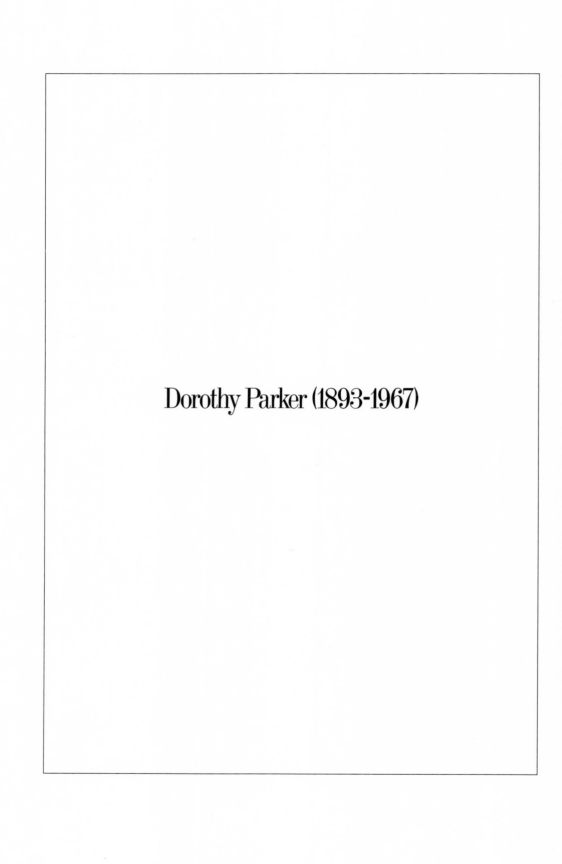

Dorothy Parker (1893-1967)

IT WAS at once Dorothy Parker's armor against the world and her entrée to it. Her childhood, as she told it to friends, was strange and loveless. She was born Dorothy Rothschild in West End, New Jersey in 1893 of a Scottish mother, who died in Dorothy's infancy, and a Jewish father. Her father soon remarried, but a bitter antagonism grew up between the new wife and her stepdaughter. Dorothy's experience at convent school, where she was sent to learn to "love Jesus," produced a life-long hatred of all religion. Luckily her parents chose to "finish" her at Miss Dana's school in Morristown, which offered its students a reasonably broad liberal arts education. A few years between her graduation and the beginning of her literary career are unaccounted for both by biographers and by Parker herself, but after her father's death she appears to have experienced financial difficulties. By the time she was twenty-three she had sold a poem and landed a job with *Vogue* at ten dollars a week. There followed a few years of cheerful hard times during which Dorothy lived in a boardinghouse with other aspiring writers and turned out clever verse after the fashion of Edna Millay.

During these years she moved from *Vogue* to *Vanity Fair*, a step upward in the magazine world, and married Edwin Parker II, a handsome young stockbroker. The marriage was weakened by their separation during the war and by Ed's drinking. As Dorothy came into her own as a New York wit, poet and journalist,

Edwin Parker drifted out of her life. The war took some talent away from the magazines, and it was during the war years that Dorothy, humorist Robert Benchley, and drama critic Robert Sherwood formed the basis of the coterie that met at the Algonquin Hotel to exchange gossip and jokes.

Dorothy's wit was sometimes coarser than that of her male companions, but she was often quoted in their columns. Her sharp tongue got her fired from *Vanity Fair*. Life was precarious. At thirty she had a tiny, dreary apartment, a failed marriage and a disastrous love affair behind her as well as an abortion and a suicide attempt. Then, at thirty-two, her career took one of its upward swings. Her first book of poems, *Enough Rope*, was published and made her an immediate success.

Genevieve Taggard, the poet, wrote the most perceptive review. She remarked that Mrs. Parker had begun in the familiar Millay manner and "worked into something quite her own. . . . Miss Millay remains lyrically, of course far superior to Mrs. Parker. . . . But there are moods when Dorothy Parker is more acceptable, whiskey straight, not champagne." If you were wallowing in love, requited or otherwise, and wished to go on, you picked up Miss Millay; if you wanted some detachment from the event you took Mrs. Parker, neat. In fact her verse is a foil to the lyrics of Millay and Wylie. They created lyrical and emotional room for a view of love in which the woman's experience was central and in control. Dorothy Parker more radically questioned the virtues of romantic love; indeed, she was one of the first modern women poets to do so. Love, in her view, has nothing to recommend it. It comes across in her verse as a nasty and ennervating disease. Not even in the most disillusioned poems by Millay or Wylie is love so despised. The tone, however, is always leavened by humor. Parker asks "For this my mother wrapped me warm/And called me home against the storm . . ." to "hear a whistle and drop my wits." Her light verse is a leech to romantic pain: she stands on a shore of turbulent emotions from which there is no retreat into the quiet life. "This level reach of blue is not my sea."

There are among her poems some fine "straight" lyrics, but more poke fun at the sentimental view of love.

I think no matter where you be,
You'll hold me in your memory
And keep my image there without me
By telling later loves about me.

Dorothy Parker said that she liked her men handsome, ruthless and stupid. Alan Campbell, whom she married twice, was a near enough fit. With him she endured a total of fifteen years in Hollywood, where they turned out a series of second-rate film scripts. Their first parting was to a certain extent brought about by Dorothy Parker's outspoken left-wing politics. In spite of her marriages and love affairs she was in important respects a loner. She could never write well in tandem. In middle and later life she drank too much and, as she herself admitted, abused her talent. Still, she wrote enough to secure a lasting reputation. The best of her short stories, "Big Blonde," documents the loneliness of a very ordinary kept woman who has no exceptional spiritual or intellectual resources. Even with such resources, Dorothy Parker's life and work suggest the fragility of the joys of liberation in a society where women are conditioned to find emotional security in love rather than work. Her pen, when she used it, was a scalpel with which she exposed her own nerves. Her verse at its best has a classical precision and a cynical distance from the tender emotion, a distance often missing in women's poetry after the seventeenth century.

Unfortunate Coincidence

By the time you swear you're his,
  Shivering and sighing,
And he vows his passion is
  Infinite, undying—
Lady, make a note of this:
  One of you is lying.

Symptom Recital

I do not like my state of mind;
I'm bitter, querulous, unkind.
I hate my legs, I hate my hands,
I do not yearn for lovelier lands.
I dread the dawn's recurrent light;
I hate to go to bed at night.
I snoot at simple, earnest folk.
I cannot take the gentlest joke.
I find no peace in paint or type.
My world is but a lot of tripe.
I'm disillusioned, empty-breasted.
For what I think, I'd be arrested.
I am not sick, I am not well.
My quondam dreams are shot to hell.
My soul is crushed, my spirit sore;
I do not like me any more.
I cavil, quarrel, grumble, grouse.
I ponder on the narrow house.
I shudder at the thought of men. . . .
I'm due to fall in love again.

Interior

Her mind lives in a quiet room,
  A narrow room, and tall,
With pretty lamps to quench the gloom
  And mottoes on the wall.

There all the things are waxen neat
  And set in decorous lines;
And there are posies, round and sweet,
  And little, straightened vines.

Her mind lives tidily, apart
  From cold and noise and pain,
And bolts the door against her heart,
  Out wailing in the rain.

Of a Woman, Dead Young

(J. H., 1905–1930)

If she had been beautiful, even,
Or wiser than women about her,
Or had moved with a certain defiance;
If she had had sons at her sides,
And she with her hands on their shoulders,
Sons, to make troubled the Gods—
But where was there wonder in her?
What had she, better or eviler,
Whose days were a pattering of peas
From the pod to the bowl in her lap?

That the pine tree is blasted by lightning,
And the bowlder split raw from the mountain,
And the river dried short in its rushing—
That I can know, and be humble.
But that They who have trodden the stars
Should turn from Their echoing highway
To trample a daisy, unnoticed
In a meadow of small, open flowers—
Where is Their triumph in that?
Where is Their pride, and Their vengeance?

Theory

Into love and out again,
    Thus I went, and thus I go.
Spare your voice, and hold your pen—
    Well and bitterly I know
All the songs were ever sung,
    All the words were ever said;
Could it be, when I was young,
    Some one dropped me on my head?

Coda

There's little in taking or giving,
    There's little in water or wine;
This living, this living, this living
    Was never a project of mine.
Oh, hard is the struggle, and sparse is
    The gain of the one at the top,
For art is a form of catharsis,
    And love is a permanent flop,
And work is the province of cattle,
    And rest's for a clam in a shell,
So I'm thinking of throwing the battle—
    Would you kindly direct me to hell?

Chant for Dark Hours

Some men, some men
Cannot pass a
Book shop.
(Lady, make your mind up, and wait your life away.)

Some men, some men
Cannot pass a
Crap game.
(He said he'd come at moonrise, and here's another day!)

Some men, some men
Cannot pass a
Bar-room.
(Wait about, and hang about, and that's the way it goes.)

Some men, some men
Cannot pass a
Woman.
(Heaven never send me another one of those!)

Some men, some men
Cannot pass a
Golf course.
(Read a book, and sew a seam, and slumber if you can.)

Some men, some men
Cannot pass a
Haberdasher's.
(All your life you wait around for some damn man!)

Fair Weather

This level reach of blue is not my sea;
Here are sweet waters, pretty in the sun,
Whose quiet ripples meet obediently
A marked and measured line, one after one.
This is no sea of mine, that humbly laves
Untroubled sands, spread glittering and warm.
I have a need of wilder, crueler waves;
They sicken of the calm, who knew the storm.

So let a love beat over me again,
Loosing its millions desperate breakers wide;
Sudden and terrible to rise and wane;
Roaring the heavens apart; a reckless tide
That casts upon the heart, as it recedes,
Splinters and spars and dripping, salty weeds.

271

Louise Bogan (1897-1970)

O F THAT REMARKABLE generation of American women poets born in the 1880's and the 1890's Louise Bogan was perhaps the most talented and, though neither the most prolific nor the best known, one of the most influential poet-critics of the last forty years. From 1931 to 1951 she served as poetry critic for the *New Yorker*, and contributed as well a steady flow of reviews and articles to other American periodicals. She served on the controversial committee which awarded Ezra Pound the Bollingen Prize for poetry in 1949, and won the award herself in 1954. For some years she was Poetry Consultant to the Library of Congress.

Louise Bogan was as hard on herself as she was on her poet contemporaries. *The Blue Estuaries, Poems: 1923–1968* is a severe pruning of her total output. Theodore Roethke, whom she encouraged as a young man and who was a lifetime friend, thought she wrote out of "the severest lyrical tradition in English. Her spiritual ancestors are Campion, Jonson, the anonymous Elizabethan writers." Her poems are spare and unsentimental although her subject is, almost always, the heart and its transformations.

In the thirties she felt herself out of tune with the vogue for public, politically-oriented poetry. She was a fiercely "private" person for whom all political feeling was immediately suspect. For a long time she refused to meet W. H. Auden, presumably because of his politics, but eventually they became good if not intimate friends. Although many of her close friends were "thirties radicals"

her own conservatism was constant,

Louise Bogan was born in Livermore Falls, Maine in 1897. She grew up in Boston and attended Boston Girls' Latin School and Boston University. Her childhood was, by her account, unhappy: "I never was a member of a 'lost generation' . . . I was the highly charged and neurotically inclined product of an extraordinary childhood and an unfortunate early marriage, into which last state I had rushed to escape the first. . . ." She and her first husband, Curt Alexander, who died in 1920, had a daughter, Maidie.

Professionally she was lucky. By her mid-twenties her poetry was being published fairly regularly in Harriet Monroe's *Poetry* and other periodicals. She had also already begun lifelong friendships with critics Edmund Wilson and Rolfe Humphries and anthropologists Ruth Benedict and Margaret Mead. For some nine years she was married to Raymond Holden, a minor novelist and poet. In spite of fairly steady success in her work, her life was marked by periodic breakdowns.

Bogan's correspondence, *What the Woman Lived*, reveals her as a passionate, unconventional, hardworking artist. Her friendships were deep and stormy. Though she knew most of the other women poets with whom she was roughly contemporary, she became close only with Leonie Adams and later May Sarton.

On the other hand she was hardly an establishment figure and looked with a dim eye on poets like Robert Frost. She viewed overambitious authors with suspicion and a certain hostility. She herself was prepared to lose a friend rather than write a neutral or flattering review of a poet she disliked. Age and possibly her own eminence mellowed her sharp tastes in poetry. In the forties, when the bite was still there, she thought Marianne Moore's poetry "decadent" though delightful. She preferred Auden to poets like Moore and Wallace Stevens who were in their lives and verse "fixed and finished."

Bogan saw herself as separate from the tradition of female sonneteers that runs from Browning to Millay, although in mood and emotional tone her poetry is similar to Wylie's. Both are lyric poets obsessed with the twists and turns of private feeling. Bogan, however, was the better technician. She said, "I care, really truly care, about the actual *writing* in a poem . . . I have given some thought to the effects of tension, sonority, etc. that language can produce." All this is apparent but seems, on reading, effortless. If Louise Bogan seems somehow blind to the public events that accompanied her life—in almost 400 pages of letters over a fifty-year span there is hardly a reference to any social or political fact that did not directly impinge on her—she made the most of her personal experience. She would not read Marx but she understood Freud; she and H.D. were among the first women to use the concept of the female unconscious in poetry. In her work, as in the poems of other "liberated" female poets of her generation, nature is revived as a positive symbol of love. Even when it signified love lost or denied, the natural imagery is controlled by the poet. As Roethke says, "Her poems create their own reality, and demand not just attention, but the emotional and spiritual response of the whole man." He speaks also of her "absolute loyalty to the particular emotion" and here he is very close to the law that bound her life and art. To a remarkably narrow range of experience she gave a comprehensive attention and considerable skill at defini-

tion. The meanings of the poems widen and begin even to include the bits of the world she has let pass. Occasionally this scope, this inclusive subject and timeless reader, exasperates. Whom is this poem addressed *to*?

Henceforth from the mind,
For your whole joy, just spring
Such joy as you may find
In any earthly thing.
And every time and place
Will take your thought for grace.

Better, much better, is "Old Countryside" or "The Dream," where the speaker is identifiable and the event precisely located. In these poems "the grandeur of generality" is placed in a firm context which matches the strong lines and high emotional tension.

In a 1954 letter to May Sarton she tells a story of her mother's inability to make custard because she didn't have "the *right kind* of double boiler." Against this helpless mystification of experience Louise Bogan struggled: ". . . I refuse to make *things symbols* of bafflement. As for spiritual bafflements, or bafflements of situation, I want to get those out of the way quick, too. To act on life; to be a *subject*, not an object. . . ." Reading through the letters it seems as if the whole life as well as the poetry was bent to those ends. What emerges is a sense of the enormous energy it took to be an independent but outgoing woman and an artist. Perhaps the failure of energy and confidence caused her breakdowns. This pattern, common enough in writers of either sex, had a particular application in women writers of Bogan's generation. They bore the strain of living unrooted, emotionally complicated lives in a milieu which, even when not directly oppressive, was hardly encouraging to women on their own.

The Frightened Man

In fear of the rich mouth
I kissed the thin,—
Even that was a trap
To snare me in.

Even she, so long
The frail, the scentless,
Is become strong
And proves relentless.

O, forget her praise,
And how I sought her
Through a hazardous maze
By shafted water.

The Crows

The woman who has grown old
And knows desire must die,
Yet turns to love again,
Hears the crows' cry.

She is a stem long hardened,
A weed that no scythe mows.
The heart's laughter will be to her
The crying of crows,

Who slide in the air with the same voice
Over what yields not, and what yields,
Alike in spring, and when there is only bitter
Winter-burning in the fields.

Women

Women have no wilderness in them,
They are provident instead,
Content in the tight hot cell of their hearts
To eat dusty bread.

They do not see cattle cropping red winter grass,
They do not hear
Snow water going down under culverts
Shallow and clear.

They wait, when they should turn to journeys,
They stiffen, when they should bend.
They use against themselves that benevolence
To which no man is friend.

They cannot think of so many crops to a field
Or of clean wood cleft by an axe.
Their love is an eager meaninglessness
Too tense, or too lax.

They hear in every whisper that speaks to them
A shout and a cry.
As like as not, when they take life over their door-sills
They should let it go by.

Cassandra

To me, one silly task is like another.
I bare the shambling tricks of lust and pride.
This flesh will never give a child its mother,—
Song, like a wing, tears through my breast, my side,
And madness chooses out my voice again,
Again. I am the chosen no hand saves:
The shrieking heaven lifted over men,
Not the dumb earth, wherein they set their graves.

Hypocrite Swift

Hypocrite Swift now takes an eldest daughter.
He lifts Vanessa's hand. Cudsho, my dove!
Drink Wexford ale and quaff down Wexford water
But never love.

He buys new caps; he and Lord Stanley ban
Hedge-fellows who have neither wit nor swords.
He turns his coat; Tories are in; Queen Anne
Makes twelve new lords.

The town mows hay in hell; he swims in the river;
His giddiness returns; his head is hot.
Berries are clean, while peaches damn the giver
(Though grapes do not).

Mrs. Vanhomrigh keeps him safe from the weather.
Preferment pulls his periwig askew.
Pox takes belittlers; do the willows feather?
God keep you.

Stella spells ill; Lords Peterborough and Fountain
Talk politics; the Florence wine went sour.
Midnight: two different clocks, here and in Dublin,
Give out the hour.

On walls at court, long gilded mirrors gaze.
The parquet shines; outside the snow falls deep.
Venus, the Muses stare above the maze.
Now sleep.

Dream the mixed, fearsome dream. The satiric word
Dies in its horror. Wake, and live by stealth.
The bitter quatrain forms, is here, is heard,
Is wealth.

What care I; what cares saucy Presto? Stir
The bed-clothes; hearten up the perishing fire.
Hypocrite Swift sent Stella a green apron
And dead desire.

Roman Fountain

Up from the bronze, I saw
Water without a flaw
Rush to its rest in air,
Reach to its rest, and fall.

Bronze of the blackest shade,
An element man-made,
Shaping upright the bare
Clear gouts of water in air.

O, as with arm and hammer,
Still it is good to strive
To beat out the image whole,
To echo the shout and stammer
When full-gushed waters, alive,
Strike on the fountain's bowl
After the air of summer.

Animal, Vegetable and Mineral

*Glass Flowers from the Ware Collection in the
Botanical Museum of Harvard University.
Insect Pollination Series, with Sixteen Color
Plates, by Fritz Kredel.*

Dieu ne croit pas à notre Dieu.   JULES RENARD

On gypsum slabs of preternatural whiteness
In Cambridge (Mass.) on Oxford Street is laid
One craft wherein great Nature needs no aid
From man's Abstracts and Concretes, Wrong and Rightness:
Cross-pollination's fixed there and displayed.

Interdependence of the seed and hive!
Astounding extraverted bee and flower!
Mixture of styles! Intensity of drive!
Both Gothic and Baroque blooms flaunt their power.
The classic *Empire* bees within them strive.

The flower is to bee a kind of arrow;
Nectar is pointed out by spot and line.
Corollas may be shaped both wide and narrow;
Mechanics vary, though the play is fine,
And bee-adapted (not for crow or sparrow).

Bush-bean and butterwort keep bee in mind;
Chamisso too (which has no common name);
Red larkspur, devil's-bit scabious are aligned
With garden violet in this bee-ish claim
(*Impatiens Roylei Walpers* acts the same).

Expectancy is constant; means are shifting.
One flower has black cloven glands that pinch
The bee's foot (on the stigma these are lifting);
Anthers with cell-hid pollen wait the clinch.
Think well on this, who think that Life is Drifting . . .

Eager quickly to free its sticky foot
The bee stamps briskly just where stamp is needed:
Motion and power attendant on this boot
Extract *pollinia*. (Here the mind's exceeded;
Wild intimations through the fibers shoot.)

Self-fertile flowers are feeble and need priming.
Nature is for this priming, it appears.
Some flowers, like water-clocks, have perfect timing:
Pistil and anthers rise, as though on gears;
One's up and when t'other's down; one falls; one's climbing.

Charles Darwin saw the primrose, and took thought.
Later, he watched the orchids. There, the bees
Enter in, one way; then, with pollen fraught,
Have to climb out another, on their knees.
The stigma profits, and the plant's at ease.

The dyer's greenwood waits the bee in tension.
Petals are pressed down: then the stamens spring
(The pistils, too) into a new dimension,
Hitting the bee's back between wing and wing.
Who thought this out? It passes comprehension.

For forty million years this has gone on
(So Baltic amber shows, and can it lie?)
The bee's back, feet, head, belly have been drawn
Into the flower's plan for history.
Nectar's been yielded for the hexagon.

Then think of Blaschkas (*père et fils*), who spent
Full fifty years in delicate adjusting,
Glass-blowing, molding, skill with instrument,
While many other crafts were merely rusting.
Two Yankee Wares (*mère, fille*) the money lent.

Cynics who think all this *bijouterie*
Certainly lack a Deepening Sense of Awe.
Here Darwin, Flora, Blaschkas and the bee
Fight something out that ends in a close draw
Above the cases howls loud mystery.

What is the chain, then ask, and what the links?
Are these acts sad or droll? From what derived?
Within the floret's disk the insect drinks.
Next summer there's more honey to be hived.

What Artist laughs? What clever Daemon thinks?

Question in a Field

Pasture, stone wall, and steeple,
What most perturbs the mind:
The heart-rending homely people,
Or the horrible beautiful kind?

The Dream

O God, in the dream the terrible horse began
To paw at the air, and make for me with his blows.
Fear kept for thirty-five years poured through his mane,
And retribution equally old, or nearly, breathed through his nose.

Coward complete, I lay and wept on the ground
When some strong creature appeared, and leapt for the rein.
Another woman, as I lay half in a swound,
Leapt in the air, and clutched at the leather and chain.

Give him, she said, something of yours as a charm.
Throw him, she said, some poor thing you alone claim.
No, no, I cried, he hates me; he's out for harm,
And whether I yield or not, it is all the same.

But, like a lion in a legend, when I flung the glove
Pulled from my sweating, my cold right hand,
The terrible beast, that no one may understand,
Came to my side, and put down his head in love.

Evening in the Sanitarium

The free evening fades, outside the windows fastened with
    decorative iron grilles.
The lamps are lighted; the shades drawn; the nurses are watching a little.
It is the hour of the complicated knitting on the safe bone needles; of
    the games of anagrams and bridge;
The deadly game of chess; the book held up like a mask.

The period of the wildest weeping, the fiercest delusion, is over.
The women rest their tired half-healed hearts; they are almost well.
Some of them will stay almost well always: the blunt-faced woman
    whose thinking dissolved
Under academic discipline; the manic-depressive girl
Now leveling off; one paranoiac afflicted with jealousy.
Another with persecution. Some alleviation has been possible.

O fortunate bride, who never again will become elated after childbirth!
O lucky older wife, who has been cured of feeling unwanted!
To the suburban railway station you will return, return,
To meet forever Jim home on the 5:35.
You will be again as normal and selfish and heartless as anybody else.

There is life left: the piano says it with its octave smile.
The soft carpets pad the thump and splinter of the suicide to be.
Everything will be splendid: the grandmother will not drink habitually.
The fruit salad will bloom on the plate like a bouquet
And the garden produce the blue-ribbon aquilegia.

The cats will be glad; the father feel justified; the mothers relieved
The sons and husbands will no longer need to pay the bills.
Childhoods will be put away, the obscene nightmare abated.

At the ends of the corridors the baths are running.
Mrs. C. again feels the shadow of the obsessive idea.
Miss R. looks at the mantel-piece, which must mean something.

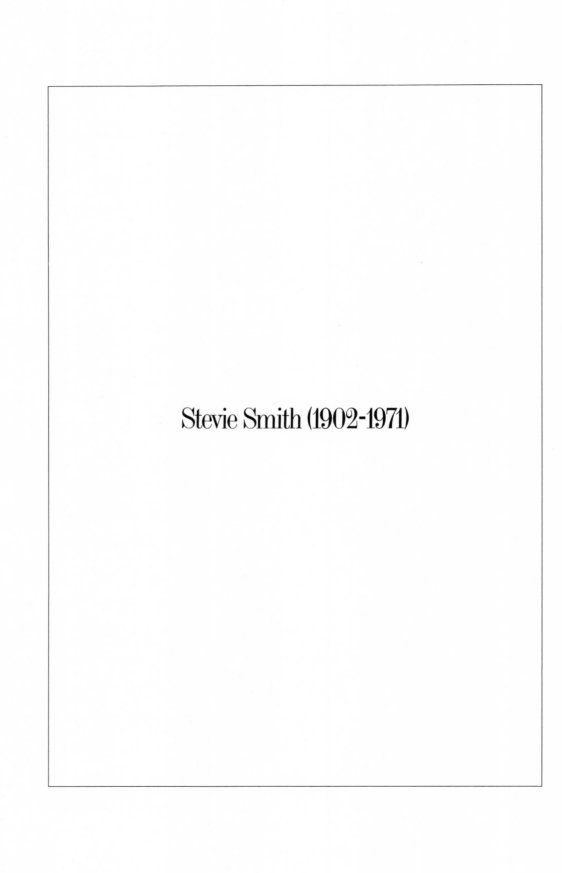

Stevie Smith (1902-1971)

STEVIE SMITH, novelist and poet, was born in Hull on September 20, 1902, but spent most of her sixty-eight years in a Victorian house in North London. She and her sister were brought up by her mother and her aunt, "two sheltered ladies" for whom she had a deep affection. She described her father, who joined the Sea Patrol after his business collapsed, as "a bore." Her attitude toward him is set out in "Papa Love Baby." Stevie was a delicate child. At five she contracted tuberculosis and spent three years in the hospital. She was educated at Palmers Green High School and North London Collegiate School for Girls. Until the early 1950's she worked as a secretary for publishers Nevil Pearson and Sir Frank Newnes, writing on her own time, and sometimes on theirs. *Novel on Yellow Paper* was so called because it was written on yellow office flimsy during working hours.

Her early poems and novels, published in the 1930's, made her famous in Britain, but she had some slack years just after the war when she seemed to have lost her audience. By the late fifties she was back in vogue, and admired not only in England but in America, where her tongue-in-cheek prose poems, accompanied by line drawings of distressed maidens and beasts fitted into a genre created by Ogden Nash and James Thurber.

Stevie Smith's mother died when she was sixteen, and she lived on with her adored aunt, whom she survived by a few years. She thought herself "too selfish" to marry. "I'm much more interested in what I'm thinking about, and I shouldn't recognize him in the street probably." Her poems contain an enormous compassion for the experience of women and children, a compassion tempered with humor rather than sentiment. Men in general, not only "Papa," come off rather badly. They are petty, egotistical tyrants who bully the frail, genteel ladies and children in their care.

Smith never read other poets, she said, but she often read with them on the radio and for schools. She had a large circle of friends, and according to one of them, Kay Dick, she had "an immense capacity for non-sexual love." In English literature she is *sui generis*. While female comic novelists reigned supreme for over a century, few modern women poets writing in England have turned the lyric form against the romantic impulse and run it out of town. A comparison of her "free" prose poems with Marianne Moore's poetry points up how differently the two poets operate. Miss Moore delights in the "art" of the sentence and the phrase; she borrows from past masters. Stevie Smith's ear picks up and transforms the rhythms of contemporary middle-class suburban speech. She emphasizes its sing-song monotony in which carefully supressed feeling is embedded. Poems like "Major Macroo" and "Not Waving but Drowning" achieve their effect by imitating the understatement of "conventional" speech; they suggest to us how the repression of emotions becomes manifest in language.

The story in "Not Waving but Drowning" contains a theme central to many of her poems. The communication we are taught by culture is, she says, too limited a code; too few gestures are meant to convey too many meanings. The man who was "too far out all his life" is simply one tragicomic victim of those who are forced by their class and education to stick to this restricted code. Watchers on the shore, says Miss Smith, are always more willing and able to interpret an ambiguous gesture as a polite farewell than as a cry for help.

A remarkable number of Stevie Smith's poems are about domestic tragedy and death, yet their total effect is funny rather than sad. The people she describes are real enough; it is the emotional clichés they live by that she renders ludicrous. There runs through her verse a kind of mad sanity that tips the world upside down. We are made to see Christianity as the particular gift of the lions, and the Electra complex from the point of view of a misanthropic three-year-old.

Stevie Smith died on March 7, 1971. She was awarded the Cholmondely Award for Poetry and, in 1969, the Queen's Gold Medal for Poetry.

Papa Love Baby

My mother was a romantic girl
So she had to marry a man with his hair in curl
Who subsequently became my unrespected papa,
But that was a long time ago now.

What folly it is that daughters are always supposed to be
In love with papa. It wasn't the case with me
I couldn't take to him at all
But he took to me
What a sad fate to befall
A child of three.

I sat upright in my baby carriage
And wished mama hadn't made such a foolish marriage.
I tried to hide it, but it showed in my eyes unfortunately
And a fortnight later papa ran away to sea.

He used to come home on leave
It was always the same
I could not grieve
But I think I was somewhat to blame.

Sunt Leones

The lions who ate the Christians on the sands of the arena
By indulging native appetites played what has now been seen a
Not entirely negligible part
In consolidating at the very start
The position of the Early Christian Church.
Initiatory rites are always bloody
And the lions, it appears
From contemporary art, made a study
Of dyeing Coliseum sands a ruddy
Liturgically sacrificial hue
And if the Christians felt a little blue—
Well people being eaten often do.
Theirs was the death, and theirs the crown undying,
A state of things which must be satisfying.
My point which up to this has been obscured
Is that it was the lions who procured
By chewing up blood gristle flesh and bone
The martyrdoms on which the Church has grown.
I only write this poem because I thought it rather looked
As if the part the lions played was being overlooked.
By lions' jaws great benefits and blessings were begotten
And so our debt to Lionhood must never be forgotten.

Louise   Why is the child so pale
Sitting alone in that sawny way
On an upturned valise
In a suburban sitting-room?
Louise
Can't you give moma a smile?
Come and say How-do-you-do
To Mr. Tease.

Why is the child so pale?
They have come overnight by rail
From Budapest,
Oh the poor child.

And the money has given out
And they've telegraphed home for more
And meanwhile they're having to stay
In a small-beerish way
With Mr. and Mrs. Tease as I have said
Of Harringay Park instead
Of having a comfortable bed
At the Ritz.

The child is pale and precocious
She knows all the capitals of Europe
She knows all there is to know about Wagons-Lits
And First Class accommodation,
But she has never been long enough in any nation
Completely to unpack:
Always her thoughts are centred
On the nearest railway station.

Moma and nurse and Louise
A hatbox a trunk a valise
And one was lost at Marseille,

  "Oh if I only could stay
  Just for two weeks in one place"
  Thinks the child of the doleful face.

Moma has had a cup of tea
She is feeling better
"Cheer up girlie" she says
"I've a letter here from your poppa
It will take him some time to raise the bucks—
Shucks child
Go and help nurse unpack
We're here for two weeks at least
Then we leave for Athens and the Near East."

In the surburban sitting-room
The poor child sits in a mazy fit:
Such a quick answer to a prayer
Shakes one a bit.

Major Macroo

Major Hawkaby Cole Macroo
Chose
Very wisely
A patient Griselda of a wife with a heart of gold
That never beat for a soul but him
Himself and his slightest whim.

He left her alone for months at a time
When he had to have a change
Just had to
And his pension wouldn't stretch to a fare for two
And he didn't want it to.

And if she wept she was game and nobody knew it
And she stood at the edge of the tunnel and waved as his train went through it.

And because it was cheaper they lived abroad
And did he care if she might be unhappy or bored?
He did not.
He'd other things to think of—a lot.

He'd fads and he fed them fat,
And she could lump it and that was that.

He'd several boy friends
And she thought it was nice for him to have them,
And she loved him and felt that he needed her and waited
And waited and never became exasperated.

Even his room
Was dusted and kept the same,
And when friends came
They went into every room in the house but that one
Which Hawkaby wouldn't have shown.

Such men as these, such selfish cruel men
Hurting what most they love what most loves them,
Never make a mistake when it comes to choosing a woman
To cherish them and be neglected and not think it inhuman.

Seymour and Chantelle or Un peu de vice

(in memory of A. Swinburne and Mary Gordon)

Pull my arm back, Seymour,
Like the boys do,
Oh Seymour, the pain, the pain,
Still more then, do.
I am thy schoolboy friend, now I
Am not Chantelle any more but mi.
Say ''sweet mi'', ''my sweet mi.'' Oh the pain, the pain,
Kiss me and I will kiss you again.

Tell me, Seymour, when they . . . when . . .
Does it hurt as much as this
And this and this? Ah what pain.
When I do so I feel
How very painful it is for you,
No I will, so, again and again,
Now stuff the dockleaves in your mouth
And bite the pain.

Seymour, when you hold me so tight it hurts
I feel my ribs break and the blood spurt,
Oh what heaven, what bliss,
Will you kiss me, if I give you this
Kiss, and this and this? Like this?

Seymour, this morning Nanny swished me so hard
(Because I told her she had the face
Of an antediluvian animal that had
Become extinct because of being so wet)
She broke her hair-brush. What bliss.
No, don't stop me now with a kiss, oh God it was pain-
Ful, I could not stop crying.

Oh darling, what heaven, how did you think
Of doing that? You are my sweetest angel of a
Little cousin, and your tears
Are as nice as the sea, as icy and salt as it is.

Not Waving but Drowning

Nobody heard him, the dead man,
But still he lay moaning:
I was much further out than you thought
And not waving but drowning.

Poor chap, he always loved larking
And now he's dead
It must have been too cold for him his heart gave way
They said.

Oh no no no, it was too cold always
(Still the dead one lay moaning)
I was much too far out all my life
And not waving but drowning.

Sylvia Plath (1932-1963)

THE POETRY of Sylvia Plath forms an appropriate end-piece to this collection. Because she died so young she stands, somewhat unfairly, as the representative here of almost two generations of women poets. Yet no better representative could be found. Her work and her life, her extraordinary achievement and its extraordinary cost, reproduce on a tragic scale the pattern of conflict which the "queer lot" of women who write poetry experience.

Sylvia Plath was born on October 27, 1932 in Winthrop, Massachusetts. Her father was a German-born academic who died when she was eight; his death looms large in her poetry. There was a coldness and lack of understanding between mother and daughter which may have caused the poet's mistrust of other women. Shortly after her father's death Sylvia started to write poetry. In high school and at Smith College, where she went on a special scholarship, she did well, even brilliantly in most subjects.

If it was slightly more feasible for a woman to choose poetry as a profession in the post-war world, it was definitely not easier to practice it in the cultural and political climate of the 1950's. Sylvia Plath wrote almost all of her published poetry in that repressive decade, and it rings with an angry alienation which is both personal and political. Smith College embodied the contradictions any young ambitious intellectual woman faced in those years. The blue-stocking faculty lectured, while the twin-setted debutantes simultaneously knitted, took exam notes and dreamt of fraternity pins and diamonds. Neither group presented a happy model for Sylvia.

In *The Bell Jar*, the pseudonymously-published autobiographical novel which she wrote "in order to free myself from the past," she tells the story of her first breakdown, attempted suicide and recovery. The novel begins in the summer of 1953, on the day the alleged atomic spies Julius and Ethel Rosenberg are executed. Esther, the protagonist, says that their death "had nothing to do with me," but she cannot stop thinking about it. The event is a preview, as it turns out, both for Esther's suicide attempt and the shock therapy—symbolic execution—with which she is cured. More than that, the death of the Rosenbergs is a dreadful warning to women against egalitarian marriage, left-wing politics and overweening ambition.

Esther goes to New York City for a hideous-fantastic month as a literary prize-winner in a *Mademoiselle* magazine contest. Caught between her literary ambitions and the demand that she also perform as a well-turned-out virgin sex symbol for the *nouveau riche* fifties, Esther cracks up and attempts suicide. Shock therapy brings her back; technology has temporarily lifted the bell jar, but it remains suspended over her. The novel ends with Esther's return to college. Sylvia, like Esther, also returned to Smith and went on triumphantly to Newnham College, Cambridge University, where she met and married the English poet Ted Hughes. She taught briefly at Smith, made a home in Devonshire, became a successful poet, had two children. The marriage failed and in 1962 she committed suicide.

The Bell Jar is too often linear and over-literal, more confession than novel. It is primarily a report of the outer landscape, while Sylvia Plath's poetry tells us what the inner one is like. Although the poems have various physical settings,—the seashore of her childhood, the Devon countryside of her marriage, interiors of houses and hospitals—as one reads through the four books of collected verse another setting emerges. More often than not we seem to be at an expensive sanitarium in which the keepers are a family of Freudian monsters, the poet's family and friends. Attentive, watchful, they reconstruct her according to the requirements of the society; at the end they are simply "Death and Co." The poetry is preoccupied with violence and weighted, sometimes over-weighted, with gothic foreboding.

It has been tempting for male critics to admire the aesthetic contours of Plath's poetry while describing its inspiration as the special and sexless pathology of the potential suicide. Some women admirers who read the poetry as explicitly feminist have tried blaming real-life fathers and husbands for Sylvia's death. Both interpretations are seriously misleading: the first fails to see that the poems are intrinsically sexual and political and the second discounts the cultural sources of the poet's malaise. If Sylvia Plath's isolation and early death were the result of an overdose of patriarchy, it was administered by archetypal fathers, husbands and gods, and by the women who collude with them. Of this last group she herself is sometimes a member. The injustice continues; on the dust jackets of her books admiring poets and critics busily deny that the poetry is "female" or "feminine" or written by another "poetess."

The period in which she wrote outdid even the present one in praising "macho" styles and postures in literature as in life. Against this oppressive patronage Sylvia Plath did not have the resources to defend herself. In Plath's mythic world, there is no protection against her demons. There are light moments, but there is no poem that is without shadows and no really frightening poem that exorcises as it frightens. "The stream that hurtles us/Neither nourishes nor heals."

Plath's poetry is not truly feminist. Other women are either agents of the maiming culture or separately stranded victims. Yet the poet herself, under the stress of her own situation, develops a consistent set of female-oriented symbols and images which succeed in making her anguish common, in some way, to all women.

Other women poets of roughly her generation—notably Adrienne Rich, Ann Sexton, Maxine Kumin—make the same attempt to construct a form and language in which to express the special condition of women. They seek imaginatively as well as ideologically to reject the centrality of male experience. In none of these poets is this revised vision so macabre, so despairingly complete, or so successfully realized as in the work of Sylvia Plath. In no other poet is love in all its guises so totally defined as cultural manipulation. In "The Stones," the concluding poem of her first book, *The Colossus*, the repaired woman rises from a sinister operating table. She cries out that "Love is the bone and sinew of my curse. . . . My mendings itch. There is nothing to do/I shall be good as new."

The women's movement and its reflection in the poetry women have been writing in the 1970's renders the particular isolation in which Sylvia Plath wrote a part of the past. From her isolation she wrenched a vision so powerful that it cannot, finally, be dismissed or disallowed for its blatant, often angry sexual bias. More than any other poet in this book, but backed by the lives and work of all of them, Sylvia Plath has made it possible for women today to "curse and write."

Watercolor of Grantchester Meadows

There, spring lambs jam the sheepfold. In air
Stilled, silvered as water in a glass
Nothing is big or far.
The small shrew chitters from its wilderness
Of grassheads and is heard.
Each thumb-size bird
Flits nimble-winged in thickets, and of good color.

Cloudrack and owl-hollowed willows slanting over
The bland Granta double their white and green
World under the sheer water
And ride that flux at anchor, upside down.
The punter sinks his pole.
In Byron's pool
Cattails part where the tame cygnets steer.

It is a country on a nursery plate.
Spotted cows revolve their jaws and crop
Red clover or gnaw beetroot
Bellied on a nimbus of sun-glazed buttercup.
Hedging meadows of benign
Arcadian green
The blood-berried hawthorn hides its spines with white.

Droll, vegetarian, the water rat
Saws down a reed and swims from his limber grove,
While the students stroll or sit,
Hands laced, in a moony indolence of love—
Black-gowned, but unaware
How in such mild air
The owl shall stoop from his turret, the rat cry out.

The Disquieting Muses

Mother, mother, what illbred aunt
Or what disfigured and unsightly
Cousin did you so unwisely keep
Unasked to my christening, that she
Sent these ladies in her stead
With heads like darning-eggs to nod
And nod and nod at foot and head
And at the left side of my crib?

Mother, who made to order stories
Of Mixie Blackshort the heroic bear,
Mother, whose witches always, always
Got baked into gingerbread, I wonder
Whether you saw them, whether you said
Words to rid me of those three ladies
Nodding by night around my bed,
Mouthless, eyeless, with stitched bald head.

In the hurricane, when father's twelve
Study windows bellied in
Like bubbles about to break, you fed
My brother and me cookies and Ovaltine
And helped the two of us to choir:
"Thor is angry: boom boom boom!
Thor is angry: we don't care!"
But those ladies broke the panes.

When on tiptoe the schoolgirls danced,
Blinking flashlights like fireflies
And singing the glowworm song, I could
Not lift a foot in the twinkle-dress
But, heavy-footed, stood aside
In the shadow cast by my dismal-headed
Godmothers, and you cried and cried:
And the shadow stretched, the lights went out.

Mother, you sent me to piano lessons
And praised my arabesques and trills
Although each teacher found my touch
Oddly wooden in spite of scales
And the hours of practicing, my ear
Tone-deaf and yes, unteachable.
I learned, I learned, I learned elsewhere,
From muses unhired by you, dear mother,

I woke one day to see you, mother,
Floating above me in bluest air
On a green balloon bright with a million
Flowers and bluebirds that never were
Never, never, found anywhere.
But the little planet bobbed away
Like a soap-bubble as you called: Come here!
And I faced my traveling companions.

Day now, night now, at head, side, feet,
They stand their vigil in gowns of stone,
Faces blank as the day I was born,
Their shadows long in the setting sun
That never brightens or goes down.
And this is the kingdom you bore me to,
Mother, mother. But no frown of mine
Will betray the company I keep.

The Stones   This is the city where men are mended.
I lie on a great anvil.
The flat blue sky-circle

Flew off like the hat of a doll
When I fell out of the light. I entered
The stomach of indifference, the wordless cupboard.

The mother of pestles diminished me.
I became a still pebble.
The stones of the belly were peaceable,

The head-stone quiet, jostled by nothing.
Only the mouth-hole piped out,
Importunate cricket

In a quarry of silences.
The people of the city heard it.
They hunted the stones, taciturn and separate,

The mouth-hole crying their locations.
Drunk as a fetus
I suck at the paps of darkness.

The food tubes embrace me. Sponges kiss my lichens away
The jewelmaster drives his chisel to pry
Open one stone eye.

This is the after-hell: I see the light.
A wind unstoppers the chamber
Of the ear, old worrier.

Water mollifies the flint lip,
And daylight lays its sameness on the wall.
The grafters are cheerful,

Heating the pincers, hoisting the delicate hammers.
A current agitates the wires
Volt upon volt. Catgut stitches my fissures.

A workman walks by carrying a pink torso.
The storerooms are full of hearts.
This is the city of spare parts.

My swaddled legs and arms smell sweet as rubber.
Here they can doctor heads, or any limb.
On Fridays the little children come

To trade their hooks for hands.
Dead men leave eyes for others.
Love is the uniform of my bald nurse.

Love is the bone and sinew of my curse.
The vase, reconstructed, houses
The elusive rose.

Ten fingers shape a bowl for shadows.
My mendings itch. There is nothing to do.
I shall be good as new.

The Applicant

First, are you our sort of a person?
Do you wear
A glass eye, false teeth or a crutch,
A brace or a hook,
Rubber breasts or a rubber crotch,

Stitches to show something's missing? No, no? Then
How can we give you a thing?
Stop crying.
Open your hand.
Empty? Empty. Here is a hand

To fill it and willing
To bring teacups and roll away headaches
And do whatever you tell it.
Will you marry it?
It is guaranteed

To thumb shut your eyes at the end
And dissolve of sorrow.
We make new stock from the salt.
I notice you are stark naked.
How about this suit—

Black and stiff, but not a bad fit.
Will you marry it?
It is waterproof, shatterproof, proof
Against fire and bombs through the roof.
Believe me, they'll bury you in it.

Now your head, excuse me, is empty.
I have the ticket for that.
Come here, sweetie, out of the closet.
Well, what do you think of *that*?
Naked as paper to start

But in twenty-five years she'll be silver,
In fifty, gold.
A living doll, everywhere you look.
It can sew, it can cook,
It can talk, talk, talk.

It works, there is nothing wrong with it.
You have a hole, it's a poultice.
You have an eye, it's an image.
My boy, it's your last resort.
Will you marry it, marry it, marry it.

Morning Song

Love set you going like a fat gold watch.
The midwife slapped your footsoles, and your bald cry
Took its place among the elements.

Our voices echo, magnifying your arrival. New statue.
In a drafty museum, your nakedness
Shadows our safety. We stand round blankly as walls.

I'm no more your mother
Than the cloud that distils a mirror to reflect its own slow
Effacement at the wind's hand.

All night your moth-breath
Flickers among the flat pink roses. I wake to listen:
A far sea moves in my ear.

One cry, and I stumble from bed, cow-heavy and floral
In my Victorian nightgown.
Your mouth opens clean as a cat's. The window square

Whitens and swallows its dull stars. And now you try
Your handful of notes;
The clear vowels rise like balloons.

By Candlelight

This is winter, this is night, small love—
A sort of black horsehair,
A rough, dumb country stuff
Steeled with the sheen
Of what green stars can make it to our gate.
I hold you on my arm.
It is very late.
The dull bells tongue the hour.
The mirror floats us at one candle power.

This is the fluid in which we meet each other,
This haloey radiance that seems to breathe
And lets our shadows wither
Only to blow
Them huge again, violent giants on the wall.
One match scratch makes you real.
At first the candle will not bloom at all—
It snuffs its bud
To almost nothing, to a dull blue dud.

I hold my breath until you creak to life,
Balled hedgehog,
Small and cross. The yellow knife
Grows tall. You clutch your bars.
My singing makes you roar.
I rock you like a boat
Across the Indian carpet, the cold floor,
While the brass man
Kneels, back bent, as best he can

Hefting his white pillar with the light
That keeps the sky at bay,
The sack of black! It is everywhere, tight, tight!
He is yours, the little brassy Atlas—
Poor heirloom, all you have,
At his heels a pile of five brass cannonballs,
No child, no wife.
Five balls! Five bright brass balls!
To juggle with, my love, when the sky falls.

Aftermath

Compelled by calamity's magnet
They loiter and stare as if the house
Burnt-out were theirs, or as if they thought
Some scandal might any minute ooze
From a smoke-choked closet into light;
No deaths, no prodigious injuries
Glut these hunters after an old meat,
Blood-spoor of the austere tragedies.

Mother Medea in a green smock
Moves humbly as any housewife through
Her ruined apartments, taking stock
Of charred shoes, the sodden upholstery:
Cheated of the pyre and the rack,
The crowd sucks her last tear and turns away.

Winter Trees The wet dawn inks are doing their blue dissolve.
On their blotter of fog the trees
Seem a botanical drawing—
Memories growing, ring on ring,
A series of weddings.

Knowing neither abortions nor bitchery,
Truer than women,
They seed so effortlessly!
Tasting the winds, that are footless,
Waist-deep in history—

Full of wings, otherworldliness.
In this, they are Ledas.
O mother of leaves and sweetness
Who are these pietas?
The shadows of ringdoves chanting, but easing nothing.

The Rabbit Catcher It was a place of force—
The wind gagging my mouth with my own blown hair,
Tearing off my voice, and the sea
Blinding me with its lights, the lives of the dead
Unreeling in it, spreading like oil.

I tasted the malignity of the gorse,
Its black spikes,
The extreme unction of its yellow candle-flowers.
They had an efficiency, a great beauty,
And were extravagant, like torture.

There was only one place to get to.
Simmering, perfumed,
The paths narrowed into the hollow
And the snares almost effaced themselves—
Zeroes, shutting on nothing,

Set close, like birth pangs.
The absence of shrieks
Made a hole in the hot day, a vacancy.
The glassy light was a clear wall,
The thickets quiet.

I felt a still busyness, an intent.
I felt hands round a tea mug, dull, blunt,
Ringing the white china.
How they awaited him, those little deaths!
They waited like sweethearts. They excited him.

And we, too, had a relationship—
Tight wires between us,
Pegs too deep to uproot, and a mind like a ring
Sliding shut on some quick thing,
The constriction killing me also.

Selected Reading List

The list which follows is a brief guide to the poetry of the poets included in this book, with an emphasis on those volumes that are available to the lay reader. It should be noted that poets published exclusively in America or Great Britain are often unavailable to readers on the other continent, or only to be found in large research libraries. *The Women Poets in English,* edited with an Introduction by Ann Stanford (New York, 1972) is the most comprehensive historical anthology which includes poets from Canada, Ireland, Scotland, Australia and New Zealand.

Two other modern American anthologies of women's poetry are *No More Masks! An Anthology of Poems by Women,* Edited by Florence Howe and Ellen Bass, Introduction by Florence Howe (Garden City, N.Y., 1973) and *Rising Tides: 20th Century American Women Poets,* Edited by Laura Chester and Sharon Barba, Introduction by Anais Nin (New York, 1973). All three of these anthologies will introduce readers of this book to the increasing number of talented modern women poets. Readers might be interested in comparing these modern collections of women poets with the anthologies produced in the nineteenth century. Three mid-century anthologies—Rufus W. Griswold's *The Female Poets of America,* Caroline May's *The American Female Poets* and Thomas B. Read *The Female Poets of America*—have been reprinted in 1972, and will therefore be more generally available in libraries.

Anne Bradstreet's *The Tenth Muse* was first published in London in 1650. It has been republished in facsimile together with other poems from manuscript, prose meditations, and letters (Gainsville, Fla, 1965). Her poetry and prose is available in various modern editions. The most recent is perhaps *Poems of Anne Bradstreet.* Robert Hutchinson, ed. (New York, 1973), but the best edition is *Works of Anne Bradstreet.* Jeannine Hensley, ed. (Cambridge, Mass., 1967).

Aphra Behn's poems can be read in *Selected Writings of the Ingenious Mrs. Aphra Behn* (Westport, Conn., 1973). Volume VI of *Works of Aphra Behn.* Montague Summers, ed. 6 vols.

(Staten Island, N.Y., 1973) contains her poetry, but it's worth browsing through the plays in the other volumes for some of the best songs and satirical verse.

Katherine Philips's verse is not available in any modern edition. Some libraries may have *Selected Poems: The Orinda booklets 1,* (Cotlinghen, 1904).

The Poems of Anne, Countess of Winchilsea. Myra Reynolds, ed. (New York, 1973) is a reprint of a 1903 edition which has an excellent introduction by the editor. Libraries may also have *Poems.* Selected and with an introductory essay by John Middleton Murry (London, 1928).

A renewed interest in Blacks and women has made the poems of Phillis Wheatley accessible once more. There are two facsimile editions: *Life and Works of Phillis Wheatley* and *Memoir and Poems of Phillis Wheatley, a Native African and a Slave.* (New York, 1973). A paperback *Life and Works of Phillis Wheatley* (Miami, 1973) is available, but the best reading edition is *Poems of Phillis Wheatley,* Julian D. Mason, ed. (Chapel Hill, 1966).

There is no modern edition of Charlotte Smith's poems, although the Oxford University Press has reprinted a few of her novels. Her poems were widely reprinted in the nineteenth century and local libraries may still have *Elegiac Sonnets and Other Essays,* first printed in 1784; and *Beachy Head, with other poems,* first printed in 1807.

Felicia Hemans's poems have not been republished recently but were published in both England and America in many editions. The most complete is *Poetical Works* (Edinburgh, 1911) 7 vols.

Only recently have Elizabeth Barrett Browning's complete poems been reissued in *Complete Poetical Works of Elizabeth Barrett Browning.* Harriet Waters, ed. (New York, 1973) and *The Complete Poetical Works* (New York, 1972) which is a reissue of the 1900 edition. *Sonnets from the Portuguese* is widely available in American editions—four were in print in 1973. *Sonnets from the Portuguese and Other Poems* (New York, 1967) gives the reader a taste of her other verse.

Mathilde Blind's poems have not been republished since *The Poetical Works of Mathilde Blind* (London, 1900).

A wide selection of Christina Rossetti's poetry has recently been published. *Poetical Works,* William M. Rossetti, ed. (New York, 1972) is a reissue of the 1906 edition. Choose from: *A Choice of Christina Rosetti's Verse,* selected, with an introduction by Elizabeth Jennings (London, 1970), *Poems,* (New York, 1973), *Selected Poems of Christina Rosetti,* Marya Zaturenska ed. (New York, 1970) and *Goblin Market* (New York, 1970).

The Complete Poems of Emily Dickinson, Thomas H. Johnson, ed. (Cambridge, Mass., 1960; London, 1970) is the authoritative edition. There are several selected editions: *A Choice of Emily Dickinson's Verse,* Ted Hughes, ed. (London, 1973); *Selected Poems and Letters of Emily Dickinson,* Robert Linscott, ed. (Garden City, 1973); and *Selected Poems of Emily Dickinson* (New York, 1973).

Libraries will have *Emma Lazarus, Selections from her Poetry and Prose,* (New York, 1944). Recently *Admetus* and *Songs of a Semite* have been reprinted (Boston, 1971 and 1970) from the 1871 and 1882 editions.

Alice Meynell was, in England at least, a reasonably popular poet in her own time. Local libraries should still have *The Poems,* (London, 1940) and *Poems,* (London, 1948).

Charlotte Mew's poems were published in small editions by the Poetry Bookshop. *The Farmer's Bride* (London, 1917) and *The Rambling Sailor* (London, 1928) are hard to find now and ought to be republished.

The Complete Poetical Works of Amy Lowell (New York, 1955) is still available. In addition, there are some selected editions of her poetry: *A Critical Fable* (Havertown, Pa., 1973) and *Selected Poems* (New York, 1971) are reprints of the 1922 and 1928 editions respectively. There is also a new selection: *Shards of Silence: Selected Poems of Amy Lowell* (New York, 1971).

Elinor Wylie is not much read now, but *Collected Poems* (New York, 1932) and *Last Poems* (New York, 1943) are available in American libraries.

It is still possible to get *H.D. Selected Poems* (New York and London, 1957) although *Collected Poems of H.D.* (New York, 1925) contains many interesting poems not included in the later selection. The trilogy consisting of *The Walls Do Not Fall, Tribute of the Angels* and *The Flowering of the Rod* which came out in 1944, 1945 and 1946 has now been reprinted in one volume (New York, 1973). A limited edition of her last poems *Hermetic Definitions* (n.p., 1971) has reached some libraries.

Marianne Moore's *Collected Poems* (New York, 1951) are still in print. *A Marianne Moore Reader* (New York, 1961) has later poetry plus some prose and a long interview and *Complete Poems of Marianne Moore* (New York, 1967) is the most comprehensive collection.

Dorothy Parker's poetry is available in *Collected Poetry* (New York, 1973) but *The Portable Dorothy Parker* (New York, 1973), which has gone through many printings, has stories and reviews as well.

Edna St. Vincent Millay's poetry can be read in *Collected Poems* (New York, 1956). There is also a good *Collected Lyrics* (New York, 1969) and a *Collected Sonnets* (New York, 1970). Both these volumes are inexpensive paperbacks.

There are two collections of Victoria Sackville-West's poetry, *Collected Poems* (London, 1933) and *Selected Poems* (London, 1941).

The Blue Estuaries: Poems 1923–1968 (New York, 1968) by Louise Bogan contains her selection of her own verse.

A complete edition of Stevie Smith's poems will be published in England in 1975. Meanwhile, American readers can find her in *Selected Poems* (New York, 1964) and *Best Beast* (New York, 1969). *Selected Poems* was first published in England in 1962. *The Frog Prince and Other Poems* (London, 1966) and *The Best Beast* (London, 1969).

Four books of Sylvia Plath's poetry are in print both in England and in America: *The Colossus* (London, 1960) reprinted in a slightly different form as *The Colossus and other Poems* (New York, 1968); *Ariel* (London and New York, 1965); *Crossing the Water* (London and New York, 1971); and *Winter Trees* (London and New York, 1971).

Index

98963

F   98963
821.009
Kl7s
1975
AUTHOR
Kaplan, Cora

TITLE
Salt and bitter and good...

DATE DUE   BORROWER'S NAME
RETURNED
05 12 9   Geo S Sweatland

F
821.009
Kl7s
1975
Kaplan, Cora
Ohio Dominican College Library
Salt and bitter and good...
1216 Sunbury Road
Columbus, Ohio 43219

DEMCO